D1614589

Organization Analysis
and Development

Wiley Series
Industrial Psychology and Organizational Behaviour

Series Editors

Professor Cary L. Cooper
Department of Management Sciences
University of Manchester Institute of Science and
Technology

Professor Iain L. Mangham
Centre for the Study of Organizational Change &
Development
University of Bath

ORGANIZATION ANALYSIS AND DEVELOPMENT
A Social Construction of Organizational Behaviour
Edited by Iain L. Mangham

Further titles in preparation:

Organization Analysis and Development
A Social Construction of Organizational Behaviour

Edited by **Iain L. Mangham**
University of Bath

JOHN WILEY & SONS
Chichester · New York · Brisbane · Toronto · Singapore

Library of Congress Cataloging-in-Publication Data:

Organization analysis and development.
  Includes index.
  1. Organizational behavior. 2. Organizational
change.   I. Mangham, I. L.
HD58.7.0669   1987   658.4′06   86–26713

ISBN 0 471 91227 1

British Library Cataloguing in Publication Data:

Organization analysis and development
  1. Organization
  I. Mangham, Iain
  302.3′5   HM131

ISBN 0 471 91227 1

Typeset by Witwell Ltd, Liverpool.
Printed in Great Britain by St. Edmundsbury Press Ltd, Bury St. Edmunds.

List of Contributors

Dr Peter Cumberlidge, *Formerly School of Management, University of Bath*

Dr Sue Jones, *School of Management, University of Bath*

Professor Iain L. Mangham, *School of Management, University of Bath*

Dr Roger Peskett, *Formerly Department of Sociology, University of York*

Dr Alistair M. Preston, *Department of Management Sciences, University of Manchester, Institute of Science and Technology*

Dr Michael Saren, *School of Management, University of Bath*

Dr David Sims, *School of Management, University of Bath*

Dr Tim Smithin, *School of Management, University of Bath*

Dr Andrew Travers, *Formerly School of Management, University of Bath*

Dr Robert Westwood, *School of Business Administration, University of East Asia, Macau*

Contents

Preface

This book started life as an attempt to bring together a number of authors who would reflect upon the nature of organizations within a perspective deriving from a broadly interactionist, social construction of reality school of thought. As will be seen from even the most cursory glance at the contents, this has not been easy to achieve and one or two of the contributions stray well beyond the boundaries of such a school, but many of them are content to remain within the grounds of a rhetoric which holds that conduct is constructed by participants within organizations rather than determined for them by the environment, technology, fate or whatever.

The purpose of this book, however, is not to give a confined view of interaction theory as applied to organizations. The book's strength lies in the diversity of approaches it represents; it is unique in that it is not an attempt to force its contributors into a narrowly defined view of organization, of conduct or of development. It is, none the less, one of the few available that seeks to apply qualitative and broadly interactionist ideas to problems and issues within organizations. There are a good many volumes exhorting us all to practise such approaches, few which document the results of such work.

There are several audiences for this book. It can be used as an advanced undergraduate or graduate course in organization analysis or development, where it will no doubt generate a great deal of discussion and a modicum of ire. It can also be used as a complementary text on courses purporting to address aspects of behaviour in organizations; juxtaposed with highly normative and more popular books which abound in this field, its contents could lead to some anxiety and, God forbid, an occasional insight. A third target audience is that of the proverbial 'thinking manager', that rare beast who is interested in the bases of management, the underlying processes which may inform action at every level of the operation. The major audience, however, is those who delight in the title of academic, be they teachers or researchers. As I propose in the introduction, they will find a great deal in this volume to delight and/or to infuriate them.

ILM
September 1986

Introduction:
Offending the Audience

This collection of essays has no theme and little or no coherence; the authors for the most part do not know each other and have shown little interest in each other's work. Their contributions are drawn from a variety of frameworks, some carefully delineated in the text, some less so. They make their points, some with wit and elegance, some with doggedness and what amounts to no more than rustic charm; some smuggle in every reference to the great and the good, some pay scant attention to the work of others; some pieces are transparent and deceptively simple, others opaque and irritatingly confused.

What little connection there is derives from a common disenchantment with what until recently has been taken to be the standard form of academic analysis: the kind of frameworks which claim association with 'scientific' truth. The growing challenge to this kind of thinking has enabled many a closet qualitative researcher to come out. There is now a general interest in 'qualitative approaches', usually taking the form of 'wouldn't it be good to do qualitative research?' The term has become almost a talisman; indeed one or two pieces in this volume do not wholly avoid using the notion as primitive incantation. Much of what is presented here, however, represents attempts to *do* something, to understand behaviour and processes in organizations rather than to become endlessly caught up in discussions about what the nature of such understanding may look like.

The bringing together of these particular pieces and their particular authors is in one sense accidental and in another inevitable. Accidental in that the one common experience that each of the authors has is some time spent in the School of Management at the University of Bath. Inevitable in that some aspect of that experience has led to each of them in his or her own style questioning the nature of the interpretations of organizational behaviour which they encountered in their research. This questioning has taken some such as Westwood into the realms of semiotics and language studies, others such as Peskett into a much narrower aspect of that field: conversational analysis. It has stimulated Jones to look at the broader issues of qualitative research and caused Travers to attempt a radical conjunction of Goffman and Freud. Each piece stands alone; no attempt has been made to yoke authors or concepts. These essays celebrate a diversity of subject matter, style and approach.

My purpose in putting them together is straighforward: I wish to give offence. Some years ago, a playwright, Peter Handke, much influenced by Brecht, confronted an audience with a 'play' which denied that it was a play. He presented four actors, unnamed, addressing the audience from an empty stage denying at each and every turn that they are present to engage in impersonation or to play even their own roles. They will, they say, offer no visual effects, no appeals to the senses or the imagination; what they will do, they say, is to recite the author's lines, which in and of themselves are without significance. *Nothing*, they assert, is being played. Reality simply *is*. Appearance is all there is, there is nothing but appearance.

The actors note, however, that the audience are playing roles. They have made preparations to attend, they have formed themselves into an audience and now expect something. To the extent that theatrical values are present anywhere in this performance, they lie not with the actors but with the audience. They are the topic and the focus. Handke's actors go on to berate the audience in a series of 'offending' speeches in which the stigma of theatricality is passed to the audience. As Barish (1981) puts its:

> We have come to watch a play, only to be told that there is no play, or rather that we are the play, that it is we who are being watched, we who 'represent' something other than what we appear, we who are insincere, inauthentic and theatrical in the worst sense.

I want to do for essay collections what Handke did for the theatre: I want the readers to be made uncomfortable by what they read, to become angry and to react sharply to the material that is presented to them. Some of what is contained in these three hundred or so pages is nonsense, some of it good, stimulating, brilliant even; some of the material is banal, some trite and obvious; but, then, some of what is contained in your heads, gentle readers, is nonsense, banal, trite and obvious, some good, stimulating, even brilliant. This collection is strung together in a manner which is calculated to cause one to think not only about what is presented, but also about what one's own frameworks are. Reading a book ought to be like going to a theatre, an opportunity to reflect upon as well as experience the thoughts of another person. I do not wish you to be seduced by the prose of the contributions, I do not wish you to agree with them, still less do I wish you to suspend judgement or disbelief. I wish you to be open to the material but also to be critical of it and in the fullest sense of yourself. Reading a collection such as this is an interactive event — a meeting of minds. The contributors have put down their thoughts (or some of them) and now invite you to examine yours in the light of what they have written. Some of you will be professional critics, hardened theatregoers as it were, stuffed full of prejudices and theories of your own; it is unlikely that you will bother to see the entire performance, preferring to leave halfway through with a few scribbled notes on your programme. I have anticipated your early departure, your anxiety to be elsewhere, and consider it no great loss. Others, more naive, will stick it out to the last page (the final curtain) and leave with mixed thoughts and emotions. This book is for you, for those not too far gone to be prepared to take the opportunity to think through their own frameworks. If these essays can provoke you into doing that, I shall be more than content.

I. L. MANGHAM
June 1986

Organization Analysis and Development
Edited by I. L. Mangham
© John Wiley & Sons Ltd.

A Matter of Context

CHAPTER 1   *Iain L. Mangham*

Over the past fifteen or twenty years there has been a growing criticism of what had hitherto been taken to be 'orthodox' approaches to the analysis of organizations (Whitley, 1977). Early shots in the campaign were fired by Silverman (1970), who criticized what he saw as the ideological basis of much of what purported to be organization theory and the attack was pressed home through a range of texts (Benson, 1977; Burrell and Morgan, 1979; Clegg and Dunkerley, 1980). The assault has been so successful that it has carried the walls of the old orthodoxy and is busy establishing a new order within the keep.

The proponents of this new order are many and various and between them they deploy a variety of weapons. It is not my purpose to muster the arguments nor to bring to bear still others in attacking the ground which has already been taken. My concern is the more limited one of stating what I take to be the broad parameters of the new order, the emergent orthodoxy, and indicating where my own ideas do or do not find accommodation with it.

I cannot do better than start with David L. Clark's (1985) piece on what he terms 'nonorthodox' theory (that which I claim is becoming the new orthodoxy):

> Suppose, for a moment, that you are sitting on a plane and overhear fragments of an apparently serious discussion among some fellow passengers. The first snippet of conversation is from Character A: 'It's okay not to know where you're going as long as you're going somewhere. Sooner or later you'll know where that somewhere is.' (Weick, 1979)

> Character B seems to be agreeing: 'I now believe that the concept of organizational goals as a major influence upon organizational behaviour is only a convenient fiction.' (Perrow, 1982)

> Character C picks up the point: 'We need a modified view of planning. Planning in organizations has many virtues, but a plan can often be more effective as an interpretation of past decisions than a program for future ones.' (March, 1972)

> Character A is back again: '[That's right], how can I know what I think until I see what I say.' (Weick, 1979)

A new voice suggests that organizations can be viewed as 'choices looking for problems; issues and feelings looking for decision situations in which they might be aired; solutions looking for issues to which they might be the answer, and decision makers looking for work.' (Cohen, March and Olsen, 1972)

Character A concludes: 'Most managers get into trouble because they forget to think in circles.' (Weick, 1979)

The smart person, Clark argues, does not take this to be the ramblings of a group of business consultants who have drunk too much but as the talk of 'nonorthodox organizational theorists whose work and thought is breaking down the dominant paradigm in organizational theory'. The potential confusion between these two groups of people is, however, quite understandable. Virtually everything that has been hitherto taken to be axiomatic for the functioning of organizations is denied by this ragged band of revellers. In effect they assert that behaviour in organizations is *not* goal directed, that people do *not* direct their behaviour by preference for one course of action over another and that there is *no* linkage between intent and action. It is hardly surprising that those who utter such sentiments should be taken as inebriated.

The headiest of them all is Karl Weick, whose writings and, more importantly, his recent editorship of the *Administrative Science Quarterly* have influenced very strongly the development of the new orthodoxy. It is to him and a recent statement of ideas (Weick, 1985) that I now turn to focus upon the overarching model of the new order: that organizations may best be considered as 'organized anarchies' or, what amounts to the same thing, 'loosely coupled systems'. In support of this contention he argues that formal rationality is in short supply in organizations, that 'organizations' are segmented rather than monolithic, that stable segments in organizations are small, that connections between segments are of variable strength and that the variable strength of connections produces ambiguity which is reduced when 'managers act as if loosely coupled units are tied together'.

Citing commentators such as Anderson (1983), Manning (1983), Staw (1980) and Starbuck (1982), Weick first questions the notion of rationality, noting that for the newer theorists action precedes planning; first action occurs and then 'reasons' are invented and retrospectively applied. Such rationalization occurs for the benefit of outsiders — organizations must be seen to be driven by reason, not whim — and also for the insiders, who need 'reasonable reasons' as much as anyone else. What happens is that once an outcome is known, the reasons for a particular action are then adduced with the inevitable result that the previous uncertainty is glossed over or, at best, but ill remembered.

In effect, since the appearance of rational action legitimates the flow of resources into the organization, those within it interested in its survival *dramatize* its planning processes, its adherence to reason, since to do otherwise would be to place in jeopardy its very existence given society's presumption that

that which is compulsive, erractic, unpredictable and unplanned is necessarily bad. Rational talk thus becomes *the* rhetoric of management and planning the ritual of legitimacy.

There is, Weick argues following March and Olsen (1976), a marked indeterminacy that inheres in adaptive action: there is no guarantee that what has happened was intended nor that it had to happen. Sometimes what occurs produces outcomes that were intended by no one and on other occasions, despite clear intentions, the firm is overwhelmed by factors beyond its control. Failure to take into account the indeterminacy of actions leads many to conclude that organizations are much more 'tightly coupled' and monolithic than is sensible. Those who adopt this perspective do so because, in looking back over a series of events, they neglect to take into account the messiness of what actually occurred.

Unity, from a Weickian perspective, is held to be impossible. The predominant organizational form is that of a 'federation, a market, a holding company, or a confederacy that tries to keep from getting overly organized'. Organizations are segmented and only the smaller segments are stable. There is a tendency for complex states to revert to 'simpler, more stable configurations'. An organization, any organization, consists of small stable structures linked together somewhat loosely to produce a semblance of orderliness. Once these structures proliferate in time and space, 'orderliness, predictability and sensibleness decline'.

Not only are organizations best thought of as being segmented, these segments are to be regarded as variably connected; some have stronger connections than others. Most organizations are neither entirely loose nor entirely tight. There are, according to Weick, four general features of organizations that affect the strength of connections: rules, agreements on rules, feedback and attention. Connections are strong the more rules there are, the more severe they are, the clearer they are and the less room for manoeuvre they imply. The more agreement there is on the content of the rules and the greater the consensus about the nature of violations and how they will be handled, the tighter the coupling. Similarly, the more constant the attention people get and the sooner they receive feedback on the effects of their action, the tighter the coupling. Loose or tight though all of these connections may be, for Weick they do constitute a *system* which 'sooner or later' completes a cycle and 'produces something approximating to what it was designed to produce'.

Ambiguity is endemic to such loosely coupled systems. Variability makes it difficult to plan, coordinate and control with any degree of confidence (McCaskey, 1982); to the extent that people in organizations are interested in planning, coordination and control, struggle to reduce ambiguity and seek to tighten the links between the segments in order to steer the whole in what they take to be appropriate directions. For Weick, ambiguity is a source of learning and adaptation. By acting as if they can change environments, for example, on occasions people do change environments. Ambiguity may also promote a change in values and ideology. When ambiguity increases, the person best able to resolve it gains power; new ideas, new values, new perspectives on organization and action may produce innovation and revitalize the institution. Similarly, continuous ambiguity exerts pressure on the organization to modify its structure so that it copes more successfully: 'when organizations face chronic ambiguity their ongoing activities can be interpreted as continuing efforts to move from a less appropriate mechanistic structure to a more appropriate organic structure'. Not that all is change and flux; to note that variable connections promote ambiguity is 'to describe a prominent background characteristic to which organizations accommodate. As they accommodate, organizations assume predictable forms'.

It follows that managers or leaders spend a great deal of their time seeking accommodation, attempting to pattern and thus predict and control events. They work 'amid a great deal of disorder' but operate as if there were 'a logic by which events cohere' and in so operating cause events to become 'more tightly coupled, more orderly, and less variable'. In other words, a manager acts on some belief of how things are or should be and in so acting imposes an order on the situation.

> The trappings of rationality such as strategic plans are important largely as binding mechanisms. They hold events together long enough and tight enough in people's heads so that they do something in the belief that the actor will be influential. The importance of presumptions, expectations, justifications and commitment is that they span the breaks in a loosely coupled system and encourage confident interactions that tighten settings. *The conditions of order and tightness in organizations exist as much in the mind as they do in the field of action.* (Weick, 1985) (italics in original)

Order is achieved through talk, action and interaction. Words are the currency of management, talk the shaper of decisions and the conduit of action. Words induce connections, direct attention and convey information; labels reduce ambiguity and direct response. To note that something is a 'problem' implies that it should be resolved, that it is a 'challenge' indicates that though difficult it should be tackled with enthusiasm, and so on. Stick a label on something and it can be managed. It matters not a jot whether the label is in some sense 'correct' or not; 'people who find a vivid label and then push it persistently often are able to redirect organizational action, because they have gained control over how the organization defines itself and what it says it is up to'.

Similarly, action may reduce ambiguity. Peters and Waterman (1984) note that successful companies have a strong bias for action: they 'wade in', take vigorous action and secure their environment. Otherse spend large amounts of time considering every aspect of the situation before initiating often much less vigorous action. Both stances have their strengths and weaknesses and both reduce ambiguity.

The third 'classic response to ambiguity' is to increase one's interaction with other people and try to sort things out. Given a degree of success in reducing the tension, the process of mutual ambiguity reduction may become reinforcing and those involved may become closer, thus tightening their connections and reducing ambiguity overall. It is possible, however, that once the variability has been reduced, those concerned will revert to solitary action, reducing the discussion and thus, eventually, promoting further ambiguity.

Such, then, are the broad lines of the new orthodoxy. A view which eschews simplicity and maintains complexity and which turns much of what has hitherto been taken to be axiomatic upon its head: 'goals are discovered by acting. Action precedes intent. Solutions search for problems' (Clark, 1985). Above all the new orthodoxy points towards 'disorderliness in ...... organizations' (Clark, 1985). A necessary corrective to previous frameworks in which the tendency has been to 'convert micro-confusion into macro-order' (Perrow, 1982).

The new orthodoxy may be criticized upon a number of grounds (Donaldson, 1985) but my concern here is to enlarge upon it and set it within what I take to be a more appropriate metaphor than it has hitherto enjoyed. Despite assertions that his concern is primarily with people rather than reifications such as 'organizations' and 'systems', Weick consistently uses the language of mechanics to describe that which he takes to be behaviour in organizations. His texts are replete with notions of scanning, feedback, links, loops, coupling and decoupling, flows, sequences, controls, regulators and the like. Occasionally he departs from the mechanistic world view and embraces the related organic one (Weick, 1979); at other times he appears to be investing in game metaphors (Weick, 1985). In the piece presently under consideration, he begins with a soccer metaphor but concludes that in the final analysis 'managing may be more like surfing on waves of events and decisions than like ... soccer .... People who surf do not command the waves to appear, or to have a particular spacing, or to be of a special height. Instead surfers do their best with what they get. They can control inputs to the process, but they can't control outcomes. To ride a wave as if one were in control is to act and have faith. The message of newer perspectives often boils down to that.'

In short, Weick is confused and confusing. His love of aphorisms leads him into some delightful areas but his basic metaphor drags him back. If we are to believe the language that Weick uses persistently throughout his analyses, life in organizations is not like 'surfing', nor is it like 'soccer', nor is it a matter of growth and 'natural selection'. Logically, rationally and in a calculated fashion, he denies the ground that his implicit (and, occasionally, explicit) metaphor then retakes. This passage on social interaction is typical:

Social interaction seems to reduce ambiguity in the following way:

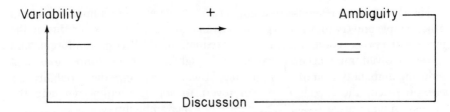

Figure 1   Social interaction/ambiguity and Inquiry.

Two things are interesting about this solution. First, ambiguity created by loose connections is managed by increased interdependence between people. As depicted, once the variability has been reduced, people will revert back to more solitary action, in which there is less discussion. That prediction may be accurate, especially if ambiguity reduction is reinforcing and people become closer to those who satisfy important needs. Thus, persistent mutual ambiguity reduction could tighten a previously loose social system.

Such a passage is a long way from talk of soccer, or surfing or, for that matter, of human beings. It has a mechanistic, functional flavour which, elsewhere, Weick appears to be at pains to deny. Essentially, Weick wishes to replace 'simple linear causality' with 'mutual causality': 'there is no simple finite set of causes for anything that happens in an organization' (1979). Nonetheless, in his view events are caused, are systematically related. The problem is that 'origins are often impossible to discover, because they usually lie at some distance from the symptom and they usually have grown out of all proportion to their beginnings through deviation-amplifying loops' (1979).

Weick, like each of us, is bound to his roots or rather, to be more accurate, to his *root metaphor*. The notion derives from Pepper (1942) and is worth quoting at some length:

The method in principle seems to be this: A man desiring to understand the world looks about for a clue to its comprehension. He pitches upon some area of common-sense fact and tries if he cannot understand other areas in terms of this one. This original area becomes then his basic analogy or root metaphor. He describes as best he can the characteristics of this area, or, if you will, discriminates its structure. A list of its structural characteristics becomes his basic concepts of explanation and description. We call them a set of categories. In terms of these categories he proceeds to study all other areas of fact ... whether uncriticized or previously criticized. He undertakes to interpret all facts in terms of these categories. As a result of the impact of these other facts upon his categories, he may qualify and readjust the categories, so that a set of categories commonly changes and develops. Since the basic analogy or root metaphor normally (and probably at least in part necessarily) arises out of common sense, a great deal of development and refinement of a set of categories is required if they are to prove adequate for a hypothesis of unlimited scope.

Some root metaphors prove more fertile than others, have greater powers of expansion and of adjustment. These survive in comparison with the others and generate the relatively adequate world theories.

According to Pepper, there are four such root metaphors: formism, mechanism, contextualism and organicism. Weick appears to favour the mechanistic variety, or at least one variant of it, 'discrete mechanism'. The basic assumption of discrete mechanism — clearly apparent in much of the new orthodoxy — is that many of the 'structural features of nature are loosely ... related'. From such a perspective, 'almost anything might have been different, because almost everything is independent of almost everything else'. The notion of connectedness, of links and causes, is perhaps odd given such a comment, but discrete mechanism contains within itself a polarity of accident and necessity. Discrete mechanism holds that space is distinct from time, every action is distinct from every other action, every 'natural law (such as the law of inertia or the law of action and reaction) is distinct from every other law'. In such a universe, since every thing is independent of everything else, any thing might have been different. If, say, an atom had happened to be elsewhere at another time, then it would not have been hit by another particular atom. Nonetheless, since the atom was in a particular place at a particular time, it was *inevitable* that a collision would occur. As Pepper puts it, 'There is this strange polarity of accident and necessity in discrete mechanism, which is understandable as soon as it is realized that the accidental comes from the conception of the independence of the details, and the necessary from the inevitability of the event's being just what it is since there is no reason to be found for its being anything different.' This kind of strain or polarity is evident in Weick's writing and, as elsewhere with those who embrace this form of mechanism, there is a tendency for the accidental to be pushed further and further back into the purely and utterly irrational and the search for the necessary — in the form of laws (in Weick's case about the reduction of ambiguity, the strength of links, etc.) — to become predominant. As Pepper notes (although the new orthodoxy is still at a distance from it), there is a tendency to move towards the more consolidated form of mechanism 'in which the details are seen so to involve and determine one another that the accidental almost completely disappears within the folds of the inevitable'.

Since most metaphors are autonomous, it follows that it is pointless to disparage one in terms of the other. I consider mechanism in whatever form to be as credible as any of the other three and as capable of generating interpretations *in its own terms*. Of course, I could argue that Weick and others are deluded, that they are prejudiced, that they are selective in their choice of facts, and so on. On the basis of careful exegesis, I could argue that their account is not in accord with the nature of things. But they could mount such an attack on any position that I cared to advance since, by definition, a good root metaphor must be able to interpret the errors of other root metaphors or world theories.

My quarrel, therefore, is not with the scope of Weick's 'discrete mechanism' – I wish, indeed, that he would stick to it — rather it is with his confused and confusing eclecticism. If, as has been argued, root metaphors are autonomous, it follows that they are mutually exclusive. It is possible that, at some point in the future, formism, mechanism, organicism and contextualism may be replaced by a single world view, but at the moment 'These four theories' [and the metaphors which derive from them] 'are irreconcilable.' There is no value in mixing up root metaphors. Weick and some of his colleagues consistently cast around for perspectives deriving from a variety of root metaphors and, as a result, end up with an unnecessary degree of confusion.

If the adherents were to own and stick to their root metaphor, the confusion would be correspondingly reduced; essentially, the root metaphor common to most of the new orthodoxy derives from the mechanistic perspective on social and organizational life. Few of the new orthodoxy can tear themselves away from conceiving of events as caused; for them, there is always — somewhere and perhaps at some distance — a cause and an effect. For me, there is an alternative way of sharing similar observations to those made by Weick and his colleagues, but avoiding the sterility of mechanism. That alternative is contextualism.

The best way to convey the notion of contextualism is to use verbs. 'It is doing, and enduring and enjoying: making a boat, running a race, laughing at a joke, persuading an assembly .... These acts or events are all intrinsically complex, composed of interconnected activities with continually changing patterns. They are like incidents in the plot of a novel or a drama. They are literally the incidents of life.'

The contextualist regards everthing that happens in the world as being composed of such incidents or episodes. In order to describe and understand what is occurring, we must take account of an act 'in and with its setting, an act in context' (Pepper, 1942). The 'historic event' is at the heart of contextualism: not in the sense of a past event but a present one, the 'dynamic dramatic active event'. What the contextualist seeks to depict is the rich, concrete act in which features interpenetrate and may never be repeated in precisely that configuration. Change and novelty are central features of social life: 'nothing shall be construed as denying that anything may happen in the world.' Furthermore 'disorder is a categorical feature of contextualism, and so radically so that it must not even exclude order. That is, the categories must be so framed as not to exclude from the world any degree of order it may be found to have, nor to deny that this order may have come out of disorder and may return into disorder again — order being defined in any way you please, *so long as it does not deny the possibility of disorder or another order in nature* also. This italicized restriction is the forcible one in contextualism, and amounts to the assertion that change is categorical and not derivative in any degree at all.'

The basic categories, therefore, of a contextualistic perspective may be said to be *change* and *novelty*. They in turn may be subsumed under notions of *quality* and *texture*. Every event has quality and texture. It is impossible to appreciate the notion of quality without contrasting it with texture. To illustrate, let me take what I am actually doing at the moment: I am writing a chapter in this book. What is quality and what is texture in this activity? The quality is the 'intuited wholeness or total character; the texture is the details and relations which make up that character or quality'. The two are not separable although, at times, one may be more prominent than the other. For a contextualist, there is no such thing as 'a textureless quality or a qualityless texture'. Indeed, contextualism denies:

> that a whole is nothing but the sum of its parts. It even denies that a whole is a sort of added part like a clamp that holds together a number of blocks. A whole is something immanent in an event and is so intuited, intuited as the quality of that very event.

In reading this passage you intuit that I am writing a chapter, even though you are now concentrating (no doubt quite hard) on the details. Normally we intuit the broad features of an event and we never notice that we are doing it. In a sense the context, although the focus of our attention, is never the focus of analysis. The quality of an event cannot be explained away by simply paying attention to its texture: 'elements, details, features, components are there and constitute the texture, but the texture has also its intuited quality, which is not reducible to these, though it is precisely the wholeness of these'.

My contention is that much if not all of the new orthodoxy can be accommodated within the contextualist perspective and that given release from the entailments of mechanism other features of social and organizational life can be described. In what follows, through adopting the contextualist approach as embodied in dramaturgical analysis, I hope to go some way to validating this somewhat rash claim. I will begin by outlining the broad features of the dramaturgical perspective and then revisit the themes of the new orthodoxy (Mangham, 1986; Mangham and Overington, 1987).

The dramaturgical model in its social psychological form arose from the thoughts and lectures of George Herbert Mead and in particular from the notions of role and role-taking which were two of his central concepts. Such concepts are potentially contextual. As Sarbin points out, not only must the social actor take into account the role of the other in determining what he or she is to do, the very performances then undertaken and the judgements made about them become the very stuff of construing the self (Mangham, 1986).

The key characteristics of the dramaturgical model rest upon a number of assumptions (Sarbin, 1982; Brissett and Edgley, 1975).

1. That 'meaning' is a guide to action and that 'meaning' arises through interaction.
2. That the self in all its aspects is a social product; that who I am arises out of interaction.

3. That we are all actors; that is, we are both affected by and affect situations.
4. That the unit of analysis therefore is not an individual or a trait but interaction within a context.
5. That as situations develop, social actors construct and reconstruct meanings with reference to the performance of others and of themselves.

but not arbr- ulott

Such a perspective is clearly contextualist:

> an ongoing texture of multiply elaborated episodes, each leading to others each being influenced by collateral episodes, and by the efforts of multiple actors who perform actions in order to satisfy their needs and meet their obligations. Contained in the metaphor is the idea of constant change in the structure of situations and in the positions occupied by the actors. Linearity is not intended. (Allen and Schiebe, 1982)

The dramaturgical perspective has no problem with the notion of order as conceived of by Weick *et al.*: small, stable 'segments'. The theatrical notion of script encompasses this aspect clearly and unambiguously; not script in the sense that every word is written down, every inflection is carefully delineated for the actor, although some theatre is of this form (as, indeed, is some of social interaction). Rather script in the sense that once we know the kind of roles to be played and the broad lines of a possible encounter, then we can run off the performance without much anguish.

A great deal of social intercourse is improvised around what Schank and Abelson (1977) have termed 'situational scripts' in which:

1. the situation is specified;
2. the several players have interlocking roles to perform;
3. the players share an understanding of what is to happen.

A script in the sense used by Schank and Abelson is 'a *structure* that describes appropriate sequences of events in a particular context .... Scripts handle stylized everyday situations. They are not subject to much change, nor do they provide the apparatus for handling totally novel situations. Thus, a script is a predetermined, stereotyped sequence of actions that defines a well known situation. (Schank and Abelson, 1977)

Below is reproduced Schank and Abelson's 'Restaurant Script' as seen from the point of view of the customer.

Much of everyday social conduct in organizations and elsewhere is of this form; more than is allowed for by Weick and his followers. Langer (1978) notes:

> Philosophers and cognitive psychologists have been concerned with the process of shifting attention from something to something else. However it may be the case that in many working instances, we shift attention from something to nothing else. At these times, we possess a normal amount of information to get us through whatever activity engages us ....

Figure 2: The Restaurant Script

Script:	RESTAURANT		
Track:	Coffee Shop	Roles:	S—Customer
			W—Waiter
Props:	Tables		C—Cook
	Menu		M—Cashier
	F—Food		O—Owner
	Check		
	Money		

Entry conditions: S is hungry Results: S has less money
  S has money   O has more money
   S is not hungry
   S is pleased (optional)

Scene 1: Entering

S **PTRANS** S into restaurant
S **ATTEND** eyes to tables
S **MBUILD** where to sit
S **PTRANS** S to table
S **MOVE** S to sitting position

Scene 2: Ordering

(menu on table) (W brings menu) (S asks for menu)
S **PTRANS** menu to S   S **MTRANS** signal to W
   W **PTRANS** W to table
   S **MTRANS** 'need menu' to W
   W **PTRANS** W to menu

  W **PTRANS** W to table
  W **ATRANS** menu to S

 S **MTRANS** food list to **CP**(S)
*S **MBUILD** choice of F
 S **MTRANS** signal to W
W **PTRANS** W to table
 S **MTRANS** 'I want F' to W

  W **PTRANS** W to C
  W **MTRANS (ATRANSF)** to C

C **MTRANS** 'no F' to W   C **DO** (prepare F script)
W **PTRANS** W to S   to Scene 3
W **MTRANS** 'no F' to S
(go back to *) or
(go to Scene 4 at no pay path)

Scene 3:   Eating

C   **ATRANS** F to W
W   **ATRANS** F to S
S   **INGEST** F

(optionally return to Scene 2 to order more;
otherwise go to Scene 4)

Scene 4:   Exiting

S **MTRANS** to W
      (W   **ATRANS** check to S)

W   **MOVE** (write check)
W   **PTRANS** W to S
W   **ATRANS** check to S
S   **ATRANS** tip to W
S   **PTRANS** S to M
S   **ATRANS** money to M
(no pay path):   S   **PTRANS** S to out of restaurant

Key to above

PTRANS   The transfer of the physical location of an object. Thus, 'go' is **PTRANS** oneself to a place; 'put' is **PTRANS** of an object to a place.

ATTEND   The action of attending or focusing a sense organ towards a stimulus. **ATTEND** ear is 'listen', **ATTEND** eye is 'see', and so on. **ATTEND** is nearly always referred to in English as the instrument of **MTRANS**. Thus, in conceptual dependency, 'see' is treated as **MTRANS** to **CP** from eye by instrument of **ATTEND** eye to object.

MBUILD   The construction by an animal of new information from old information. Thus, 'decide', 'conclude', 'imagine', 'consider', are common examples of **MBUILD**.

MOVE   The movement of the body part of an animal by that animal. **MOVE** is nearly always the ACT in an instrumental conceptualization for other ACTs. That is, in order to throw, it is necessary to **MOVE** one's arm. Likewise **MOVE** foot is the instrument of 'kick' and **MOVE** hand is often the instrument of the verb 'hand'. **MOVE** is less frequently used non-instrumentally, but 'kiss', 'raise your hand', 'scratch', are examples.

MTRANS   The transfer of mental information between animals or within an animal. We partition memory into two pieces: the **CP** (conscious processor where something is thought of) and the **LTM** (long-term memory where things are stored). The various sense organs can also serve as the originators of an **MTRANS**. Thus, 'tell' is **MTRANS** between people, 'see' is **MTRANS** from eyes to **CP**, 'remember' is **MTRANS** from **LTM** to **CP**, 'forget' is the inability to do that, 'learn' is the **MTRANS**ing of new information to **LTM**.

ATRANS   The transfer of an abstract relationship such as possession, ownership or control. Thus, one sense of 'give' is: **ATRANS** something to someone else; a sense of 'take' is: **ATRANS** something to oneself. 'Buy' is made up of two conceptualizations that cause each other, one an **ATRANS** of money, the other an **ATRANS** of the object bought.

INGEST   The taking in of an object by an animal to the inside of that animal. Most commonly the semantics for the objects of **INGEST** (that is, what is usually **INGEST**ed) are food, liquid and gas. Thus, 'eat', 'drink', 'smoke', 'breathe', are common examples of **INGEST**.

The condition of the actors well into their runs; all danger long since overcome; virtuosity is exhausting so we all settle on many occasions for much less. The danger remains nonetheless; something may cause us to become very much aware of what we are about:

1. When encountering a novel situation, for which, by definition, we have no script.
2. When enacting scripted behaviour becomes effortful.
3. When enacting scripted behaviour is interrupted by external factors that do not allow for its completion.
4. When experiencing a negative or positive consequence that is sufficiently discrepant with the consequences of prior enactments of the same behaviour.
5. When the situation does not allow for sufficient involvement. (Roloff and Miller, 1980)

In such circumstances, each of us is forced to cast around for a new script or to take action to reduce the ambiguity such that events can be run off with less anxiety. We are forced, that is, to *improvise*, to seek to bring order out of disorder.

'YOU'RE THE DOG; YOU'RE DAD; YOU'RE MUM — IMPROVISE'

The notion of improvisation in the theatre has recently received a less than ecstatic press, associated as it often has been with the image of shambling, inarticulate actors casting around for something less than memorable to say.

The manner in which the parts were dictated to the young actors he describes as 'you're the dog; you're the dad; you're the mum — improvise'. Once the parts had been distributed ... there followed 'dozens of brief improvisations in which we created, at a very superficial level, the relationships and problems of the characters'. Some of the improvisations were about little more than the generation of dialogue. (Clements, 1983)

That which we take for improvised theatre nowadays, although often superficial and embarrassing, derives from the origins of drama itself. Its strongest manifestation was in the school of performance referred to as *Commedia dell'Arte*.

The *Commedia* flourished in the sixteenth and seventeenth century, most notably in Italy and France, but remnants of the style still exist today. Performers had in their command a large store of speeches and bits of 'business' which they would exchange with their fellow players within a known framework. *Commedia* is an extempore art form played by professional actors, 'off the cuff' (*a bracchia*) against a theme or scenario (*canovaccio*). What is most needed for players is the theatrical intuition which enables them to support or feed, whether by words or by actions, the other actors in the drama.

Nonetheless, it requires a discipline and a degree of preparation; it has form and yet at the same time allows the individual actor scope for invention and spontaneity. Through the process we are told the comedy is 'borne along to a gay and sprightly conclusion. It is apparent that these actors (those within the tradition of *Commedia*) penetrate to the very core of their subjects, establishing their scenes on different bases with so many varieties of dialogue that, with each performance, the interpretation seems to be quite new, yet inevitable and permanent' (Gozzi, 1890).

The scenarios were well known to the performers:

> The Italian comedians learn nothing by heart; they need but to glance at the subject of a play a moment or two before going on the stage . . . .
> The subject which serves as guide for these excellent players is written entirely on a small slip of paper and posted under a little light for the greater convenience of the troupe.

Gozzi illustrates one such slip of paper:

ACT I

Leghorn

Brighella enters, looks about the stage and, seeing no one, calls:

Pantaloon, frightened, comes on.

Brighella wishes to leave his service, etc.

Pantaloon recommends himself to him.

Brighella relents and promises to aid him.

Pantaloon says (in a stage whisper) that his creditors, especially Truffaldino, insist on being paid; that the extension of credit expires that day, etc. . . .

And so on. The actors need to know only who they are as characters and a limited number of script headings, as it were, to enable them to give very creditable performances. There is no question of their work being scripted in the commonly accepted meaning of the term. In other words, in this kind of theatre the performers approach the conditions of ordinary social intercourse, in which the 'ordinary person continually modifies the presentation of an idea in response to the reactions of the listener' (Hare, 1985). In effect I am putting forward the argument that the metaphor is appropriate on two counts: because the practice of improvisation can accommodate the notion of a continually adjusting performer and, the obverse of this as it were, that in many social circumstances the room for improvisation is relatively limited. In social life as in the theatre, given the characters we are to play and the broad headings, we can each make a pretty good fist of it, always providing we cooperate. A point known to commentators of both theatrical and social life:

The actor who improvizes plays in a much livelier and more natural manner than one who learns his role by heart. People feel better, and therefore say better, what they invent than what they borrow from others with the aid of memory. But these advantages are purchased at the price of many difficulties; the actors are presupposed to be clever, and they are also presumed to be of equal talent, for the drawback of improvization is that the success of even the best actor depends upon his partner in the dialogue. If he has to act with a colleague who fails to reply exactly at the right moment or who interrupts him in the wrong place, his discourse falters and the liveliness of his wit is extinguished. (Riccoboni, 1728)

Within the walls of a social establishment we find a team of performers who cooperate to present to an audience a given definition of the situation .... Among members of a team we find that familiarity prevails, solidarity is likely to develop, and that secrets that could give the show away are shared and kept .... We find that performers, audience, and outsiders all utilize techniques for saving the show, whether by avoiding likely disruptions or by correcting for unavoided ones, or by making it possible for others to do so. To ensure that these techniques will be employed, the team will tend to select members who are loyal, disciplined, and circumspect, and to select an audience that is tactful. (Goffman, 1959)

I am in danger of starting too many hares. It is perhaps appropriate to enumerate the points I am seeking to make:

1. Much of what passes for ordinary everyday social intercourse approaches the conditions that apply to the *commedia*. Once we know the character to be played and the script headings, most of us most of the time can perform adequately.
2. Our performances are sustained by others who are more or less skilled in ensemble playing; in many circumstances we sustain each other and cooperate to save face.
3. It is important to remember that within the broad constraints of character and headings, each actor is free to improvise his or her response. Such patterns are the very stuff of social and organizational life; all is not spontaneous interaction *de novo* on each occasion that performers meet. It is not a case of 'You're the dog — improvise', since each of us knows not only what is expected of us in particular circumstances but who we are to be in it. For the most part we play our parts smoothly and without reflection upon what it is we are doing or why we are doing it.
4. Nonetheless, on occasion, the script is interrupted and virtuosity is demanded of each one of us. Disorder is seen to be the normal condition and we struggle to bring order from it through testing out possible scenarios.

I need to say something more about this last point. As was noted elsewhere, the dramaturgical model rests upon a number of assumptions, the most notable of which was and is that 'meaning' is a guide to action and that 'meaning' arises through interaction. The essence of improvisation is that one discovers what one is about by doing something (echoes of Weick are likely to become deafening at this point). The creative person in any sphere — art or social — does not anticipate meaning, he or she *realizes* it:

> I usually produce a blueprint which is there to be destroyed ... the anarchic process is very important.... (Peter Wood, director, 'On The Razzle', National Theatre, 1981)

The process of arriving at order — be that a play, an opera or a music programme for TV — is one of improvising or running things up provisionally, taking a look at them in light of standards deriving from experience and knowledge, modifying, rejecting or accepting the whole or aspects of it before moving on to develop other ideas out of that which has so far been achieved. A process, that is, of discovering the problematic and rendering it less so through provisional, cobbled-together attempts to come to terms with it (Briskman, 1981).

Improvisation consists of a process of proceeding by trial and error in a necessarily indeterminate manner to render the problematic less so, ceasing when an appropriate meaning has been established. This final stage is the most difficult to define and to account for — perhaps the words of a composer best sum up the sort of notion I am trying to encapsulate: 'I recently spent three months collaborating with Peter Porter on an opera on the subject of Orpheus. I then literally had to tear the whole lot up and start again (the second time round I finished it in five weeks). It wasn't right. Often it can be very nearly right, but it's when it's most nearly right that it's most difficult because what you've done, although it's wrong, is all you've got .... And of course you may find at the end that you've pretty well written what you did the first time, but with a few, tiny, crucial changes' (Burgon, 1982).

The process of improvisation can be rationally accounted for (even though stages in it may appear to be non-rational) and may be retrospectively described, but it is, at the same time, unpredictable and relatively free from rules and routines; the kind of 'foolishness' March and Simon (1958) talk about: 'Treating action as a way of creating interesting goals.' The envisaged end is likely to change as the work already done reveals an unexpected character and suggests unforeseen possibilities. Picasso tells a story that illuminates emergent but, in this case, unwelcome features about a painting by the cubist artist Braque:

> I remember one evening I arrived at Braque's studio. He was working on a large oval still life with a package of tobacco, a pipe, and all the usual paraphernalia of Cubism. I looked at it, drew back, and said, 'My poor friend, this is dreadful. I see a squirrel in your canvas.' Braque said, 'That's not possible.' I said, 'Yes, I know, it's a paranoiac vision, but it so happens that I see a squirrel.' ... Braque stepped back a few feet and looked carefully and sure enough, he too saw a squirrel .... Day after day, Braque fought that squirrel. He changed the structure, the light, the

composition, but the squirrel always came back .... However different the forms became, the squirrel somehow managed to return. Finally, after eight or ten days, Braque was able to turn the trick and the canvas became a package of tobacco, a pipe, a deck of cards .... (Gilot and Lake, 1964)

Improvisation is a struggle to reduce confusion; to impose order upon disorder; to make sense out of nonsense. Recourse to the dramaturgical metaphor enables us to capture the flux of events, the notion of performers creating events by performing, shaping them as they perform, guided throughout their endeavours by some sense of wholeness.

Such a perspective is explicit in the work of people such as Weiss (1980) who argue that much of what occurs within organizations is improvised: 'Many moves are improvisations. Faced with an event which calls for response, officials use their experience, judgement and intuition to fashion the response to the issue at hand. That response becomes a precedent, and when similar — or not so similar — questions come up, the response is uncritically repeated .... Soon what begun as an improvisation has hardened into policy.' It may harden into a script or a text, but it is always open to change through further improvisation (Mangham and Overington, 1987).

Let me return to Schank and Abelson's restaurant script once again. Here is what may justifiably be termed a system in operation, the kind of occasion where all concerned know what is expected of them and, normally, perform in line with expectations. A system (or, in my terms, a performance) which has been developed to reduce all forms of ambiguity concerned with eating out. Assume now, if you will, that the system 'breaks down', that the performance does not go as planned. What follows is a description of the missing scene in Schank and Abelson (2a 'Preparing the Food'):

> Within the kitchens, all hell was let loose. The chefs had decided to punish one of the kitchen porters for reasons which were not very clear to me at the time. The three of them pursued him around the kitchen, pelting him with eggs. There must have been upwards of a couple of dozen eggs used. Eventually they cornered him and really let fly at him. The waiters stood around and watched as though this were nothing unusual. Indeed they paid little attention to it, preferring to gossip amongst themselves. I was amazed by what was going on; outside, beyond the swing door, a number of customers, sitting decorously at their tables, sipping their sherry or whatever, and in here, pandemonium, violence and mayhem. (Fieldwork report, Jonathan Dudley, 1986)

The connection between any of the scenes which precede this one and those which follow is of the most tenuous nature. The customers will, no doubt, eventually be served, but nothing they have done or will do is likely to have any relation to that which has been described as occurring within the kitchen. What has been depicted is an *episode* in the life of those involved in performing in this particular theatre and is in no sense *caused* by those sitting quietly at their tables.

To be sure, they are all involved in the restaurant system or script, but the mechanistic flavour of Schank and Abelson's analysis cannot and does not do justice to such a scene (nor, to be fair, was it ever intended to; it is designed to handle stylized interactions).

In order to understand what may be happening in such a circumstance, the contextualist looks to the idea of emplotment (Sarbin, 1982); human beings carry on their commerce one with another episodically; the episode, or scene, is a changing one influenced by the performers and performances which occur within it but is describable by the notion of plots. The theatregoer, as well as the participant in any social interaction, must be able to 'frame' any given episode of scene in order to separate it from other episodes or frames (Bateson, 1972; Goffman, 1975). As I have noted earlier, the setting helps in the process of framing in the theatre (and elsewhere), as do the costumes, the properties and the demeanour of those present. Such artefacts and signals help us to work out 'what is going on here' and to behave accordingly.

> In everyday behaviour, frames have to be constructed, ... for purposes of emplotment, in order to make sense of the complex of happenings ... and the doings of persons. A clear-cut example of constructing a frame for social behaviour is the shift from serious goal-directed activity to play. The message 'This is play', no matter how delivered, whether by word, gesture, facial expression, or contextual marker, frames one scene from another. The communication 'This is play' signals a particular context, the condition for special kinds of role enactment. (Sarbin, 1982)

The chefs may be seen as indulging in 'play', or in 'revenge', or in 'initiating the porter into the routine of the kitchen'. The writers, the porter, the chefs and the observers may, in fact, all differ in their 'framing' of the event and some considerable ambiguity may result. Assume the porter regards it as 'revenge' whilst the chefs regard the attack as an initiation ceremony, the former retaliates with a knife or a pan of scalding water; some rapid redefinition, some revised interpretation of what is going on in this episode is likely to occur.

The root metaphor of the new orthodoxy, the machine or mechanism is 'feebly inappropriate as a trope to convey the complexity of human episodes and the effect of a constantly changing milieu' (Sarbin, 1982). Episodes, scenes, acts, entire lives and performances are describable without the notion of cause and effect. What is occurring in the kitchen may be described as a plot and, as such, may be seen as part of a catalogue of plots. As Sarbin points out, there have been a number of attempts to classify plots in drama and in folk tales (Polti, 1916, Aarne, 1964; Propp, 1968) but, to date, little has been done to describe the functions of dramatis personae in everyday encounters. Eric Berne (1964) identified some of the 'games people play' in their efforts to solve their problems and he did so from a contextualist and largely dramaturgical perspective. For the most part, he eschews linear causality and considers human interaction as deeply embedded in historical contexts.

In discussing the idea of emplotment, one further issue remains to be noted: that of emotion. The new orthodoxy ignores emotions and feelings just as the old did. Anger, aggression, pride, grief and the like, particularly when allied to conceptions of *wilful* individuals, are particularly difficult for those of a mechanistic persuasion to handle. It is hardly surprising, therefore, to find that such notions receive short shrift in the writings and comments of the new or the old priesthood. I have argued elsewhere that theatre emblematizes feelings and relationships, that what we see unfolding before us on the stage is a plot which is informed by emotions (Mangham, 1986; Mangham and Overington, 1987). What is true of the theatre may, since theatre is an attempt to reproduce and reflect upon social life, be true of ordinary intercourse. It is possible to argue that emotions are not simply somatic conditions that happen to us, 'I am overwhelmed by grief', 'I am consumed by anger', and the like, but are in fact 'transitory social roles' (Averill, 1980), performances like any other performance. Emotions may be conceived of as expressions of motive and purpose: anger and love are replete with intent. Shame and pride are projections into the world, they are about something. Emotion is a judgement or set of judgements (Solomon, 1976) which may or may not be justified (if challenged, one may acknowledge that one's emotion is excessive or unwarranted) and may or may not be expressed.

Let me seek to illustrate with a further example; below I reproduce a brief exchange between two senior executives:

Brian: Of course, if Eric wants to do it that way, then it is up to him to do it that way. It's eventually his responsibility.
Eric: That's just the kind of support I would expect from you.
Brian: Hold on. Hold on. I'm simply saying it's your baby, that's all ....
Eric: And implying that I'm wrong to take the line I'm taking.

Out of context, it is probably difficult to get the feel of what is going on, but it should be reasonably clear that Eric reacts with hostility to Brian and is not placated by Brian's admonitory 'Hold on. Hold on'. Indeed his anger appears to escalate as a consequence of these remarks. The episode seems to have a trajectory something like the following: (1) Brian makes his remark, which may or may not have had the intention of putting Eric down; in any event (2) Eric *judges* this to have been the intent, considers this offensive and, in reacting with feeling as he does, *constitutes* the offence. Consequently (3) Brian points up the hostility, decides that it is inappropriate and conveys that message to Eric who (4) considers these comments not sufficient to abandon his own hostility. At one level, both social actors pay attention to the content of what is being said, but at another, in seeking to frame what is happening, they interpret and perform temporary emotional roles. In other words, the developing plot, the 'what is the encounter about', is as much conveyed by emotional roles as it is by more explicitly cognitive considerations.

The emotion that is experienced in a particular situation is, as with other forms of conduct, constructed and improvised. The definition of the situation is the key process. By interpreting what is going on through the process of role-taking, identities are defined for self and others and performances are constructed in line with these attributions. Eric considers that he *should* feel slighted by Brian's words and, having chosen to be angry, experiences anger. Such an outline of the process is, of course, too mechanistic by half; it rarely happens like that. Strategic interaction is possible, but it is not the norm. Brian and Eric run off their emotional performances as they run off many of their other performances, without conscious reflection and deliberation. Eric enacts his anger rather than reflects upon it and he does this because he, like each of us, has a great deal of training in emotional performances: 'Don't let him get away with saying that to you', 'If I were you, I'd feel pissed off about that', and so on. Everyday scripts imply emotional performances; indeed we characterize circumstances lacking such characteristics as 'empty' or 'shallow'.

The notion of emotion as 'transitory social roles' is relatively new and, as yet, not fully developed in the literature. The feature of the dramaturgical perspective which has been much more extensively used is that of role, simple and unadorned. It can be held that all social interaction is a form of drama, the workplace no less than any other setting. Berger and Luckmann (1967) highlight a key aspect of the dramaturgical perspective in the observation that:

> Only through . . . representation in performed roles can the institution manifest itself in actual experience. The institution with its assemblage of 'programmed' action is like the unwritten libretto of a drama. The realization of a drama depends upon the reiterated performance of its prescribed roles by living actors. The actors embody the roles and actualize the drama by representing it on a given stage. Neither the drama nor institution exists empirically apart from this recurrent realization . . . .

Ralph Turner (1981) makes a similar point, with the stress upon actors frequently checking with each other that they are — as it were — in the same play:

> Actors will behave as though they and others with whom they interact are in particular roles as long as the assumption works by providing a stable and effective framework for interaction. They test the assumption by continuously assessing one another's behaviour, checking whether that behaviour verifies or validates the occupancy of a position by corresponding to expectations and by demonstrating consistency.

The emphasis here, as in the piece cited from Berger and Luckmann and as in a great deal of literature which purports to advance the dramaturgical perspective, is upon roles and role enactment. The argument is that each of us in our time plays many parts; that role pluralism (Parsons, 1968) is a central feature of all human societies but is more important to complex developed ones than to more traditional ones. As drama involves 'parts to be played', it follows that 'roles implicit in the parts must be conceived and performed in ways expressive of the role. The construction of social conduct involves roles and characters, props and supporting casts, scenes and audience' (Stryker, 1980).

Note the perspective involves 'roles *and* characters, props and supporting casts, scenes and audience' (emphasis mine). In fact in the heroic overuse of the notion of role, generations of those claiming adherence to the perspective have done a disservice to it. The dramaturgical metaphor is predominantly contextualist in principle if not yet in application. Let me illustrate, briefly, the kind of wholeness that I wish to highlight. On a visit to a theatre (or to a social setting that is new to us), the first thing we observe is the scene. When the characters (or social actors) appear, we hear what they have to say against the scene, within the setting. In fact, more often than not the setting will become a vague surround to the talk and the action, the context will be subsumed within the particular activity. It is nonetheless possible to argue that our perceptions, actions and reactions are occasioned by a form of double stimulae; that in a sense we hear the scene and see the talk. As States (1985), following in the footsteps of Merleau-Ponty puts it, in the theatre (and I would argue in everyday social intercourse) 'the speeches become a kind of metaphysical light cast upon the setting, while the illuminated setting encompasses the speech and gives it a kind of environmental meaning .... The scene "permeates" the speech and the speech illuminates the setting.' Theatre makes a complex appeal to the senses, we understand what is occurring before us by intuiting a wholeness, not by paying attention to the details; action occurs within a setting and our response to it is a combination of the literary and pictorial images. As Merleau-Ponty (1970) says, 'The senses interact in perception as the two eyes collaborate in vision .... The senses translate each other without the intervention of any idea.' The full use of the dramaturgical metaphor enables us to consider action in context and context in perception and action.

I digress merely to point up that — to date — the metaphor has not been fully exploited (Mangham and Overington, 1987). A further example: even the massive amount of work on roles has, for the most part, failed to exploit the distinction between character and performer. In the theatre, our involvement with the characters is attested by another largely subliminal empathy arising from the possibility that the illusion may be shattered by a mistake or an accident. Hamlet's costume may burst apart, he may forget his lines, be overcome by stage fright or whatever. To be sure, at the end we applaud the skill of the actor in 'becoming' Hamlet, but we are also impressed by the virtuosity with which the characterization was achieved; we do not forget that undertaking the part is not without danger. At any step, the performer can *fall out* of character and wreck the illusion. This, I would argue, is as much a feature of social life as it is of the theatre; each of us can and does carry off our everyday performances with skill and conviction but in some circumstances — interviews, love affiairs, business deals — there is a distinct sense of danger. Something can go wrong, the performer may be spotted beyond the character, we may fall out of role with disastrous consequences. The danger the actor experiences, that which gives the edge to his or her performance, is the condition of us all *in extremis*. Life in and out of the theatre demands virtuosity.

I could go on and demonstrate further that the metaphor is 'fertile', capable of 'expansion' and adjustment, but that is not my purpose. I began with an outline of what I took to be the new orthodoxy, particularly as proclaimed by Karl Weick and his followers. On the one hand, he asserts that the 'universe is not sufficiently connected to make widespread change possible' and, on the other (actually on the same page — 121), that 'if people watch the system long enough, they will see that the components are connected and that everything gets processed'. Elsewhere he proposes that individuals control what it is they are about, 'research goes the way the researcher wants it to go' and 'people can create a reality', yet also proposes that nearly everything is determined, 'to ride a wave as if one were in control is to act and have faith. The message of newer perspectives often boils down to that.'

I have argued that the new orthodoxy is caught up with the old in that it too is concerned with causality. At one level it accepts that situations are variable but goes on to argue that somewhere, somehow, everything is linked. The contextualist approach holds that one can describe episodes of human interaction without recourse to the idea of causality. The dramaturgical perspective derived from this world view holds that order is enacted, that disorder surrounds the actor and that a condition of our existence is the virtuosity each of us displays in reducing ambiguity and performing our parts. Weick advises the scholars and the administrators interested in the study of human behaviour in organizations to 'complicate yourself .... Whatever additional ways we can find to complicate observers should also be adopted because the primary thrust of organizations is toward simplification, homogeneity, and crude registering of consequential events' (1979). Contextualism certainly complicates the description but accords well with our common observation that events are continually in flux. Neither fate nor mechanism is valuable as a guide to understanding our condition; I am in accord with Harré in considering that: 'The activities of a playwright offer a better mode for a social scientist to follow than does the work of physicists. At least a playwright has the authenticity of his recreation of social reality checked every night in the theatre by a multitude of people. Intuitively he has a profound nature of the principles of social behaviour' (Harré, 1974). The success of dramatists, novelists and those who view life as theatre lies in their ability to construct plots and characters that hang together. I suggest that social science in general and organizational analysis in particular could well reflect the wholeness of human interaction by attempting to learn something from them.

Organization Analysis and Development
Edited by I. L. Mangham
© John Wiley & Sons Ltd.

Choosing Action Research:
A Rationale

CHAPTER 2   *Sue Jones*

Over the last few years a central interest of mine has been to understand the processes of complex, strategic problem-solving by individuals and groups in organizations — not the neat, linear, 'rational–objective' activity prescribed in many texts about problem-solving, but the untidy, cyclical, often highly charged and political processes most of us go through when we attempt to tackle what we see as complicated problems in the social contexts of our organizations.

The main methodology I have used to pursue this inquiry has been that of action research. I have sought to learn about the processes of complex problem-solving by working with people as they experience and address specific problematic issues, doing so usually in the explicit, negotiated role of researcher/facilitator.

In this chapter, I shall discuss the rationale for this choice of methodology. I want to talk in less general terms than often presented by the advocates of action research. Instead, I shall explore the particular theoretical and practical questions which have absorbed me in trying to get the data and understanding I want about the topic, for example: the particular experiences of construing and addressing complex problems, not as seen through retrospection or prospection but as far as possible 'as they happen'; the social and political processes of trying to get things done through and with other people in the organizational setting; the thinking about such processes, which is often regarded as too illegitimate or threatening to reveal to some outside researcher who can offer no particular benefit in return.

My intention is not to assert that action research is always possible or appropriate. I shall suggest, however, that the issues raised by an action research philosophy are important for anyone who wishes to do research through which, to address the theme of this book, 'organizational analysis' can lead to 'organization development'.

A QUALITATIVE METHODOLOGY

When I think of action research I think less of large-scale public programmes than of face-to-face, intensive, longitudinal involvements with particular individuals and groups within particular organizations, with the intention of understanding how these people experience, give meaning to, act and interact with respect to particular situations. Action research is a *qualitative* methodology.

As Filstead (1970) asserts:

> Qualitative methodology refers to those research strategies... which allow the researcher to obtain first hand knowledge about the empirical social world in question. Qualitative methodology allows the researcher 'to get close to the data', thereby developing the analytical, conceptual and categorical components of explanation from the data itself — rather than from the preconceived, rigidly structured, and highly quantified techniques that pigeonhole the empirical world into the operational definitions that the researcher has constructed ... qualitative methodology advocates an approach to examining the empirical social world which requires the researcher to interpret the real world from the perspective of the subjects of his investigation.

The arguments for a qualitative philosophy of research are well rehearsed in numerous writings (see, e.g., Glaser and Strauss, 1967; Blumer, 1969; Diesing, 1972; Bogdan and Taylor, 1975; Lofland, 1976; Van Maanen, 1979; Silverman, 1985). Here I shall only summarize what I take from these in my own position, involving, in particular, a concern with the meanings of action, individuality and multiple meanings, and the generation of grounded theory.

My starting point is a phenomenological, 'social constructionist' perspective which seems human action not as a given response to some external stimuli, but arising out of the meaning and significance persons construct in events. Bringing to bear the personal frameworks of beliefs and values they have developed over their lives (variously labelled as a 'system of expectations' (Parsons, 1951), a 'construct system' (Kelly, 1955), a 'scheme of interpretation' (Schutz, 1970) or as 'mental schemata' (Neisser, 1976)), persons subjectively and selectively define situations. In Thomas and Thomas' (1928) famous words, 'If men define situations as real, they are real in their consequences.' As Ball (1972) asserts:

> ... What Thomas is basically arguing here ... is that ... in order to understand social conduct, we must look to existential causality, that is to the meanings of situations and the situated meanings within them as they are phenomenologically experienced by the actors located within them.

These meanings are created, communicated, sustained, and modified through the processes of social interaction. Many actions are intended to signify particular meanings within a particular social code. Yet an actor's meanings cannot be treated as non-problematically 'given', or accessible to a researcher simply by virtue, for example, of her sharing the same broad cultural context. Berger and Luckmann (1966) have pointed to the paradox that we live in a social world which is nothing other than a human construction and yet we experience many of its institutions as external objectivities which are something other than a human product. Central to this objectification is the language through which we are socialized. Language is the 'objective repository of vast accumulations of meaning and experience', the substance of a 'social stock of knowledge'. We operate as social beings on the basis that we, and the others with whom we interact, share, at least in part, a social stock of knowledge. However, as Ball (1972) also asserts, although we operate within cultures which tell us 'what to know and what to know that [our] partners know', and this is the basis for generalization and prediction:

> such predictions are always probabilistic and therefore never completely given; social location determines the statistical probabilities of sharing situated meanings. (in the aggregate, not the particular)

Indeed, the potential for individuality, the way two persons may differ markedly in the meaning and significance they attribute to the 'same' situation, is part of our everyday experience. Thus, although the very possibilities of interpreting the world 'from the perspectives of the subjects of his investigation' is predicated on the existence of social constructs with which to do so, nonetheless what is involved in qualitative research is a theoretic stance which self-consciously seeks to suspend careless assumptions about shared meanings and significance. It is a stance which looks for what is common but remains open to individuality and multiple meanings. It does not destroy these in the pursuit of the statistical average. Qualitative research also seeks to explore others' meanings in ways, and in contexts, which do not rigidly structure the direction of inquiry within the researcher's *a priori* assumptions, hypotheses and operational definitions.

This last point is the fundamental argument underlying Glaser and Strauss' notion of grounded theory. Rather than forcing data within logico-deductively derived assumptions and categories, research should be used to generate grounded theory, which 'fits' and 'works' because it is derived from the concepts and categories used by social actors themselves to interpret and organize their worlds.

Of course, there is no such thing as presuppositionless research, nor does theory simply emerge from data. One of the reflexive features of this model of human beings is the recognition that a researcher also gives meaning to what she sees and hears. In making her own sense and structure in the data, a researcher inevitably constructs 'second-order' meanings about the others' meanings (see, e.g., Kaplan 1964; Geertz, 1975). Indeed, there may be a negotiation of accounts (e.g. Harré and Secord, 1972) between a researcher and research participants about the meaning of the latters' actions.

However, the power and appeal of Glasser and Strauss' notion of grounded theory is its emphasis upon building understanding about the social world which is embedded in the personal theorizing of the persons concerned. Any second-order theorizing must be firmly linked to the social world it is intended to illuminate. As Lofland (1976; see also Blumer, 1969) argues, our concern in qualitative research is with developing 'disciplined abstractions':

> An empirical science is constructed... out of the interplay of data and perplexed perception that *gives rise* to concepts yet contains and *constrains* them by a context of concrete empirical materials.

PHENOMENOLOGICAL EXPERIENCE

My aim is to build theory from an understanding of the situational definitions and meanings constructed by the actors themselves in a social arena. Where, however, do I start? With the understanding persons have of particular events and their own actions when they theorize about these retrospectively or prospectively, in contexts divorced from the events concerned? Or when they are, for example, actually experiencing a complex problem and acting with respect to it? These are not the same. All retrospection involves some reinterpretation of history in the light of its place in the new sequence of events available for consideration and the different knowledge and interests with which to construe it. All prospection addresses an as yet unknown future, even if one which may be a close approximation to similar events in the past and/or is significantly affected by the very process of mentally preenacting it. In retrospective or prospective accounts, a conceptual logic will inevitably be placed on past or future events which may tidy, simplify, complicate or otherwise find a plausible and legitimate description and explanation of them.

This is not invalid data; on the contrary. But I crucially want, as far as possible, to get near to the immediacy of experience and construal in the sense outlined earlier by Ball, that is, 'the meanings of situations and the situated meanings within them as they are phenomenologically experienced by the actors located within them'. I want, as far as possible, to understand the experience of addressing a complex problematic situation for the persons concerned as they do so — why some situation is problematic for them, the key elements with which they characterize the situation, what actions they deem appropriate to move the situation in a preferred direction.

I say 'as far as possible' because, of course, a distinction between how persons construe a particular event 'as it happens' and the meanings they give to some past or future situation is not a theoretically or practically clear-cut distinction. Any process of articulation about an experience in some way reorganizes and changes that experience. I will seek to be involved in conversations with the research participants about things that have happened in the past and are likely to happen in the future. I will ask people about why they said and did particular things in meetings about which it would be quite inappropriate to ask for further explanatory commentary within the meeting itself. As often an actor in the proceedings myself, I do not have some all-seeing eye. I forget, take for granted, become caught in the flow of social dynamics within a meeting in which I attribute particular significance to certain events and miss the significance of others, including their significance to the other participants. I must ask about these.

Yet I want such conversations and reflections with research participants about, for example, the meanings given to past and future events, to be part of, and made sense of within, the context of their construing the relevant unfolding present as they tackle their issue. The kind of data acquired in this way, which explore and relate, in Harré and Secord's (1972) terms, persons' retrospective, monitoring and anticipatory commentaries about unfolding events, are likely to be importantly different from those which come from, let us say, a one-off qualitative interview focused around some such question as 'Tell me what happens, what you do and why, when you construe a situation as problematic and try to tackle it in your organization.'

A LONGITUDINAL INVOLVEMENT: PROCESS AND STRUCTURE

I want to be around and involved as far as possible at the time when particular issues are construed and addressed. I want to be involved in such a way and in such a role that the persons concerned do not find it odd to talk to me about their constructions of past, future and current events. I also want to be around and involved not just at the time but for a time.

I am interested in the processes of problem-solving. I want to understand the personal and social processes through which problems are constructed, negotiated and resolved in the organization. The data we obtain through longitudinal research are never 'complete'. Even in organizations within our own society (rather than, say, Bali or Papua New Guinea), learning about what meanings are being constructed and communicated in patterns of social action is often:

> . . . like trying to read (in the sense of 'construct a reading of') a manuscript —foreign, faded, full of ellipses, incoherences, suspicious emendations, and tendentious commentaries, but written not in conventionalized graphs of sound but in transient examples of shaped behaviour. (Geertz, 1975)

Nevertheless being around for a time, observing, participating, talking about events and other people in a detail which persons would find strange were I not sharing some important parts of their experience, checking my understandings in these discussions; in these ways I can begin to gain the range and richness of data I need to help me construct, and make sense of, the various meanings of what is going for the actors concerned and myself. I can develop something like the 'intimate familiarity' without which, as Lofland (1976) argues, the concepts and analyses of a researcher are prone to be 'ethereal and empty' (see also Geertz on 'thick description').

The wish to be around and involved for a time is also related to a concern to understand something of the impact of structural contexts on the ways persons define problems and try to influence outcomes. We can consider a number of levels of analysis in organizational research. The first of these focuses on the micro-processes of interpretation and interaction among any particular group within the organization. Yet these dynamics cannot be fully understood without an understanding of their wider organizational context and history. These include, for example, the wider interpersonal and political relationships in which a group's members are embedded and the perpetuating power structures, history and culture which crucially affect the way in which particular situations are defined. At yet another level of analysis, we can also be aware that particular organizational structures and cultures are themselves predicated on a set of external social, political and economic forces which are indeed frequently experienced as a set of external objectivities, existing independently of our interpretations of them.

The complexity of synthesizing micro and macro perspectives is addressed by Silverman (1985). I am less ambitious than his recommendations for research practice, based on the work of Foucault, would require. Nevertheless, at the cost of simplification, it seems to me that the qualitative researcher must constantly move (as her research participants do) in the space between the negotiability and the apparent immutability of the social reality in which she and the others operate. It is not a fixed space. Rather, in understanding this space, she must pay attention both to the debates between social actors about the meanings and significance of particular social and environmental forces and to the apparent impact of those structural forces upon the way in which those debates are framed and the 'rules of the game' for action are construed. The researcher who is rooted in actors' meanings, debates and actions is continually reminded of the multiplicity of perspectives for construing reality, of how what is 'given and immutable' is indeed often a matter of differential interpretation and human ingenuity, that historical cultural and social structures may define the parameters of vision and action but do not totally determine outcomes. She is also, however, led to confront, as her researcher participants do, the impact of macro social forces which are clearly often beyond the power of any single individual, group or even institution to significantly affect — or see beyond.

What also seems to me the case is that I am most able to get at something like this contextual and 'macro' understanding by being around and involved with people when they are seeking to understand their worlds and to act to influence them. As Lewin (1947) argued in his original formulation of the notion of action research, the best way to try and understand social structures is to try and change them — and to sometimes succeed and often fail to do so.

THEORY FOR PRACTICE

It may seem that much of what has been said so far could relatively easily be related to a traditional participant observation method, involving spending a period of time as a researcher in a particular setting and combining observation with interviews.

At this point, however, I find myself confronted with two key, interrelated questions. These are: 'What do the research participants in a particular setting get out of this research, other than perhaps the vague sense that they are "contributing to the stock of social science learning"?' and, 'On what possible basis can I expect them to give me the kind of data I want, particularly those which are sensitive and potentially threatening to reveal, unless they can see some personal benefit from doing so?' Both questions relate to the 'pragmatics' of relationship-building and data-gathering within specific research situations. They also implicitly touch on the more general issue of the aims and outcomes of research in organizations. Both foci represent crucial components in my choice of an action research methodology.

Thus the practical usefulness of the research I do is of considerable importance to me. My interest in processes of complex problem-solving is not simply in understanding what they are 'really-like', but also in developing approaches and techniques which can help them in some way to be done better — for example more explicitly, analytically and creatively. Thus the notion that social science research should contribute to practical knowledge and that 'there is nothing as practical as good theory' lies at the heart of the action research philosophy. Sandford (1981) has argued that:

> the categorical separation of research from practice has made it very difficult for a social scientist to study phenomena that cannot be experimented upon in the laboratory or social structures that can only be understood through attempts to change them. Likewise it has laid the social sciences open to the charge of irrelevance, not only by students but by men of affairs. It would hardly occur to a college president to look to the social science literature for help with his problems and ... social scientists are among the last people state legislators would consult about the problem of drug abuse.

Of course, particularly in the field of organization research, the exhortation to practical relevance has something of the character of 'motherhood and apple pie'. The management literature, for example, is littered with prescriptions about what managers ought to do in order to be better managers. The central weakness of many of these prescriptions is that they appear to bear little relation to what managers actually do, and why. They are not sufficiently grounded and tested in the world of organizational life as it is experienced and enacted. As such, they can only be of limited relevance and use. As Mintzberg (1983) cogently puts it:

> ... much of the 'descriptive' research about organizations has set out to prove some prescription, for example that a participative managerial style is more effective than

an autocratic one. . . . It is the literature of management that often emerges as naked, since much of what it says becomes transparent when held up to the scrutiny of descriptive research.

The original formulation of action research by Lewin (1947) emphasizes the process of understanding through initiating change. This raises the question of the nature of the change we wish to understand. Organizational life is naturally characterized by both stability and change. The action researcher is concerned with understanding the impact of interventions intended to affect the way in which changes occur. When I work with people on their complex, problematic issues, and experiment with particular approaches to assist the process, I am learning about a process which would have been different without that intervention. Nevertheless, I am trying to do this in such a way that I can learn, from the content, processes and outcomes of the intervention, what is or is not possible, what does or does not 'work', because this is the way things, and people, *are* in a particular setting. The action researcher must constantly work with and towards a sense of things as they are, and as they might be. Nor is there any neat distinction between generating theory and testing theory. It is through cycles of interpreting what is, trying for what might be, rigorously testing and refining her ideas, that the action researcher can weave some of the interlaced patterns of theory for, and theory about, practice and change.

WHAT DO THE RESEARCH PARTICIPANTS GET OUT OF THE RESEARCH?

If a general concern with practice outcomes orients me to action research, scarcely less significant for me are ethical and practical concerns about my research relationships with particular people. Thus, when I ask the question, 'What do the research participants get out of the research?', this reflects my own sense of discomfort at treating the individuals concerned simply as data-providers. I am aware that some of them may well enjoy being observed and being asked to talk about aspects of their organizational lives. I am also aware that, for some, the process of explication can involve a useful form of self-reflection. However, I do not find this thought sufficiently comforting. Nor am I reassured by the notion of a contract promising that, at some remote future date, the participants may receive a research report in which there may be some useful learning for themselves.

Secondly, I have to consider the implications of my role and relationship with the research participants for the kind of data they will give me about the research topic. For example, it seems clear to me that there is little point in trying to do action research with people for whom the research issue, as reflected in the particularity of their own experience, is of no interest. As Rapoport (1970) suggests, there may well be negotiation about the specific focus of the research.

It is also the case that some persons may resist the idea of research in a particular area as highly threatening. However, if a researcher has failed to persuade a substantive core of potential participants of the relevance of the research, if the outcome of negotiation is a resigned acceptance that the researcher must pursue some additional research inquiry which is of little relevance and interest 'in exchange' for pursuing that which is of interest, then she must question what quality of data she will obtain about that additional inquiry. Of course, understanding why a research topic is of little interest is itself useful data. Were I to find a wide level of apathy about a particular topic, then this would lead me to ask myself whether the research was worth pursuing at all.

However, I must go further than finding some general level of interest, in considering the personal and political context of my research. The model of human beings which brings me to qualitative research is also one which orients me to a political model of organizational life. The worlds I wish to enter and understand are characterized by complex political relationships which are inevitable among persons who bring to their organizations their own beliefs about the workings of their worlds, their personal ambitions and agendas and their own conceptions of what is right and best for the organization as a whole. In pursuit of these, they must seek to influence those others who see the world differently or compete for the same scarce and valued resources.

The stakes attached to influencing how problems are defined and managed are high (Pettigrew, 1973; Pfeffer, 1981), as are the stakes attached to sustaining and presenting particular personas in order to do so most effectively (Mangham, 1979). I *must* ask myself on what basis I can expect the persons concerned to tell me about the personal ambitions, concerns, vulnerabilities which may be crucial elements in their problem definitions but are also deemed as illegitimate and potentially damaging to reveal. I must ask why persons should bother to tell me about a problem they find complicated, perhaps confusing, perhaps difficult to articulate? Would I reveal these kinds of data to somebody who wanted to investigate the way I address my complex problems in my own organiztion? Not unless I could see the possibilities of some learning and benefit to myself from doing so, except perhaps in some odd bits of data which were unlikely to be substantially revealing to her (although she might then construct some great edifice of unchecked — with me — interpretation on the basis of these).

Clearly, a researcher who is around for a while has more opportunity to develop some level of trust and rapport with the research participants than one who only meets them once for a single interview. However, again, I do not have confidence that this is enough of itself, particularly when dealing with socially skilled and powerful managers whose survival in an organization depends on being careful about what they say to whom. If they so choose, these persons can readily deflect a researcher with some well-rehearsed scripts within the legitimate public language and ideology of the organization.

This view is not an intendedly cynical one. It simply acknowledges the social and political complexity of the organizational setting, and the way my research topic impinges directly on this complexity. Although I do believe that trust can be developed, at least at a reasonable level with some people, I also believe that it must be earned by a researcher, through a research process which the persons concerned can believe has, or is likely to have, some direct personal relevance and use.

The issue of the personal relevance of research is graphically addressed by Maruyama (1974) when he describes the attitudes of prison inmates in his studies:

> Inmates are frequently interviewed by psychologists, sociologists, students, newspaper reporters, etc, whose purposes are irrelevant to inmates, such as proving a theory, writing a book, getting a degree, obtaining promotion or prestige. On the other hand, the purposes relevant to inmates are, for example, food made edible, vocational training updated, harassments reduced, etc. There is no relevance resonance between the inmates and the usual interviewers. The inmates feel exploited by the interviewers. In order to keep the intrusion of the exploiters to the minimum, inmates use sophisticated phoney answers which make the interviewers happy.

It is not necessary to presume that all research respondents will feel exploited by researchers, and deliberately develop phoney answers, to acknowledge that a person for whom research has no intrinsic relevance may see little reason to provide a researcher with good data. Above all, I am interested in a research relationship in which the persons concerned articulate their images of their worlds not primarily to please (or deflect) me but because doing so is part of a process of reflection and analysis about their issue which is of relevance and use *to themselves*.

A VARIETY OF ROLES

At this point it could be argued that there is a certain arrogance and presumption in the posture I have been describing, particularly in the notion of the researcher as a facilitator or helper. The answer to this charge seems to me that it depends on how the researcher interprets and enacts this role, in what circumstances and with whom. What does seem to be important, however, is the explicit integration of methodological theory and research practice.

Thus, as suggested earlier, there seems little point in embarking upon action research among persons most of whom have little interest in the research. However, once a community of interest is established, the particular role and relationship of the action researcher with the research participants may vary considerably. She may act quite clearly in the role of consultant/helper, or the relationship may be one of collaborative inquiry in which the research participants do not expect her to take an independent role as facilitator of the process.

Indeed I would use the term action research in relation to the wide range of different labels that various researchers have constructed for their work — for example, experiential (Heron, 1981), endogenous (Maruyama, 1974), participative (Brown and Kaplan, 1981), and so on. What is common to these approaches are processes in which researchers and research participants are working together, although perhaps in different ways and at different points, to develop understandings which both parties want and expect to have an impact on the way they conduct aspects of their lives. It is the notion of involvements by researchers and research participants in *working* on an issue of shared interest that differentiates action research from other forms of qualitative research; and from those programmes called action research because traditional forms of enquiry such as observation, questionnaires and interviews without feedback have been used to collect data about certain issues of interest to paying but remote sponsors.

A variety of action research roles and relationships is both inevitable and proper in research which must respond opportunistically to the possibilities for research and negotiatively to the particular expectations, interests and power of potential research participants. This variety also reflects the particular models of human beings and organizational life which the researchers bring to their research.

For it is important to note that, while the various approaches to which I have just referred tend to share a phenomenological perspective, their emphasis within this is different. Thus, for example, the experiential model of research described by Heron (1981) is one in which understanding human action must involve participating in that action, and:

> ... knowledge of persons is most adequate as an empirical base when it involves the fullest sort of presentational construing; that is, when researcher and subject are fully present to each other in a relationship of reciprocal and open enquiry, and where each is open to construe how the other manifests as a presence in space and time.

Within this paradigm of research, those involved are coresearchers. The subjects of the research contribute to the creative thinking which generates research conclusions while the researchers also participate in the activity which is being researched. It is a paradigm drawn from humanistic psychology, in which openness, trust and mutual caring between those involved are crucial.

Rejecting the frequent lack of 'relevance resonance' between researchers and researched, Maruyama's (1974) endogenous research also emphasizes the central role in the research process of those whose lives are being studied. In endogenous research academic researchers act as helpers to the 'insiders' — the endogenous researchers — who are themselves not only the data collectors but also the conceptualizers, focus selectors, hypothesis makers, research designers and data analysts.

The participative research of Brown and Kaplan (1981) stresses joint investigations by researchers and subjects to produce solutions to specific problems and new understandings of organizational realities. However, they point not only to trusting and open relationships, but also to the potential for political conflict among persons whose particular inquiry objectives and conceptual frameworks may be very different. The outcome of participative research may be misunderstanding, ambiguity and conflict, or there may be a helpful dialectic as one perspective leads to the clarification of others. Above all, 'participative research' leads to complex and often competing perspectives being brought to understanding and acting in organizations

> Participative inquiry does not produce unambiguous explanations of a reality; on the contrary, it often produces *competing* explanations that reflect the *multiple* realities experienced by different parties to the inquiry.

My own perspective of action research is closest to that of Brown and Kaplan. Tackling complex problems in organizations is a social, political process. By being involved in this process I expect to learn about and work with different visions and concerns. These impact both at the level of the specific issue being addressed by the organization members and upon second-order theorizing about the nature of organizational realities and problem-solving within these. Sometimes these multiple perspectives can be negotiated to build a new superordinate vision, sometimes they cannot.

My orientation to multiplicity of perspectives profoundly affects the way I approach a researcher/facilitator role. It is an approach in which there is no clear distinction between 'being a consultant' and 'being a researcher'. Learning, as a researcher, about the way individuals give meaning to their worlds is also integral to my activity as a facilitator. My concern is to facilitate individuals make explicit, analyse and, in a group, build upon their complex and diverse beliefs and values about situation. It involves developing and using process and qualitative modelling methods designed to assist persons:

> ... see as legitimate knowledge their own subjective understanding of their organizational life and then to self-consciously reflect upon this knowledge so that they may learn to know what they know and learn from its implications, and thus learn by enquiring in a relevant way. (Eden, Jones and Sims, 1979)

This is an activity in which the careful exploration and checking of personal meanings is central. My own understanding of these is continually tested in terms of their ownership by the persons concerned. However, the process is also one which recognizes that the relationship between a researcher and research participants can become a *dialogue* without this destroying the integrity of the research process. The meanings persons construct are sustained but also created and modified within the processes of social interaction. I wish to develop a relationship in which the persons concerned can say to me 'No, things are not like that, and it is not helpful for me to think in these terms', or 'Yes, that is a helpful perspective, although I had not thought in precisely those terms before, and therefore I now propose to do this rather than that', and so on. I wish to learn about and from my own role in what is occurring, and how the research participants see that role. I cannot achieve this by not knowing what 'questions the others are answering' when they try and second-guess my own interests and intentions; by pursuing some impossible aim of avoiding 'contaminating' the proceedings.

AN EXAMPLE

At this point I shall illustrate some of the themes discussed so far by describing aspects of one particular action research project with which I was involved. It is not the most typical project I have undertaken since it was with members of a voluntary group rather than a formal organization. It was, nonetheless, one of the most personally rewarding in terms of its outcomes.

The Project

The outlines of the story can quickly be told. Two of us decided that we would like to become involved in work in a less traditional setting than the large, formal organizations we were mostly accustomed to. We wanted to do something which could be helpful to those who do not normally have consultancy help available to them (although we did not wish to take on an expert role). We assumed that any such activity could well become an 'extra' to our other activities, just as we might have chosen to become involved as individuals in any voluntary work. However, we also resolved to treat it seriously as a research opportunity to develop and test ideas about the processes of complex problem-solving.

From this starting point came an involvement which lasted for approximately three years, of which the most intensive period was the first eighteen months. The two key actors with whom we were primarily involved were members of a voluntary group formed to find ways of helping the unemployed school-leavers of their area, particularly within the black community. During that initial eighteen months these individuals left their original group, formed a new group and were the driving force in obtaining the necessary support to establish an independent community training workshop for unemployed youth. This eventually received official funding under the aegis of government job-training schemes. Our role during the project was to help our 'clients' work through the complexities and ramifications of their issue and devise appropriate actions as events unfolded.

My own focus of theoretical interest during the project centred on its politics, including the process of 'other definition' in the context of complex problem-solving. I was, and still am, interested in how people think about those they define as the significant actors, or 'stakeholders', in an issue. For example, how is it, and on what bases, that persons come to define some particular actors as significant and not others? What is that they pay attention to in these significant others? How do they categorize them? How do they explain and predict the others' attitudes and actions, and in what way do these explanations and predictions affect their own actions towards the others? What methods can be developed to assist the identification and analysis of the key actors implicated in a particular issue?

The impetus for this inquiry is the gap in theory and method about the psychological processes of other-definition in the context of complex problem-solving. There is, of course, a body of social–psychological research about person perception. Most of this, however, is outside the context of problem-solving in the work setting, and indeed, as Cook (1979) has pointed out, 'Too much person perception research has studied opinions formed by people, who have no pressing need to form them, about people they have little contact with, and will never meet again outside the laboratory.' There is also an important and still growing literature on organizational politics, but much of this is at a relatively 'broad brush stroke' level rather than addressing the personal cognition of how individuals mentally model their 'problem-significant' others. Furthermore, at the level of practice, most of the prescriptions and techniques for problem-solving ignore the political and interpersonal aspects of problems altogether. Thus individuals are offered little assistance with what is likely to be an important part of their thinking to understand and tackle their problems in the social contexts of their organizations.

The Politics of Problem-Solving; 'Those Who Have the Power to Help or Hinder the Attainment of Preferred Outcomes'

Throughout this project, the central characters were exercised by how to identify those who could help them achieve their objectives and then with how to manage their relationships with these others in order to influence them most effectively. In considering the question 'on what bases are others defined as significant in an issue' a crucial factor for these individuals was others' perceived power of various kinds to help — or hinder — the attainment of preferred outcomes.

Thus in relation to the objective of establishing a training workshop, central to their effort was the need to obtain the material, primarily financial, resources they required. They needed to identify and influence those who had the power to dispose such resources. Others then became significant in terms of their power to help them do this. They paid attention to those who could provide them with access to 'those who can dispose needed resources'. They were particularly interested in those who could help them influence the others, using, for example, what they called 'official post power' and/or 'respect power'. They sought for themselves 'connection power' (Hersey Blanchard and Natemeyer 1979) through their association with powerful others. They were highly exercised by their relationships with those who occupied such central positions within the community networks that they had, in our clients' own terms, 'the power to make or break'. They also expended considerable energy upon considering their allies and opponents within the internal politics of their own group, where the competition to define the agenda of what the group should do, and how, was intense.

The practical issue posed by this was to help our clients work through the strategies and tactics of building relationships with these others and of managing the complex dynamics of their developing networks of relationships. It required addressing their 'mental models' of others, their power attributions and the sharing and negotiation of differences between them in their constructions of others. However, if power represented one 'core category' for understanding their construction of the significance of others, another key dimension related to their beliefs and values about self and social image, and it is this which I shall briefly elaborate here.

Self and Social Image in Construing 'Problem-Significant' Others; Some Examples

In the context of organizational norms that proposals should be couched in terms of a concern with the 'good' of the organization, or at least some substantial part of it, it would be unsurprising for persons to declare that their pursuit of a certain end was to serve the needs of some other group. Such declarations may reflect genuine commitments to others or represent no more than legitimating rhetoric.

In this case, the participants were indeed driven by an image of a preferred future which centred around helping certain other groups — the unemployed youth of their community, their parents, and their community as a whole. These others comprised for them a category of significant others which we may label as 'those for whom I have a conception of a preferred state of existence (which I am committed to pursuing)'. Their image of a preferred future involving the others was central to their conceptions of themselves, and a 'call to action' which dominated their lives during the period concerned.

It was a concern which raised important questions, particularly in relation to some of the youngsters, about the relationship between seeking to help and seeking to impose a personal vision about a preferred state of affairs. Attention to the needs, wishes and expectations of these others also illustrated their crucial significance as, additionally, 'significant audiences for performance in an issue' with the power to reward or punish by recognition or rejection.

This aspect of the significance of members of their community became most evident in periods of crisis, when delays and setbacks led to high levels of anxiety about the consequences of failing to meet the others' expectations. Our clients did not deliberatively seek self-advancement, but their values about image with their key audiences became pressing 'defined problems' for them, in circumstances of threat. This was most particularly so for one of them, clearly distressed by any threat to his position as a leader in the black community. In terms of the construction of significant others, his value about this position also, therefore, defined the significance of 'those who can undermine my standing with significant audiences'.

So it was that there were several actors who sought to become involved in the project about whom he expressed a level of anxiety and hostility which was initially difficult to understand in terms of the task of mobilizing support for their efforts. That is, until it became clear that these others were perceived as potential rivals for the trust and respect of his key audiences, whom he saw as able, and willing, to undermine his position with the latter.

Our clients' concerns about self and social image were also manifest, in a somewhat different way, in terms of their broad attention to others' evaluation of themselves. Thus, for example, two subsets of the actors defined as significant as 'those who have the power to help or hinder the attainment of preferred outcomes' were clearly defined as allies or opponents; in their language, those who 'are 100 per cent with us' or 'are trying to nullify what we are doing'. These were the people who, on the one hand, had shown themselves fully committed to supporting our clients, or, on the other, were seen as attempting to sabotage their efforts.

This definition of allies and opponents can readily be accounted for in terms of the power politics of the task at hand. Yet our understanding would be importantly incomplete without further attention to the role of their self cognitions and values in constructing the others' meaning and significance, in particular their need to be seen as individuals of competence, significance and worth.

These persons began with little other than their own resources of energy and determination. They were conscious of their relative powerlessness, certainly at the outset of the project. They felt isolated and ignored in their own group. As they described the others they encountered it became clear that crucial constructs in the frameworks they brought to bear in considering and evaluating the others were those which assessed the others' evaluation of their own worth and competence — whether, for example, they 'listen to us', or 'take us seriously' or 'respect us'. It became clear that those 'who are 100 per cent with us' were defined in this way not only because, as they declared, 'they really care about the kids', but also because they saw our clients as worthwhile, competent people with a central role in the prosecution of any shared attempt to help the youngsters. In short, their allies were people seen to share their values, and *to value them*. In contrast, those 'who are trying to nullify what we are doing' were described as having no real interest in the 'kids' although they might have some self-serving reason for being involved; as trying to prevent them from having any influence either within their own group or elsewhere; and, crucially, as *rejecting* their worth and competence.

In some cases, those initially construed as allies came, after a time, to be defined as opponents. In this process it was our clients' conclusions about the others' negative evaluations of themselves which appeared to be the central 'pivot' in the reconstruction. This then allowed a reinterpretation of history, with assertions such as 'We realise now that he was never really interested in the kids. He was only in it for himself.'

Turner's (1968) distinction between 'task-directed' and 'identity-directed' interactions is relevant here. The latter are those in which attention is '...primarily directed by each member's concern about how others feel toward him...validation of a particular self-conception becomes the guiding consideration'. Turner points out how what begins as a task-directed interaction can shift into the other kind when a person:

> ... perceives a discrepancy between self image and self-conception which threatens to call into question his self-conception. *We assume that self-consciousness is like a lens that brings the stimuli from the passing social situation into focus, so that they become recognizable as self-imagery.* (my emphasis)

In this case also, so-called task relationships to do with helping unemployed kids became relationships in which others' affirmation or denial of important aspects of our clients' self-concepts became of crucial importance. Their values about themselves were indeed an ever-present 'lens' for construing the attitudes and actions of others with respect to themselves. This had profound implications for some of their relationships, involving cycles of interpersonal dynamics in which our clients' mistrust and antagonism towards certain others frequently exacerbated the others' own defensive and hostile responses.

More generally, the importance of persons' self and social images in their thinking and acting is, of course, well recognized in social psychology. Thus, for example, Shibutani (1961) has argued that:

> Everyman acts, then, for some kind of audience and it is important to know what this audience is and what kind of expectations are imputed to it... [the person's]... *line of activity depends on the real or anticipated reactions of the other people for whom he is performing.* (my emphasis; see also McCall and Simmons, 1966)

It is also a commonplace that persons care about how others evaluate their own worth and significance, and will generally seek social support for their preferred conceptions of themselves. This is captured, for example, in Cooley's (1902) famous concept of 'the looking glass self', where 'the thing which moves us to pride or shame is not the mere mechanical reflection of ourselves, but an imputed sentiment, the imagined effect of this upon another's mind' (see also Goffman's impression-managing actor, e.g. 1959; Mangham, 1978).

Given this base of existing theory, what was important learning in this case was to see the impact of our clients' self and social image concerns unfold in the day-to-day dynamics of their politics. The world they inhabited was not only far from the aseptic, harmonious picture of working relationships presented by much organization theory but also from the 'rational–instrumental' model of organizational politics we are often presented with, peopled by strong, calculating and relatively autonomous individuals. This was a political world of elation and dejection, of strong loyalties and passionate hostilities. It was a world which our clients often found confusing, stressful and hurtful and one which was a focus of intense cognitive and emotional energy.

Levels of Analysis

I have chosen, in this brief description of some of the findings, to concentrate primarily on aspects of the micro processes of other-definition in this case. However, the project could be examined at a number of different levels. Thus the issue of unemployment among black youngsters raises major sociological questions about, for example, racial discrimination, the nature of the educational experience for young blacks, and so on. The enormity of the structural political, economic and social forces militating against significant change can barely be overstated. This was the framework which our clients sought to understand, and within which they operated in trying to locate points of feasible action in their local community, seeking to use these as a lever to address, in the longer term, such issues as the attitudes of local employers and liaison with local schools.

At yet another level, the project also illustrated facets of the perpetuating formal and informal power structures within the local community. These included, for example, the way in which certain key figures could be found to be significant in a range of different community arenas.

Learning About and Learning For

Returning to the micro political processes at the personal and small group level, it is, of course, relatively easy to use a case to exemplify the more general points one wishes to make. I shall, nonetheless, assert my belief that it would not have been possible to obtain the richness of data that was obtained about the unfolding phenomenological experience of politics of the persons concerned without the action research role of working with them on their issue over a relatively extended period of time. The articulation, for example, of their thinking about their significant others, with its complexities, confusions, anxieties and vulnerabilities, was not primarily to provide data to researchers but in order that this thinking could be then worked on to devise the most appropriate courses of action to take.

Relatedly, the action research involvement was, I believe, crucial to the learning about the interrelationships between 'data about' and 'data for practice'. One aspect of this has to do with judgements about 'what matters' — what matters for the choices people make, the actions they take, what needs to be addressed if processes are to be improved in a way which is helpful. For example, although it was possible to draw out, as suggested above, certain patterns and similarities in the way the research participants categorized their significant others, there were also, on a day-to-day basis, some important differences between them — in their understanding of the mechanisms of power, in the predictions they made about others' likely attitudes and actions in particular circumstnaces. These differences were a source of both creativity and mutual learning, and also conflict (see Jones, 1985, on intersubjectivity in the definition of powerful others). It required us to find methods of facilitating the sharing and negotiation of their mental models and predictions about others in ways which frequently required some form of formal modelling, albeit of a crude kind. In this case the practical implications of individuality had to be addressed; they were not simply a question of a researcher noting the patterns of 'similarity and difference in the data', as for example in the data from a series of interviews with different individuals.

The same applied to the impact of self-cognitions and values in the construction of others. So, for example, it was necessary on occasions to address and redress the potentially destructive consequences of 'self as the central figure' (Heider, 1958) getting in the way of an accurate interpretation of others' perspectives and of the circumspection which was frequently necessary to their political survival.

I am not, of course, suggesting that these sorts of judgements about significance cannot be made through more traditional methods of research. I am, however, suggesting that there is a particular contact with the practical implications of data which comes from being involved in working through those implications, for choice, for action, for the most effective means of achieving preferred ends.

Because of this, an action research role also confronts a researcher most directly with the points at which her own theoretical 'hobby-horses' clash with what is significant or useful to the research participants. To take one small example from this project, there was a particular aspect of their construction of significant others to do with the details of their predictive thinking about the others about which I felt I needed more data. I suggested that we explore this arena in more depth. However, it soon became apparent that while they were willing to be helpful, beyond a certain point I was not touching on an issue that was significant to them. I therefore abandoned this attempt, not because I could not have pursued it, drawing upon their goodwill and trust, but because I would not have believed in the quality of the data I was getting.

Similarly I learned about what methods were or were not helpful in this case for the explicit analysis of the politics of the issue. Again there was a confrontation with my own theoretical ideas. While certain formal but relatively crude methods for political analysis were found to be useful (and were repeatedly asked for by the clients on this basis), the costs of time and energy in constructing the more detailed and sophisticated models I wanted to experiment with were seen by them to outweigh the benefits for analysis. Another prescription had to be abandoned, at least in this case.

The outcome of working with the participants, for example on their politics, was, of course, that their thinking and action was likely to have been different from that which would have occurred without the intervention. I also believe that the reflection and analysis involved importantly contributed to our clients' eventual success in establishing a training workshop. Yet the impact of the involvement was precisely a central focus of the research learning, balanced with those judgements about the relationship between the processes and outcomes of intervention, the inherent personalities and perspectives of those concerned and the structures within which they operated.

Beginning and Ends

One of the 'inconveniences' of action research is that its pace, progress and outcomes are not as easily controllable by a researcher as some other forms of research. Relationships are established and, as in most relationships, unanticipated demands may be made in response to particular events suddenly confronting the research participants. The development of relationships may mean that exit at the point when research needs have been fulfilled may not always be easy. On the other hand, there may be an undesired 'accelerated' exit if the research does not meet expectations about its relevance and usefulness.

The nature of an extended involvement with a small number of people or a single organization can also raise issues of scale and therefore generalizability. For example, on what basis can I claim that the findings from the case just described have any wider applicability? This issue is shared by all intensive, longitudinal approaches to research, and taking each research setting individually there must, of course, be limits to claims for generalizability. Nonetheless generalizations can be developed through qualitative research methods, not only by reference to the existing research canon within the literature but most particularly through incremental processes of comparison across a range of different settings. As Diesing (1972) suggests, 'The basic solution is to move from the particular to the general in small steps rather than one grand jump.'

Such an approach must be central to the development of theory through intensive and extended research methods approach. I can compare, for example, the project just described, another with the three directors of a small building company and various projects over several years within a large publishing company, here concerned with strategy development behind major, multimillion pound products. Here we can point to a number of key differences, including the size and nature of the business, the numbers of persons directly involved and the skills and experience of those persons. It is through working within a range of setting in this way that it is possible both to test the robustness for understanding and acting of various concepts and ideas for practice, and to elaborate the empirical contingencies surrounding the application of those concepts.

Thus, to take some of the themes about the politics of problem-solving touched on in this chapter, it has been consistently useful — that is, theory has 'earned its living' as a basis for understanding and action — to try and understand the nature and impact of any personal stakes of self and social image which may underlie the 'legitimate' problems people present. It has been consistently useful to explore the roles and significance of the significant actors in the power politics of implementation (e.g. Jones, 1986), and to develop a repertoire of 'categories of significance' for discussion and use with research participants. Yet there are differences which emerge in every setting, for example from the experience and skills of those concerned, their sensitivity to and experience of politics (including their relative autonomy from the evaluations of others), the degree of conflict between the participants, and the internal/external focus of the issues being addressed. Indeed, building in the facility to take account of individuality has been a central feature of the developments in problem-solving method, as well as the basis for judgements about the conceptual distinctions between, or within, particular phenomena.

Each setting also brings new learning. Thus, for example, in the building firm mentioned earlier, addressing the presenting problem of a strategy to increase turnover and profitability yet again uncovered major issues surrounding the politics of the relationship between the three main participants. There were some fundamental conflicts of values about lifestyles; a central question surrounded the role of the founder of the company and the conflict between his espoused commitment to sharing power and his barely self-acknowledged reluctance to cede control; there were deep, previously repressed resentments about apparent differences of input, commitment and style. The outcome in this case was not only a business plan for expansion but also a resignation of one of the team and a restructuring of the firm. I confirmed some existing ideas about the complexities, confusions and passions surrounding the politics of persons addressing complex, personally significant problems and also extended my understanding of the processes of 'team destruction' — its precedents, its value in certain circumstances as well as its dilemmas, and its aftermath in business and personal/social terms for those involved.

The work in the publishing company has involved confirmation and extension of theory about, for example, managing problem-solving processes in large groups, seeking to introduce more participative modes of strategy formulation involving a number of hierarchical levels, and the impact of changes at the top level on the likely success of such efforts.

Thus theory development through extended action research involvements rarely has the 'completeness', neatness, tidiness of the kind of research project which involves, for example, a series of one-off interviews with a number of managers, after which a researcher can look at the mass of data, carefully make her conceptual categories, find the points of similarity and difference and then, with appropriate obeisance to the 'need for further research', move onto some new topic that can be addressed in the same self-contained way. Theory development though extended action research involvements is a gradual, incremental process. Identifying points of closure, the sense that one 'knows enough' in a particular arena, is likely to come, if it does, after a lengthy accumulation of evidence of different kinds, and may indeed be difficult to articulate in a clear-cut fashion based on the representativeness of one's sample.

CONCLUSION

To take this last point, however, the thrust of this chapter has been to present a rationale for an action research methodology which suggests that such 'disadvantages' (if they are seen as such) as the lack of tidiness in theory development are outweighed by the depth and nature of the learning which can be acquired through action research. The impetus for writing was that much of the advocacy of action research has tended to be couched in general terms regarding the importance of relating research to practical social problems. Significant as this message is, I have additionally sought to ground action research within some key theoretical and practical issues raised by a qualitative approach to research.

Committed as I am to action research in relation to my own research interests, I do not want to argue that an action research mode is appropriate for all research topics and all circumstances. For example, we can envisage situations where the initial contract about the research cannot be phrased, however loosely, in terms of working together on the issue, particularly to powerful people who would jib at any implication that their own management activities needed 'improving'. A set of more traditional qualitative interviews, with a wide range of respondents, can provide a useful starting point to developing ideas about the parameters of a research arena which can then feed into the design of a more intensive and longitudinal action research involvement.

However, I do believe that action research is more often appropriate and more often possible (even with the powerful and highly skilled) than some researchers would allow. Above all, I suggest that an action research philosophy raises crucial questions which any researcher should consider who wishes to penetrate the social and political complexity by which organizational life is characterized. It brings to the forefront the key issue of the link between theory and practice, and the need to ground and test ideas for practice within that most exacting of testing grounds, organizational life as it is actually experienced and enacted by its members. It suggests the need for a research role which relies on more than comforting assumptions about 'developing rapport'. It underlines the possibilities of multiple, competing perspectives on how organizations are and might be. These issues seem to me to touch the very heart of organization research.

Organization Analysis and Development
Edited by I. L. Mangham
© John Wiley & Sons Ltd.

Analysing the Production of Meeting Talk:
'Multiple Solicits' and their Treatment*

CHAPTER 3   *Roger Peskett*

Assemblies under names such as meetings, conferences, classes, workshops or seminars may occur in the course of an organization's work. These kinds of setting share a degree of 'institutionalization'. For instance, some pre-arrangement of the encounter is usually implied, in contrast, for example, to a chance meeting between two persons passing in a corridor. There will also generally be some degree of prespecification of what is to occur in the interaction: a meeting may have an agenda and a school class will usually have a predetermined field of subject-matter which may be discussed as part of the lesson. Like all social actors, participants in such settings face identifiable problems at the interactional level. Some such problems may arise from the fact that more than two persons are present in the setting. For instance, an interactional problem for participants in a meeting might be: how do you raise an issue if your contribution has not been sought or solicited by someone else present? Or, what design of action should you employ in getting someone to volunteer to do some particular task? Or, how might you get a meeting started without using instructions or directives? Here, I will be seeking to examine how participants in meetings address a particular sort of problem in the design of the actions they produce, and at the same time how the actions of different participants coordinate to generate sequences of action.

I shall be examining a number of instances of a type of action sequence which frequently occurs in meetings and other settings where a number of interactants are present together. For the purposes of describing the analysis, transcripts of data extracts will be presented. A guide to the transcription conventions used is provided at the end of the chapter. This method of transcription is employed generally by researchers in what has come to be known as *conversation analysis* or CA, a useful review of which is to be found in Levinson (1983, Chapter 6).

*I am grateful to Tony Wootton, John Heritage and other members of the British Sociological Association Sociology of Language Study Group for their comments on earlier versions of some of the work presented here.

I shall begin by considering the following data, which are from a recording of a meeting of a self-help group at which nine people are present.

Extract 1 (SHG:1:A)

1	Colin:	Well (.) is anybody er (1.2) *tek*kin' it then
2		(2.0)
3	?:	(hh)
4	Dave:	heheh
5		(1.8)
6	Colin:	Does anybody (.) *want* to open t'meetin'
7	Bill:	Wha' ya *open*in' wi' anyway
8		(3.0)
9	Colin:	Aah ya mean *theme*
10	Bill:	Mm
11		(1.0)
12	Colin:	wella tellya wha' I tho' we' do 's we'd get
13		somebody t' read fir (.) this (0.7) First Things First
14		(2.0)
15	Malcolm:	'n how long d'z it go *on* for
16		(0.8)
17	Colin:	'bout one full pa:ge=
18	?:	=('bout five minutes)
19	Bill:	Go on (I'll)=
20	Colin:	= ⌈See First Things First its all right init
21	?:	⌊( )
22	Bill:	Mm
23	Robert:	*I*'ll read i' out if ya like
24	?:	( )
25	Colin	Eh
26	Robert:	I'll read i' out ifya like
27	Colin:	*Will* ya. Anybody else wanto open t'meeting

An initial reason for focusing on this sequence was an interest in ways in which a meeting could get under way — how whatever joint business that was to be attended to could begin in a setting and how a state of joint attentiveness was created (see Atkinson and Drew, 1979; Turner, 1972; and Atkinson, Cuff and Lee, 1978, for work on 'beginnings' in different settings). It becomes clear from this sequence that such a beginning may occupy an extended sequence of interaction, in spite of the availability of standard formulae such as 'I declare the meeting open'. Line 1 of the sequence appears to involve some kind of attempt to begin the meeting, but the joint business does not appear to be fully under way even by line 27. What then is happening in the course of the sequence?

Considering line 1 first, the 'it' in Colin's utterance refers to the meeting itself. It appears that Colin's utterance here might be asking about what prearrangement has been made about who is to open the meeting, or alternatively Colin might be asking who now is prepared to take the meeting, offering the opportunity to 'any' of those present.

Looking at how the utterance is followed up shows us the analysis which participants in the setting make of what Colin is doing. We see that a two-second gap, laughter from Dave and then another gap follow Colin's turn at line 1. The utterance has been followed by non-response. Colin reformulates what he is saying at line 6, with 'Does anybody (.) *want* to open t'meetin''. By reformulating what he had said, Colin addresses problems which coparticipants may have had in interpreting his prior utterance. That is, Colin can be heard to treat coparticipants' hearings of his prior solicit as having led to non-response and laughter, and thus as exhibiting misunderstandings of his original intentions.

Schegloff and Sacks (1973) have described the structure of what they call 'adjacency pairs' in conversation. These are pairs of action the first of which makes the second expectable or 'conditionally relevant'. For example, when a question is asked, an answer becomes expectable as a next turn. However, it is important to see that something other than the answer to the question may actually come next. For instance, there may be a gap or non-response; or quite properly there may be an 'insertion sequence' (Schegloff, 1972) such as the following (from Levinson, 1983):

A: May I have a bottle of Mich?
B: Are you twenty-one?
A: No
B: No

In this instance, another question–answer pair is inserted or embedded within the question–answer pair initiated by A. Other examples of types of adjacency pair are summons–answer, or request–granting/rejection sequences.

Colin's utterance at line 6 makes certain kinds of response conditionally relevant. Most clearly, it creates a relevance for an *offer* to perform the specified task — the task of opening the meeting. The set of potential doers of such an offer is proposed by Colin as 'anybody'. C's turn seeks to solicit something, and proposes a multiple set of potential respondents, or doers of what is solicited.

There are a number of interesting aspects of turns such as these which invite a number of people to do something. Such turns and their treatment by participants in meetings form the topic of this chapter. Before developing the first data extract further, it will be useful to define our ground more clearly.

Although our particular concern here is with interaction in meetings, the phenomenon we are concerned with can, in a formal sense, occur in any interaction involving three or more coparticipants. In such 'multiparty' interaction, a speaker may address to more than one recipient an utterance soliciting some next action which is to be produced by one (or more) of those recipients. Solicit turns which thus address multiple potential respondents will here be called 'multiple solicits'. Multiple solicits are first parts of adjacency pairs, but they project the possibility of the second part coming from any of a number of recipients. They produce what will here be called an environment of 'multiple respondency'.

Data extracts 2 and 3 below provide further examples.

Extract 2 (SWT:1)
          ((B has explained that there are two items on the agenda))
     A: ⌈ A:w
     B: ⌊ So d'z anyb'dy 'av 'any (.) pref'rence for order (.) in which we deal
                 wi ⌈ th'em ⌉
     C: ⌊ hh: : :⌋

In extract 2, B's utterance is formed as being addressed to 'anybody'. B is asking if coparticipants in a meeting which is in progress have any preference for the order in which the items of the meeting's agenda are dealt with. His utterance makes relevant a next action from 'any' of the multiple recipients addressed: it solicits a response without specifying from which of a number of recipients that response is to come. Kinds of response made relevant by B's solicit in extract 2 might include, for example, a proposal by one of the recipients of an order in which to deal with the business items or a stating by a recipient that s/he has no preference.

Extract 3 was recorded in a meeting in which participants deliver fairly lengthy statements or 'stories' in turn.

Extract 3 (SHG:2:00)
          (0.9)
     C: Righ' thanks Bill
          (0.8)
     C: 'th anybody that 'asn't *spo*ken wan'to come in

In extract 3, C first thanks Bill for his contribution to the meeting which has just been completed. He then invites any number of coparticipants to 'come in' (i.e. to speak or contribute next). The set of such potential respondents to C's solicit is characterized by C as 'anybody that 'asn't spoken'. Some of those present *have* spoken, so the set of recipients to whom C's invitation to speak is addressed constitutes a subset of those copresent with C.

An alternative way of soliciting the 'coming in' of a next interactant would have been to specify some particular candidate from among the participants in the meeting and to solicit a response from that candidate. C, the speaker in extract 3, did in fact use a turn of this sort — a one-to-one solicit — a number of times in the course of the same meeting:

Extract 4 (SHG:2:A:58)
     C: F-Fred do you wanna-
     F: Er eh yeah hh
     F: I'm F- *Fred*. . . .

Extract 5 (SHG:2:B:24)
    C: Bill do you wanna come in now please=
    B: =Yeah. . . .

Meeting talk provides a framework in which many persons may be ratified participants (on which see Goffman, 1981) in whatever joint business is going on, and therefore it provides an environment in which multiple solicit turns can become routine occurrences. Yet as we shall see from a number of data extracts, the circumstances they create become problematic for coparticipants in the setting in ways in which one-to-one solicits are not.

I now return to data extract 1 to examine in detail how C's multiple solicit turn was treated. I have already considered what occurs up to line 6. While Colin's utterance at line 6 is formulated as seeking offers, the talk which follows immediately after it is not such an offer: Bill's 'wha' ya *open*in' wi' anyway' is a question about what is involved in the task which Colin has referred to. In that it preserves the relevance of subsequent offers being produced in response to Colin's solicit turn, Bill's question can be characterized as an insertion sequence between Colin's solicit and a potential response to it.

After the turns at lines 9 and 10 in which Colin seeks and gets confirmation of what Bill is asking, at lines 12 and 13 Colin answers Bill's question. Interestingly, this answer refers to 'we' getting 'somebody' to do the reading, and thereby to open the meeting ('First Things First' is the title of a passage from a book). A hearing of this is that 'we' is supposed to include Bill (who is one of the more established members of the group) while the 'somebody' is intended to exclude him: in other words, 'we' are going to get one of 'them' to do this reading. By means of this hearing, Bill is excluded as a possible candidate to open the meeting without that being explicitly stated by Colin.

After two seconds (line 14), another participant, Malcolm, makes the enquiry, "n how long d'z it go *on* for', which is answered by Colin and someone else. Like Bill's earlier enquiry, this preserves the continuing relevance of a response to Colin's multiple solicit: the project of finding someone to take the meeting is still in the air.

Eventually, at line 23, Robert does an offer, '*I*'ll read i' out if ya like'. The construction of this offer proposes a certain position on whose interests are being served by Robert performing the task. Colin's original turn sought as a performer of the task someone who 'wanted' to do it. Robert's eventual offer proposes that Robert performing that task himself might rather be in accord with what *Colin* might like ('if ya like').

The design of Robert's response to the solicit can also be examined for what it proposes about the period following the solicit. This period has provided interactional positions in which recipients could have taken up the solicit. Robert is putting himself forward as someone willing to perform the task to help out Colin rather than to serve his own wants. Robert's response can thus be heard to propose that recipients' non-responses in that period indicate that they are taking a position of *declining* to take up the offered opportunity: if anyone else had wanted to take up the opportunity, they would have done. Robert's analysis contrasts with an analysis that there may be recipients who want to perform the task but are *withholding* taking up the opportunity. These alternative analyses of non-response will be illustrated further later in the chapter.

Examining the data illustrates how a speaker who is taking up a multiple solicit can propose an analysis of the character of a prior non-response and thereby make the taking up accountable: Robert's taking up becomes a favour to help the meeting along, rather than a claim to do something which others want to do. To see how participants' actions structure what is happening, we do not need to make an appeal to what participants' wants or psychological states are independently of what is in the data.

We have seen some of the ways in which participants' action designs seek solutions to the problem that an environment of multiple respondency has been created in which people are not coming forward with responses. We have also examined how a response can be produced which is sensitive to the environment into which it emerges — an environment in which a number of participants have been invited to do something.

The meeting from which data extract 1 is drawn continues as follows:

Extract 6 (SHG:1:B)
```
27   Colin:     Willya. Anybody else wanto open t'meeting
28              (1.5)
29   Bill:      ((coughs))
30              (1.5)
31   Colin:     Just makes a change you know (.) if we er (.)
32   Bill:      What with (.) jus- just a preamble init
33              (2.0)
34   Colin:     Yeah I'll get the (  )
35   Bill:                       (what) about the Serenity Prayer as well
36              (0.8)
37   Colin:     No just (go over that)
38   Malcolm:              (  ) finish off wi' that Bill
39   Bill:      Yeah
40   Colin:     Just welcome t'meeting and have a moment's silence (.)
41   Bill:                                          Yeah
42   Colin:     An' then say that 'n (2.0) I'm sorry eh (1.2) be a bit
43              erm (1.0)  (  )
44   Malcolm:              Disorganised
45   ?:         heheheh
```

This second sequence from the meeting also shows how interaction proceeds in circumstances where there is a failure to get a response to a multiple solicit turn. We shall examine how subsequent actions deal with those circumstances.

Colin's '*Will*ya' at line 27 acknowledges Robert's offer to do the reading which we have already considered. Colin then says 'Anybody else wanto open t'meeting'. First of all, this may seem odd because Colin has already asked for anybody to open the meeting in the previous extract, a task which was supposed to involve doing a reading which Robert has just offered to do. And here is Colin looking for someone *else* to open the meeting. However, it appears from what happens later in the sequence that opening the meeting is to involve not just this reading but also certain other activities. That Colin should now seek another person to perform certain tasks in opening the meeting may be tied up with the fact that Robert is a newcomer to the group and therefore cannot be entrusted with the whole task — but this need not concern us here.

Colin's utterance is constructed as offering an opportunity to 'anybody else' who *wants* to take it up. It thus makes relevant a 'taking-up' of that opportunity by one of a number of recipients. First, we can consider how Colin's turn at line 31 exhibits an analysis of the gap which precedes it.

Colin's initial solicit at line 27 is followed by non-response. An opportunity is being offered to recipients, but none of them are taking it up. Colin follows up this period of non-response with 'Just makes a change you know (.) if we er (.)'. Although this utterance is done as incomplete, the 'change' to which Colin refers can be heard to concern a change from whatever previously used procedure might have been employed to select a person to open the meeting. Colin holds the office of secretary of the group. It may well be that Colin usually opens the meeting himself, or that someone is selected from a restricted group of established members, or perhaps some other procedure might be used.

By following up his initial solicit in the way that he does, Colin can be heard to propose an analysis of the intervening non-response as indicative of a problem which recipients are having in dealing with the prior solicit. In saying, 'Just makes a change', Colin is minimizing the issue of who specifically performs the task. To propose yourself as the doer of the task is to claim an opportunity which others might want. Colin's follow-up utterance attempts a solution to this problem by taking the heat out of the issue of who should perform the task, and addresses the problem that in not responding recipients may be withholding responses.

Before considering Bill's turn at line 32, I shall examine what happens in subsequent actions. At line 35, Bill asks, '(what) about the Serenity Prayer as well'. Colin's response at line 37 to this second question is interesting in that Colin appears to be taking it that Bill is going to do the opening of the meeting. Malcolm also responds, saying 'finish *off* wi' that Bill'. (The Serenity Prayer routinely comes at the *end* of meetings in the self-help organization in which this recording was made.) By line 40, Colin is even more clearly instructing Bill about the task of opening the meeting which it is being taken that he will perform. We can, then, see that in these ways Bill's questions are treated as indicating his willingness to open the meeting.

Looking back to Bill's turn at line 32, he says, 'What with (.) jus- just a *pre*amble init'. In this turn, he shows himself to be checking what he already supposes to be the case. One reason for checking what you already suppose to be the case would be that you want to make use of your knowledge for the purpose of doing some activity. For example, before opening the meeting you might want to check that your knowledge of the procedure is correct; the fact that you might want to open the meeting accounts for your asking of the question. It is thus that Colin can subsequently treat Bill as being prepared to do the opening of the meeting.

If Bill had done an explicit taking-up of Colin's solicit — for instance, by offering or volunteering to open the meeting with words such as 'I'll do it' — he would have been overtly claiming an opportunity to do a task for which others also have been treated as potential candidates. Instead, Bill uses a turn design which can be and is treated as implying an offer to do the task but which avoids 'officially' offering. An outright explicit offer may be seen as a 'dispreferred' action in an environment where many have been given the opportunity to offer (on 'dispreferred' action designs in other contexts see Pomerantz, 1985 and Wootton, 1981).

A further feature of Bill's utterance is that Bill describes the opening of the meeting as involving *just* a preamble. Bill thus belittles what is involved in the task, and thereby belittles the part which he is proposing to play. In this way, Bill constructs the opportunity offered — the opportunity to open the meeting — as an opportunity to play only a minor part in the proceedings, and thus as an opportunity which others would not want.

I have above considered one particular stretch of interaction in fairly close detail. Merely the length of the two extracts 1 and 6 is indicative of the problematic nature of environments of multiple respondency for participants in the meeting. It might be argued that in this and other cases where participants are failing to respond to multiple solicit turns it is simply that participants do not want to take up the opportunity: an explanation in terms of the motivation of participants might be proposed. I have not appealed to such an account above, but have seen participants' wants and mental orientations or states as analytically pertinent only insofar as the social actors involved themselves make reference or appeal to them in the design of their actions, for instance by implicitly proposing that others do not want to take up some offered opportunity. Examining various data showed that, whatever participants' psychological orientations might be supposed to be, turns which offer some opportunity to multiple recipients are almost always followed by something other than a take-up or a declining of the offer in the next position in the interaction sequence. Other kinds of interactional object are occurring in next position, including gaps, pauses and 'inserted' talk. In the rest of this chapter, I shall broaden the discussion to consider general features underlying the ways in which participation opportunities are, one might say, 'negotiated' in meeting talk where multiple respondency occurs.

What I have termed 'multiple solicits' can of course occur in various different kinds of sequence. In extracts 1, 2, 3 and 6, they occurred in what may be called an 'openings' environment — where a meeting was being started or a discussion got under way. In other instances, a 'closing' of some kind is occurring. Thus, in extract 7, 'any questions' are sought as a way of clearing up a discussion which has been going on:

Extract 7 (BM:2:1:37)
```
        G:      Right
                (1.0)
        G:      So if anyone's got any questions on eh
                (4)
```

In extract 8, a break in a discussion is explicitly proposed:

Extract 8 (BM:1:2:29)
```
        B:      Do you think we could sort of break this great discussion now and have
                some coffee (actu'lly)
```

In extract 9, as in extracts 1 and 6, someone is sought to perform some task:

Extract 9 (BM:2:1:22)
```
        A:      ....there's this working party 'n so we need someone from here who
                would be prepared to be our (1.0) member on that
                (1.2) eh on that working party
```

In the course of a discussion, opinions may be sought from among a group of coparticipants (extracts 10 and 11):

Extract 10 (BM:1:1:39)
```
        C:      So that I think we ought to look for some sort of an organizational type
                mm of a first year (.)
        C:      Donno whether anybody else shares that feeling
                Probably not
```

Extract 11 (BM:1:4:09–11)
```
        B:      Do we accept (.) on the B 2 outline as presented=
        B:      =the outline (I think) (    )
```

Where a speaker uses a multiple solicit turn to solicit something which is to be of value to the speaker rather than recipients, a recipient may properly respond immediately. In extract 12, D seeks information about Michael's whereabouts:

Extract 12 (FN:1:86)
```
                ((D approaches three people who are seated))
        D:      Has anybody seen Michael this morning?
        A:      No I 'aven't
```

```
        ((D turns round as if leaving))
D:      Has anybody seen Michael?
B:      No I 'aven't
```

But to jump in immediately with a response when recipients are being offered an opportunity as being of potential value to them in some way appears inappropriate. A participant in a meeting told me as an anecdote that someone had asked if anyone had any questions to ask; someone else had responded immediately by saying 'Certainly not!' Even though this speaker was declining the opportunity to ask a question, her immediate claim over the interactional space following the soliciting of questions seems 'pushy' or insensitive in the setting of an adult meeting. In contrast, the occurrence of immediate and sometimes simultaneous claims by a number of interactants to take up an opportunity offered to them is probably common in adult–child interaction, in which an object or an opportunity offered to two or more children would paradigmatically be responded to with a chorus of 'Me! Me! Me!'

Jules Henry (1966) noted the following observations:

> The observer is just entering her fifth-grade classroom for the observation period. The teacher says, 'Which one of you nice, polite boys would like to take (the observer's) coat and hang it up?' From the waving hands, it would seem that all would like to claim the title. The teacher chooses one child, who takes the observer's coat. The teacher says, 'Now, children, who will tell (the observer) what we have been doing?'... The usual forest of hands appears, and a girl is chosen to tell.... (Henry, 1966)

Thus, in the classroom, the problem of multiple potential claims to be the one to perform a task can be resolved by the raising of hands by potential respondents to indicate their position and the selection of one of these respondents by the teacher. This solution is not usually part of the repertoire of meeting talk.

My own data suggest that participants are dealing with non-response in environments of multiple respondency by making use of two principal constructions of coparticipants' positions. What I mean by this will become clear below. Consider the two following extracts 13 and 14, which provide examples of gaps (NR = non-response) occurring in next position following multiple solicit turns (S).

```
Extract 13 (BM:2:3:40)
                (1.0)
       Barry:   So we've finished with ( ) are we getting on to the ( )
                (1.2)
S      Barry:   Any other items
NR              (3.0)
→      Barry:   Wa ( ) if there's no other ⌈ items
       Keith:                              ⌊ aw
```

Extract 14 (BM:2:1:43)

	Martin:	I've said all that I need to say
		(1.4)
S	Barry:	Right is ther' any (.) further
NR		(0.8)
S	Barry:	Anything further on that
NR		(0.9)
→	Barry:	Um we come to any (.) other (.) business

What participants make of such gaps can be examined by looking to subsequent turns and actions for the analysis which they propose of them. In extracts 13 and 14, Barry's turns (→) subsequent to recipients' non-response move on to next business items in the meeting. These turns are produced following periods which are thus constructed by Barry as spaces in which recipients could have taken up the opportunity to put forward 'other items' or 'anything further' respectively, but did not. Such spaces are here called 'take-up spaces'. In the sense that any of a number of people could appropriately produce the second part of the adjacency pair which the solicit initiates, these silences or take-up spaces following multiple solicits 'belong' to a number of cointeractants. Anyone who has attended meetings will appreciate some of the special problems which such an interactional environment can involve. For example, suppose that you are chairing a meeting and ask (as in extract 2 quoted earlier) if anyone has any preference for the order in which items of the agenda should be dealt with. If your question is then followed by a pause, do you make a further attempt to solicit a response or do you take the gap as indicating that no-one minds what order is adopted and proceed accordingly? In other words, do you take coparticipants' silence as implying that they don't have a preference?

In extracts 13 and 14 above, by moving on to next business, Barry treats the recipients of his solicit as having indicated through their silence that they have a particular position *vis-à-vis* the solicit — they don't have items to raise. Thus we see that, following a multiple solicit, non-response is being taken as '*position-implicative*' — as implying the non-responder's position. Rather than non-response being simply a troublesome feature of interaction in meetings, it is apparent that interactants can make a positive construction out of its occurrence.

It is, however, also evident that hearers often treat takings-up of multiple solicits as delayed or withheld.

Extract 15 (BM:2:1:37)

1 George:	.... both by staff and by (1.2) and by students
2 George:	((Coughs))
3	(2.5)
4 George:	Right
5	(1.0)
6 George:	So if (anyone's) got any questions on eh

```
7                (4)
8 George:       °(   )°
9                (2.5)
10 Barry:       (Item-) any questions (on it)
11               (1.5)
12 Barry:       On to item (.) seven
```

In extract 15, a pause of some length occurs following George's solicit at line 6. Barry's utterance at line 10 starts with what appears to be a moving-on to the next item. If this is what Barry starts doing, he subsequently abandons it. Instead, he produces a renewed soliciting of questions on the previous business by saying, 'any questions (on it)'. In moving on to a next item, Barry would be treating recipients as having no questions to ask about George's report. By renewing the solicit which George had previously made, Barry reveals an analysis of recipients' non-response as indicating that they may have questions to ask but have not yet produced them. In pausing, recipients may thus be treated by others as *withholding* responses to a solicit.

Looking at what happens next in extract 15, there's a pause of 1.5 seconds after which Barry says, 'On to item (.) *seven*'. This talk too can be looked to for the analysis which it proposes of the immediately prior pause. In moving on to the next item of business, Barry can be heard to propose that the immediately prior pause is one in which recipients had an opportunity to propose questions but chose not to. Barry is thereby now treating this prior non-response as 'declining-implicative' with respect to what has been solicited — as implying that recipients are declining. Recipients' non-response is now being taken to indicate that they don't have questions to ask; this then warrants moving on to a next item of business. The two principal constructions identified here are both being made use of in this sequence: first, that recipients may have positive responses to produce but have not yet produced them; and secondly, that in not responding verbally recipeints may be taken as implying that they decline to take up the opportunity.

We have seen how non-response can be constructed by participants as position-implicative or as a withholding of a response. The idea that recipients are withholding responses seems consistent with the notion that participants should not jump in to claim an opportunity which has been offered to others as well. One might even suggest a maxim which prescribed that recipients should delay responding in order to give others an opportunity to do their responses. But the puzzle then arises that if all of the recipients of such a solicit are to follow the rule, and know that everyone else is to follow it too, how can one be supposed to have given others an opportunity to take up a solicit if others too are supposed to be 'withholding' a taking-up of it in order to give *you* an opportunity to take it up? Alone, the maxim produces an interactional problem for which it provides no solution. It proposes a practice of 'withholding' by recipients to provide opportunities for others which it alone cannot allow to be realized. Such a rule does not direct how the interaction should proceed. Participants themselves must resolve the resultant 'impasse' and do so in ways I have discussed in this chapter.

Finally, I want to mention another kind of solution adopted in environments of multiple respondency. I noted earlier how classroom interaction can involve the teacher selecting a respondent from among a number of pupils. In meeting talk, a person may be 'nominated' by others to take up an opportunity offered instead of having to take it up themselves:

Extract 16 (VHC:0210)
```
    A:      =Anybody wanto dy' wanto raise anything now anyone
                        ((D turns to E, F & G))
            (1.5)
            ((D puts bag on lap))
    A:      Eric=
    E:      =No I don't think so
```

Extract 17 (SHG:2:00)
```
    C:      'th anybody that 'asn't spoken wan'to come in
            (0.6)
    D:      Aretha=
    B:      =Aretha
            (3.8)
    C:      Or you can pa:ss it:s (.) entirely up to you° y'know°
```

In extract 16, A, the producer of the original solicit, follows the 1.5 second gap by inviting a single participant (E) to take up the offered opportunity. In extract 17, B and D, neither of whom produced the solicit turn, both 'nominate' Aretha as someone to 'come in', i.e. to speak next.

The practice of withholding responses favours the possibility that others may nominate you as a candidate to take up an opportunity offered. 'Other-nomination' stands as a type of solution to the interactional environment created by a multiple solicit turn which can usefully be considered in the context of the techniques available for allocating turns at talk in interaction.

In their seminal study of the organization of turn-taking for conversation, Sacks, Schegloff and Jefferson (1974) identify two central techniques by which turns at talk in conversation are allocated. First, a current speaker may select a next speaker, as for example when a speaker addresses a question to another party. Or a party may begin to speak at some point in an interaction to produce some talk which has not been solicited by another party: in other words, a party may 'self-select' when initiating a turn at talk. The environment which has here been described as 'multiple respondency' is a space in which a speaker has in a sense 'allocated' a next turn without specifying which participant is to accomplish that turn. Whoever responds would be producing something which has been solicited by a prior speaker — they would be producing the second part of the adjacency pair initiated by that other speaker. But they would also be 'self-selecting' in that they would be selecting themselves as speakers from among the multiple addressees of the solicit. The solution of 'other-nomination' involves a return to the (less problematic) turn-allocation technique by which one speaker selects another.

The phenomenon of multiple respondency thus merits consideration in any general account of turn-taking in face-to-face interaction. Something which has remained outside the scope of our discussion is a full consideration of the part which non-verbal actions can play in the type of sequence we have examined. For instance, other data show how participants' glances can indicate that they have no response to make. Making such an indication by means of a glance contributes to the resolution of the problem whithout occupying a turn at talk. Or, a participant who produces a multiple solicit turn may select particular recipient(s) as respondents by directing gaze towards those particular respondents.

The analytic approach adopted in this chapter has viewed meeting talk as accomplished by its participants as the interaction unfolds, and has avoided appealing to criteria which are beyond the scope of an empirical analysis of the data at hand. Such an approach reveals interactionally generated mechanisms and techniques which may be potentially very powerful in structuring interactants' participation opportunities, and therefore in determining outcomes in the decision-making processes which form the business of meetings and other assemblies occurring in organizational settings. Tracing the impact of these influences on decision-making has, however, been beyond the scope of this chapter.

TRANSCRIPTION CONVENTIONS

The conventions used in the data extracts for transcribing recordings are similar to those used generally in conversation analysis. The following is a brief guide to the symbols used in this chapter:

[	Points of overlap in speech or action, or speakers beginning utterances simultaneously
( )	Words not clear
° °	Words spoken softly
italics	Emphasis
:	Extension of prior sound
(2)	Pause (in sec)
(.)	Pause under 0.5 sec
hh	Audible outbreaths
heheh	Laughter
=	No gap between turns or units of a turn
–	Cutoff of prior word or sound

Organization Analysis and Development
Edited by I. L. Mangham
© John Wiley & Sons Ltd.

Argument in Organizations

CHAPTER **4**   *Tim Smithin*

INTRODUCTION

This chapter is concerned with the study of argument as a means of persuading others, in particular with the role of argument in contributing to influence and change in organizational life. The ideas put forward are primarily based upon an in-depth study of the practice of argument and debate in different organizational settings but are also motivated by a feeling, and it is no more than a feeling, that there is something about 'having a good case' that makes its pursuit a worthwhile activity. This feeling was captured by Thorndike many years ago in his discussion of argument:

> For certain types of questions at least, there is a certain inherent logic and plausibility in the right choice which makes it more possible to build up a good argument on that side ... (Thorndike, 1931)

Anyone who has had to put forward a case in public, who has seen a cherished argument wither under criticism, whose opponents have taken great delight in 'picking holes' in the arguments, will have some feel for the need for a 'good case'. This is not solely a matter of avoiding personal embarrassment, for in many situations the consequences for the arguer of his case looking ill-considered or fallacious have significant implications for his future ability to persuade others in that setting. In the studies described below most individuals were aware of the importance of 'having a good case' and spent a significant amount of time preparing and rehearsing arguments, for instance one of the major speakers in the parliamentary debate studied was reported to have spent several hours preparing a 20-minute speech. Yet if someone were to cast around for help on this aspect of organizational life he would find very little guidance within the boundaries of most research into organizational behaviour and within the field of argumentation studies he would find a preponderance of texts on logic and reasoning which have only minimal contact with the reality of working life.

Theories of organizational behaviour sometimes give the impression that the act of persuading others by reasoned argument is the last and most naive resort of the skilled organizational politician. This neglect of argument is probably due to the association of traditional argumentation studies with issues of logic, and the linking of human thinking to rules of logic and the identification of human problem-solving with logical manipulation. This neglect is also encouraged by the close links between the definition of argument and of reason, so that argument is often bound up with rationalist and empiricist philosophies and their approaches to founding knowledge, approaches which are themselves open to question in the context of much research into organizational behaviour. Perhaps too the sheer scope of the subject of 'persuading others by reasoned argument' deters investigation, for if we were to follow Cicero's definition of rhetoric as 'speech designed to persuade' then the study could 'reasonably' encompass much of human activity from the rhetoric of poets to the logic of mathematicians, and the art (or science) of persuasion may include both the 'Quod erat demonstrandum' of Euclidean geometry and the wiles of dishonest politicians (Cicero, *De Oratore*). In tackling this subject I had in mind a study of much smaller scope than this, a study of occasions when it is possible to present arguments to others, and where there is some hope that those arguments will be listened to and be influential. Some years ago as a junior member of a team implementing a computer-based information system I was asked to outline to our clients the case for a particular development strategy, one which we thought would not be very popular with them (which is probably why I got the task). During the few short minutes of my presentation a remarkable transformation overtook the meeting. At first there was a polite air of listening to an 'end of agenda' item, but as I gradually presented the case for this option there was a growing interest in the arguments, and nods of agreement soon became an energetic discussion of the proposals. Overcoming my fright, I realized later that here was a source of organizational power which I had somehow accidentally tapped. In the words of Thorndike, there was a something about the case that I presented which made it possible to generate convincing arguments. It is possible to imagine a variety of other explanations for this event: perhaps people were just trying to be kind, perhaps no-one cared what happened and so would accept anything that was put forward. Certainly my persuasive powers did not lie in my political contacts or abilities, nor in the eloquence of my rhetoric; it seemed that I had with this set of arguments in some way captured a commitment to act. There was something here worthy of further study.

I am not proposing that all organizational life can in some Utopian way be ruled by reason alone, or that this is necessarily desirable or possible, or that the argument can be separated from the whole web of influences that make up a complex social event of this kind. But I am proposing that the 'marshalling of arguments' can be a powerful weapon for those involved in persuading others. It is this activity of putting together a case and presenting it to others that this chapter tackles in the light of some recent research. Throughout the chapter I have attempted to describe a theory and ideas which can be of practical use and are within a framework which can make sense of man as both a reasoning and a valuing animal. For I have often felt that many recent theories of organizational life have shied away from a study of arguing man, almost in a belief that reason and argument necessarily fall prey to the political and social whims of powerful actors, but whenever I have been involved in organizational change the gap between reason and value was rarely as clear as this. In other fields too there is a growing interest in studies of argument which are not primarily logic-based, so I am motivated to look at 'arguing man' and the study of argument as a means of persuading others, and so add to our armoury of aids for coping with organizational life (Perelman and Olbrechts-Tyteca, 1969; Reardon, 1981).

SOME EXPECTATIONS OF ARGUMENT

If argument fails then the arguer may well storm out of the meeting and say:

'It was all sewn up before I went in ....'
'We were right but they won't admit it ....'
'He's just totally irrational, he won't listen to reason ....'

Although such reflections are sometimes a way of explaining failure to others and reveal the arguer's concern with his lack of influence (Meltsner, 1979), they also point to expectations that the arguer has about the nature of the event in which he was involved. In argument and debate there is often an expectation that arguers will behave as 'reasonable men'; this implies not only the criteria on which the argument should be decided but also the way in which the debate is to be conducted. 'Reasonableness' implies that the argument be decided by reference to its content and structure alone and that the audience should behave as objective and non-involved participants, 'non-involved' in the sense that participants do not take into account the consequences of the argument for their personal values and beliefs (Rokeach, 1973). In an organizational context this expectation was put most succinctly by Ackoff, who distinguished between the qualities of 'scientific' man and 'ethical–moral' man.

The prevailing concept of objectivity is based on a distinction between ethical–moral man who is believed to be emotional, involved and biased, and scientific man who is believed to be unemotional, uninvolved and unbiased. (Ackoff, 1979)

In the light of a broadly interactionist perspective on the nature of organizational life, which contends that reality is to some extent the product of social interaction and is the viewpoint which informs this chapter (Mangham, 1978), the notion that organizational actors might behave without regard to their personal values in this 'objective' way is distinctly odd, unless of course part of their construction of 'how to argue' contains this idea of objectivity. There is considerable evidence that those involved in situations which are clearly defined as calling for reasoned debate are influenced by this idea of the non-involvement. For example, studies of mock juries (Baldwin and McConville, 1979) suggest that individuals take very seriously the role of unbiased observer and make stringent and explicit efforts to be impartial. In a similar way, senior managers are often anxious to describe themselves as people who take advantage of rational decision-making procedures, and within the realms of decision theory a variety of such rationally based decision calculi exist (Raiffa, 1968; Phillips, 1984) for use by senior managers. A less obvious illustration of the prevalence of a need to be 'rational' is the way in which experts from outside an organization are used. For experts are often cast by the manager (and by themselves) as unbiased observers whose advice, as a consequence of this lack of bias, must be given extra weight (Sims and Smithin, 1982). A description of the psychological effect of the implementation of a new budgeting system within an American governmental agency also echoes this 'rational wish':

> The experience appears to have satisfied a longing to believe that they were proceeding according to the canons of rational methods of calculation. (Wilensky, 1967)

In each of the research settings on which this chapter is based the influence of this rationalist wish was clearly evident. It is not within the scope of this chapter to consider the influence of rationalism as a cultural theme on western thinking (Holton, 1973; Heidegger, 1977), yet it is clear that where analysis of argumentation is considered as part of an organizational study this desire to be rational, whatever it means, lurks in the background even if only as a way of legitimizing decisions taken. Frequently the analysis of argument is confined to the examination of arguments as logical entities even in an organizational context (Mitroff, 1984), and many argumentation texts urge potential managers to examine arguments for the logical connections between the statements, suggesting that errors in argument arise from logical errors and common fallacies in the use of syllogisms (Bell and Staines, 1979; Kirwan, 1978; Geach, 1976). The lack of persuasive force of an argument is attributed to logical inadequacies of this sort rather than to any other cause. The recent growth in the use of computer-based decision support systems and expert systems is the most modern manifestation of this rational wish. In these systems the arguments of experts, such as an engineering consultant or market advisor, are encoded as primarily logic-based arguments, and the inferences made and new knowledge developed through the application of a logical calculus. Whilst to the user such systems appear to handle more qualitative and judgemental aspects of a decision-maker's work, their internal rules are entirely logic-based (Smithin and Eden, 1985; Duda and Gaschnig, 1981). The examples above are intended to illustrate the notion of a 'rationalist wish' which runs through much of our thinking about argument and decision-making. It is not a well-defined philosophical position but a theme which permeates our culture and provides a setting against which arguments proceed (Abrahams, 1968; Goodwin and Wenzel, 1979). It is important therefore to examine the source of attraction of this theme in more detail, to look at the compulsive appeal of rationality.

THE APPEALS OF RATIONAL ARGUMENT

Rational decision-making has frequently been described as a prescription of how decisions ought to be made rather an account of how they are actually made. There is similarly a moral element to the appeal of rational argument — this is how arguments should be conducted and decided — and this morality is echoed in the statements quoted earlier from those who had been involved in agrument; it is the 'summons of a civilized dialogue'. A 'civilized' man must argue in a particular way, and qualities are demanded in him of candour, patience, emotional coldness, self-cotrol and detachment. Scientists are well known for this sort of thing:

> The scientific man has above all things to strive for self-elimination in his judgements, to provide an agrument which is as true for each individual mind as for his own. (Pearson, 1937)

This paradoxically is the rhetorical appeal of rationality. For here the persuasive power lies in the rhetorical device of identification, of the association between moral and good behaviour and a particular way of arguing (Burke, 1950). It is also an assertion about the nature of knowledge. What is to count as true knowledge is defined in a particular way, so that pre-scientific, or non-scientific knowledge is inferior to knowledge gained through the process of rational inquiry. Similarly, arguments which have a basis in personal experience have less validity than properly rational arguments. It is only necessary to observe, or feel, the emotions aroused when someone is accused of being irrational in the course of an argument to realize the social power that this appeal of rational argument carries. The 'merely subjective' (note the merely) has apparently no place in the ontology of rational thought (Ayer, 1936; Koyre, 1965).

The rational wish is also a quest for a certain kind of knowledge and seems to offer the self-same fruits of endeavour that have lured many into lifelong work, the bait of sure and certain knowledge. A quest for knowledge which rests on certain foundations, for knowledge which is as secure as numbers (Roszak, 1972). This has been described as the Euclid myth, for 'starting from self-evident truths, and proceeding by rigorous proof, Euclid arrives at knowledge which is certain, objective and eternal'. Similarly, the philosopher Bertrand Russell described his motivation to work on mathematics and logic as a need for certainty: 'I wanted certainty in the kind of way in which people want religious faith' (Davis and Hersh, 1981). The management of complex organizations may be more prosaic than the realms of *Principia Mathematica*, but even here the appeal of techniques and methods and above all facts which can in some way make policies and strategies more certain is an expression of this appeal of rationality; for example, a study of managerial decision-making showed that managers were prepared to seek out rational decision-making methods, and prepared to change their views when logical inconsistencies were pointed out (Dickson, 1981).

This emphasis on the appeal of rationality especially in the context of argument should not be taken as a proposition in favour of rationalism or even of scientifically based empiricism — after all, whilst we may aim to ultimately secure our knowledge the evidence of success to date from Plato onwards is rather thin, and in working life in organizations it is clear that rational argument is not the empirically dominant mechanism of debate. The analysis of argument necessarily faces what has been called the paradox of psychological logic: how do we account for our conceptions of rationality, reason and logic within an environment in which plans for action finally rest upon political and value-laden judgements (Stein, 1977).

ARGUMENT AND VALUING

So far in this chapter arguing man provides reasons which renounce self — he is not involved in the argument even if he is affected by its consequences — yet when individuals argue, when they are asked to provide reasons for doing this or that, they are likely to make explicit some of the values that they hold. Which is to say that:

> Humans as rhetorical beings are as much valuing as they are reasoning animals. (Fisher, 1978)

The adequacy of an argument may also be judged in terms of the values on which it is based:

> A good reason is a statement offered in support of an ought proposition or of a value judgement. (Wallace, 1963)

But what is implied by man as a valuing animal? The following definition of value has been widely used in social science research.

> To say that a person 'has a value' is to say that he has an enduring belief that a specific mode of conduct or end state of existence is personally and socially preferable to alternative modes of conduct or end states of existence (Rokeach, 1973)

However, it remains difficult to develop and use the concept of value operationally (Eden, Jones and Sims, 1979) and it is easy to sympathize with those who despair of the task of ever getting to grips with man as a valuing animal (Bowen, 1979). Some operational pointers which have been suggested include statements which might apply to values, such as:

'It represents an internal commitment'
'Difficult to justify — can't say why, it just is'
'It is a criteria for judging outcomes'

'Can't say why, it just is' — it is here that we are starkly confronted by the difference between rational argument (as we have supposed it to be) and arguing people. Yet these disjoint elements appeared in each of the research settings studied; arguments are both personally based and rationally debated. Whilst the audiences may have been predisposed by their values to one argument rather than another, this was rarely sufficient for them to be persuaded to act.

The definition of values given above presents the idea of having a value as similar to the possession of an object which a person either has or does not. Argumentation studies usually follow a similar path when considering the interaction of argument and values; the identification of the aims of the argument with the supposed values that the audience hold is often taken to be a sufficiently persuasive force but persuasion is more complex than this because the nature of value is not fully captured by this notion of possession. The possession of any value, for example 'happiness', 'abolition of nuclear weapons', tells us nothing about the possessors at all, since it all depends upon what they mean by 'happiness'. To describe man as a valuing animal is not to describe particular values that he has, but to make a statement about human activity, to point towards a 'striving' quality that characterizes human life. This aspect is captured in what has proved in this research to be a very fruitful approach to understanding the pshychology of individuals — the theory of personal constructs, developed in the mid-fifties by the American psychologist George Kelly and others. The dynamic nature of values is enshrined in their essential conception of human thinking:

To our way of thinking there is a continuing movement towards the anticipation of events, rather than a series of barters for temporal satisfaction, and this movement is the essence of human life itself. (Kelly, 1963)

For his metaphor of man Kelly looks to another aspect of the scientist, not the scientist as a rational detached observer but the scientist as an inveterate inquirer into the world of his experience. Valuing man behaves purposively. Such an activity may sometimes be described as a striving towards an explicit end state even though that end state is not thought to be attainable (Ackoff and Emery, 1972), or it may be described as a less focused desire to move away from a given current state of affairs (Eden, 1978). Within a broad framework of personal construct theory it is possible to recast the notions of value and reason and provide a more helpful description of argument which can to some extent cope with the paradox of psychological logic. This is by no means a complete or the only approach to resolving issues in argumentation analysis but has been useful in practically examining the arguments put forward in the research setting and in explaining events which might otherwise be difficult to understand.

Personal construct theory accounts for individual behaviour in terms of the ways in which an individual makes sense of his experience. In the rather arcane, formal language of the theory a person's fundamental psychological processes are described thus:

> A person's processes are psychologically channelized by the way in which he anticipates events. (Kelly, 1955)

A person's fundamental psychological act is that of placing an interpretation on experience; this is called by Kelly the process of construing. This interpretation is 'channelized', that is to say it is continually guided by what has gone before, thus for the individual experience is something which is gradually constructed rather than directly perceived. This process of placing an interpretation on experience, of construing, arises from the individual attending to the replicative nature of experience and differentiating one aspect of that experience from another. This differentiation, or construct, then forms part of a larger construct system, which guides the construing process (Kelly, 1977). For example, from the experience of knowing Peter, Stefan and Mary, an individual may construe that Peter and Stefan are friendly whereas Mary is aloof. The construct 'friendly...aloof' forms a basis for placing an interpretation on other aspects of experience, for instance other friends.

The utility of any construct system lies in its ability to make sense of experience for each individual, to provide the person with a way of making experience predictable and hence controllable. In this way the construct system is not in any sense chaotic but represents a particular sort of order in relation to experience, and also determines to some extent the type of experience that an individual may have. In construing the person is paying attention to the replicative nature of experience at various levels of abstraction, and in creating an internal picture of what it is that seems certain and what it is that seems to change there is a coherency to the individual construct system which explains experience (Bannister and Fransella, 1971). To look at a construct system as an internally ordered way of making sense of experience provides a basis for understanding a more widely based interpretation of rationality and argument. It is important to stress that the phrase 'making sense of experience' should not be interpreted as everyone interpreting the same experience (the 'real' world) differently so that there is a rational basis for deciding between interpretations, but that experience is genuinely different for each individual and understanding would arise from a knowledge of the individual's construct system and not from empirical knowledge of a 'real' world. A construct system is therefore a way for an individual of representing experience to himself, of making sense (Young, 1977; Eden *et al.*, 1981).

The quote from Fisher earlier in this chapter emphasized in relation to argument a familiar dichotomy of approach between argument as a rational activity, concerned with objective criteria, and argument as a social event, concerned with the communication of individual values (a split which can be seen in much of the literature on argumentation: Fisher and Sayles, 1966; Miller and Nilsen, 1966). In the preceding paragraphs I have suggested that in order to usefully aid arguers the divide must be bridged, for emphasis on a value-laden interpretation of argument is not really able to explain the powerful and compulsive influence of rational inputs to debate, and conversely the techniques of traditional argumentation analysis resting on a foundation of rationality can make little contribution to arguments which rest in part on personal values.

A FRAMEWORK FOR THE STUDY OF ARGUMENT

It was argued above that the process of construing is an individual activity and particular to that individual, indeed it is a focus on understanding the differences between individual interpretation of experience which informs many of the clinical and organizationally based uses of personal construct theory. But argument, as described above, essentially involves communication between individuals: it is in its broadest sense the coming together of construct systems, it is an intersubjective activity concerned with the interaction of subjective worlds (Reardon, 1981). The possibility of argument therefore depends upon the extent to which there can be an interaction between these private worlds. These possibilities are covered by two further postulates of construct theory, namely the sociality corollary and the comonality corollary:

To the extent that one person employs a construction of experience similar to that employed by another, his or her processes are psychologically similar to those of the other person. (Commonality corollary)

To the extent that one person construes the construction processes of another, he or she may play a role in a social process involving the other person. (Sociality corollary)

These corollaries give two distinct meanings to intersubjectivity. The commonality corollary is concerned with 'having the same experience as someone else' through employing similar constructions of experience, but the judgement of similarity lies with the individual and not with any external observer. The notions of rationality and reason seem to fall into this category of construing. For example, at the simplest level my construing of mathematical addition (however it has been arrived at) I can confidently take to be the same as most other people's for the circumstances in which I need to think about it. In this view the 'taken for granted' nature of addition lies not in any objective or rationalist compulsion coming from the 'real' world but in my interpretation of this aspect of experience as something which everyone else would similarly construe. This is to give a psychological interpretation of objective knowledge and rationality and such knowledge might be defined as that on which we employ constructions similar to those of other people, and moreover constructions which are relatively stable over time. Any rule, such as a rule of logical reasoning, can be seen to act as a means of ensuring that psychological constructions within the context delimited by the rule have a feature of commonality. Intersubjective commonality can thus be seen as a basis for understanding the interaction between arguers in relation to rationality. Another aspect of intersubjectivity is represented through the sociality corollary, which defines the subjectivity of others in terms of the individual's own subjectivity. Thus it is possible to understand the construction placed on experience by another without necessarily accepting or adopting aspects of that system.

> It may be that members of the team find it useful to have a deeper awareness of their colleagues' views, and a richer view of the team, and this additional understanding leads to changes in the way the team operates which are beneficial in the longer term. (Eden, *et al.*, 1981)

A persuasive argument might be described as something which is agreeable, plausible and realistic (Gilbert and Mulkay, 1982). These terms can be given a fuller meaning in relation to the aspects of construct theory that are outlined above. Commonality between construct systems expresses the influence of culture on the individual; this is now widened to include aspects of experience which are more often described as things which we know for certain, apsects of experience that are the same for everyone; argument must realistically link to these. In construing the construing of others the individual gains some measure of the commonality between his own interpretation of experience and that of others. The aspects of experience which are judged to be commonly held are frequently very firmly placed within the construct system such that the tensions produced for individuals who are artificially placed in an environment where such beliefs are open to doubt are considerable (Asch, 1955). For these elements of the construct system it would be very difficult to play a social role with someone who did not share this commonality.

In contrast, an argument may be plausible in that it forms a coherent and linked network of ideas but is not one which we can incorporate within our own construct system. This argument may, for example, be construed as applying to particular groups of people, such as a set of arguments in favour of nationalization. In this case it may be possible for an individual to play a social role in respect of someone who does not agree with these arguments, but in extreme cases (e.g. an argument between an atheist and a devoutly religious person about the existence of God) no sociality is possible (Trigg, 1973). Finally, an argument may be agreeable, it may in some way fit in with constructs that we take to be particular to ourselves, with our values, to mesh with or support our very specific way of interpreting experience; in this case we construe the arguments as possibly being common to only a very few people.

At these different levels argument can interact with our construct system and exert a particular kind of persuasive force, a force of rationality if it is linked to commonly construed aspects of experience, a force of value if it links to our particular way of explaining experience. This analysis of argument in terms of personal construct theory provides a way of looking at these influences and a common basis for understanding rationality and value in this context. In conjunction with the technique of cognitive mapping it also provides a way of representng argument which has some significant advantages over logic-based methods. The idea of man, proposed by personal construct theory, as a being who is continually trying to create for himself an explainable world lies at the heart of a redefinition of rationality and reason which can help to make the analysis of argument a more fruitful tool of organizational inquiry and practice. Perhaps part of the compulsion of a 'good case' lies in its ability to better explain experience. The following sections describe some examples of good and bad cases taken from my recent research and attempt to show how this framework for argumentation can be used.

REPRESENTING ARGUMENT

The research was designed to study three different settings in which it was likely that reasoned debate would be a significant way for the participants to influence each other. The settings were: a study of a debate over a planning decision described in the *Diaries* of Richard Crossman, the Minister of Housing and Local Government in the 1964 UK Labour Government; an action research study of policy debates amongst senior officers in three major UK national charities; an observation of the 1983 parliamentary debate on the reintroduction of capital punishment in the UK. Each study provided a rich source of data on the arguments used by a small number of individuals and a mix between arguments to which the researcher only had public access and those which were privately rehearsed (Smithin, 1982; Crossman, 1975; Hansard, 1983; Smithin and Sims, 1982).

The method used is fully described in the literature cited and is briefly covered below. It offers a new way of describing and analysing the structure of argument in contrast to methods used in traditional argumentation which are tied to logical analysis and suppose a rationalist or empiricist view of knowledge and the nature of argument. In this research I was anxious to build representations of the arguments employed which are grounded (Glaser and Strauss, 1967) in the construct systems of the arguers themselves. In this method each argument is represented as a series of linked constructs showing the threads of the arguments used, in the form of a cognitive map. A cognitive map attempts to represent an individual's thinking as series of linked statements (Eden *et al.*, 1980; Smithin, 1982; Axelrod, 1976). Each statement is a personal construct which differentiates an aspect of experience like the construct 'friendly rather than aloof'. The constructs in a cognitive map are operational and relate to a specific issue and context rather than being more general abstractions from experience. For example, one of the constructs used by a charity officer in debates on policy was represented as, 'this charity consists mainly of volunteers ... charity has a substantial number of professionals'. The first part, or pole, of this operational construct represents the current state of affairs and the second part represents an alternative or possible future state of affairs, and taken together they form a construct about the charity. A simple part of an argument which followed from this construct is shown in Figure 1, which forms part of the cognitive map representing this officer's arguments (they are slightly modified in the context of this chapter to make the meaning clearer).

Figure 1   Example of a cognitive map

In the central thread of argument shown in Figure 1, the first poles form an argument following from the first part of the construct 'this charity consists mainly of volunteers', leading to the first part of the next construct 'appeals officer cannot wield a big stick', and so on through to the effect of the first construct on raising income. This 'side' of the argument is a description of problems with using volunteers; the complementary argument shown through the chain of second poles is an argument which is a possible alternative to the first. There are some important features of cognitive maps which make them a very useful technique for recording argument in contrast to methods based on logical networks.

The constructs can be expressed in the language used by the arguer and thus remain relatively transparent representations. The assignment of links between constructs implies that there is a causal link between the constructs but it is more loosely defined than a logical or quantitative link — the focus on a construct as two contrasting poles provides a richer indication of the meaning implied by a phrase and consequently makes the internal 'logic' of the argument clearer. This latter point can be demonstrated without recourse to theory by considering the meaning of a simple phrase such as 'working hard'. The meaning of this phrase for an individual is made much clearer by attempting to identify where possible the contrast he uses in a particular context, so that 'working hard rather than doing nothing' means something very different to the construct 'working hard rather than doing sixty hours a week'. In the first case we perhaps construe the person as a '9 – 5' person in the second case we tend to think of him as a workaholic. Understanding the contrasting arguments makes their intended meaning clearer and provides potential starting points for counter argument strategies.

Cognitive maps were also used in conjunction with computer software called COPE, which assists with recording and provides facilities for the analysis of maps. The use of computer software becomes important when the size of the maps increases and the number of interacting maps multiplies. In the study of the arguments employed by charity officers, the volume of data eventually grew to maps of several hundred concepts for each participant. The analysis can provide a sensitivity analysis on the effect of changing arguments, identify conflicting arguments and explore potential outcomes from a series of connecting arguments (Eden, Smithin and Wiltshire, 1985). In all, cognitive mapping provides a robust and friendly technique for representing argument which in conjunction with the computer software can cope with more complex sets of data than might otherwise be possible. For use in a practical organizational setting this is very important. In comparison, techniques such as those described in argumentation texts typically deal with no more than a paragraph of text, and the coding techniques to structure the data into specific parts of argument such as warrants evidence and conclusions require a significant rewording of the original text and an imposition of the analyst's structure at a very early stage of the investigation, such that the data are potentially significantly different from the original meaning intended (Toulmin, Rieke and Janik, 1979).

So far this chapter has discussed the nature of argument and suggested a framework for representing argument and analysing it. Broadly speaking, these ideas have something in common with the use of construct theory to examine argument described by Reardon, and cognitive maps are not dissimilar to the technique and theories of argument networks used in the analysis of scientific argument (Law and Williams, 1982). The following sections illustrate the use of these ideas employing examples from my research. They are necessarily oversimplified in this presentation but hopefully show how the ideas can be of use in making sense of some very surprising events.

EFFECTIVE ARGUMENT?

In the introduction to this chapter I suggested that there were occasions when argument might be powerfully influential and that when it was so the effect was often dramatic. This was most noticeable during the parliamentary debate, because it was widely expected before the debate that the motion to reintroduce capital punishment for all types of murder and a series of amendments to reintroduce capital punishment for specific categories of murder (such as the murder of a police officer) would probably succeed; as the *Guardian* reported on the day before the debate, this was a 'House of Commons where opinion is more evenly divided than ever before'. Two factors seemed to support this opinion: the recent general election has introduced into the Commons a much larger number of Conservative MPs than for many years who were thought to be in favour of reintroduction; secondly, the past few months had shown a swing in public opinion in favour of taking more drastic action in relation to terrorist murders and injuries to the police. The result when the debate started was considered to be very much in the balance. However, in the event all the motions supporting the reintroduction of capital punishment were lost by large majorities, the smallest being 81 votes. It was the size of the defeat not the fact of it that was such a surprise and it meant that a future debate on this issue was unlikely for several years if at all. It became apparent that many of the new Conservative MPs had changed their minds during the course of the debate and many agreed afterwards that the arguments put forward during the debate had been persuasive. It was generally felt that 'fluent and forceful' speeches by opponents and a weak case put forward by the Home Secretary in support of the motions were the key elements of this change. How is it possible to create such a dramatic turnaround through argument?

A second striking example of the power of argument, in this case the destructive power that a 'poor case' may have, was seen in the argument studied from the Crossman diaries. This concerned a planning decision to build a model village of some 5000 homes on designated Green Belt land at Hartley in Kent. In the early stages Crossman describes some of the arguments for and against a decision to build and plumps for a decision not to build. A little later, however, he reports that he has been persuaded by his departmental officials to allow the building to go ahead and he reiterates the case they made. At this point he seems certain that he has a 'well-argued' case and writes that although there will naturally be some protest from the 'Green Belt lobby' he feels that his arguments are strong enough to prevail. It seems that at this stage Crossman regarded this as no more than a rather tricky planning decision and later admits that he was in no way prepared for the violent 'storm of protest' which greeted his decision and dogged his attempts to explain it. At one point he clearly felt that his political future was in jeopardy as a result of the outcry. How is it possible for a skilled debater to so misjudge the capabilities of his arguments?

It would be naive and contrary to the findings of other research into organizational life to suppose that the argument was all that there was to these situations; for instance it is clear from other parts of the *Diaries* that the planning issue and how to tackle it formed part of a wider political battle between Crossman and his officials. However, in each situation the arguments presented do seem to have been central to the outcomes and to have played a particularly important role in contributing to the dramatic nature of events.

Crossman reports that he feels he has very little knowledge of the issues involved because his primary interest is in social services; he describes himself as casting around for arguments and ideas to help make this sort of decision. In a sense the constructs that he has available are inadequate for dealing with this new environment and do not enable him to make sense of his new world. This prompts a search for arguments to elaborate his construct system and make him better able to predict and control the situation. In doing this Crossman is susceptible to the 'ready-made' arguments provided by the Department. It is interesting how readily Crossman abandons his original arguments in favour of an entirely different case; this suggests that he does not have arguments to adequately reject the case put forward by his officials. Here argument can be interpreted in a role of making the world more explainable and hence more under the arguer's control, and this is also strongly supported by work on the effect of novel argumentation in policy debates, which showed that arguments which were new to the audience had most effect in terms of persuading them to the arguer's point of view (Axelrod, 1979). The debate on the reintroduction of capital punishment presents a similar need in the audience for arguments to cope with a relatively new situation. The new MPs had to come to a decision on a topic which is only rarely debated, and where, perhaps for the first time, they would need to be able to support their individual decisions publically. The need in each of these cases seemed to be for a linked set of ideas, for additional explanatory power rather than for simply more information. These examples show an important link between the nature of argument and our need to create an explainable world, and the role that others' arguments may play in this, but they say little about the persuasive power of argument — after all, Crossman eventually adopted a quite disastrous set of arguments which seemed to persuade no-one but himself. The concepts of sociality and commonality provide some insight into the nature of persuasive power.

SOCIALITY AND ARGUMENT

Within a broadly interactionist perspective the tenet of the sociality corollary is perhaps unexceptional, in the context of argument it is extraordinary. Traditionally the entire notion of a reasoned argument implies that arguments even as explanations of personal experience may be judged against objective criteria: they are either right or wrong. The remarks of those who had just 'lost' arguments seem to support this view of arguments relating to a single explanation of the world. For an arguer this may also be conceit, or such a notion can be itself used as a polemical device, but generally our expectations of rationality relate to finding the one argument with which no reasonable man can disagree. A surprising feature of this research was the extent to which this view informed the way in which arguments were prepared and the extent to which possible counter arguments are imagined from the point of view of the arguer rather than that of his audience. Crossman's discussion of his case and the likely counter arguments was very like this and he never seemed to get to grips with the world as it might be construed by the 'Green Belt lobby'. More recent and widely publicized planning enquiries also seem to reflect the inability of either party to adequately construe the opponents' construing (Wynne, 1982; Nelkin, 1979), to enter into a social role with respect to them. There is a very important distinction here between knowing at a surface level the arguments put forward by opponents and understanding how these arguments link to their view of the world, to their values, and it is at this deeper level that a rationalist wish can lead arguers astray. Crossman never seemed to appreciate that concerns about the amenity value of Green Belt formed part of a well-elaborated construct system which is an alternative explanation of experience and provides different predictions as to the impact of a model village on the environment, and that this is a coherent view of the world.

In the debate on the reintroduction of capital punishment, the Home Secretary similarly failed to enter into a social role with the rest of his parliamentary colleagues in the context of his relatively new role as Home Secretary and this seriously weakened the case that he put forward. Time and again MPs of all political persuasions rose to say that the arguments put forward were not appropriate for a Home Secretary, a different kind of argument was expected of him in this role; as one member put it, 'with all respect to him, that is not something that should come from the Home Secretary. It might come from me or one of my right hon. or hon. friends on the back benches . . . .' The argument is weak not because of its content or structure but because it is not the sort of argument that a senior member of the Government can put forward. Effective argumentation clearly requires the ability to enter into the construal of others and to play a social role with respect to them.

It might be expected that in a debate which aroused deep emotions the values of the audience would have a significant impact on the course of the debate. In the parliamentary debate, however, a detailed analysis showed that the majority of speakers focused upon 'instrumental' arguments for or against capital punishment and typically emphasized the effectiveness of capital punishment as a deterrent to potential murderers. Views which were morally based, for example arguments which stressed the importance of retribution and conversely those that pointed to the fundamentally barbaric nature of the punishment, were not prominent. This seems to be because those whose minds are capable of change by reasoned debate will not hold very strong values in relation to the issue; they are therefore more likely to be persuaded by instrumental arguments than value-laden ones. The effectiveness of one opponent in this debate seemed to lie in his ability to enter into the sociality of the undecided and whilst expressing a moral commitment against capital punishment to be able to provide other instrumental arguments as his main case. To the extent that construal expresses values, sociality is important in constructing arguments since values arise within a complex network of ideas which is intricately woven into a personal explanation of experience. Therefore arguments which attempt to change values may be less persuasive since they more fundamentally challenge the way in which the world makes sense to the individual.

Perhaps the most important feature of an argument which prevents us from entering into a social role with the arguer, and which is at the root of the compulsive power of arguments, is the 'bothersomeness of inconsistency'. Undoubtedly the most damaging feature of the arguments that Crossman eventually adopted is that they were seen to contain a major inconsistency. A few months previously a senior Labour Party MP had argued for the preservation of Green Belt as part of a commitment to the preservation of the amenity value of land surrounding London, a view which is contradicted by the authorization of the construction of a model village on Green Belt land. Once this was pointed out by opponents, Crossman was continually forced to tackle this single inconsistency and all the other arguments that he had carefully built up were useless. Suddenly Crossman's case did not seem to make sense and it could not be used to predict what was going to happen on this and other planning issues. More seriously, we are forced to reconstrue our interpretation of Crossman's thinking in order for it to make sense again. Perhaps Crossman has bowed to the pressure of property developers rather than upheld the principles of socialism (as one line of argument proposed), or perhaps he is just incompetent (as opponents in the House of Lords argued). The seriousness of the issue for Crossman relates to the extent to which we have to rethink our construal of him in order to accommodate this inconsistency. Consistency is not here solely related to logical consistency, but is concerned with our ability to enter into a social role with another, through his arguments. In order for us to do this, then, that must be a predictable system that we see; it does not of course have to be a system which we own ourselves, but it must be plausible. But for this blatant inconsistency it would have been much more difficult for opponents to sustain a forceful attack. Crossman seemed to accept the contradiction as an unalterable flaw in his case and consequently made little effort to argue the case which so convinced him but instead attempted to defuse the issue in a variety of ways, by arguing that Hartley was a special case and that it was badly presented by the Department.

COMMONALITY AND ARGUMENT

An argument may be plausible in that it presents a consistent network of ideas and it may be agreeable in that it accords with our interpretation of experience, but is this enough for argument to be persuasive? A feature of the parliamentary debate was the extent to which arguments were related to any 'facts' that were available. It was as if debaters were attempting to align their case with aspects of the physical or natural world or at least with something which was commonly agreed, so that the audience are then presented with arguments which seem to lead inevitably to a particular conclusion. The arguments are persuasively strengthened since they conform to or stem from aspects of the world which are 'certain'. For example, those in favour of the reintroduction of capital punishment often supported their arguments through reference to the increase in the number of murders since abolition in 1965. This was very neatly and effectively transformed by opponents into strong support for their case since the statistics were ambiguous in a variety of aspects, for instance the rapid increase in crimes of murder began well before abolition and also it was not clear that this kind of deterrent would apply to terrorists or have any effect on 'crimes of passion'. So opponents argued that although evidence existed its uncertainty argued for a preservation of the *status quo*; as one MP put it, 'we ought to reintroduce hanging on more than a hunch'. A very influential phrase was used by one member referring to recent cases where innocent individuals had been wrongly convicted.

> the only certain fact is that if hanging was not abolished in 1965 then five innocent men would be dead today.

The instrumental arguments revolved around issues of the certainty of evidence, the likelihood of deterrence and the size of the effect. The size of effect was an important factor in defeating the arguments in favour of reintroduction for the murder of prison officers, for in the last 40 years only two officers had been killed therefore it was difficult to make a judgement about the deterrent effect of capital punishment. Thus in argument commonality of construal, which I have argued includes our construction of the physical world, significantly influences the persuasiveness of argument. In scientific argumentation that is seen even more strongly where:

the actor (audience) is presented as being forced either by some invariant rule of conduct or by the natural world itself to come to certain conclusions. (Law and Williams, 1982)

Commonality extends from the physical world to the 'world taken for granted' by a group of individuals. For example, charity officers when talking about volunteers and their use in fund-raising produced a suprisingly common picture of how volunteers behave and how they should be used. This acted as a significant influence on debate and argument on policies for the use of volunteers, and the social 'facts' were as much facts as the sticks and stones of the natural world. Thus arguments designed to influence policies on the use of volunteers were inevitably bound up and constrained with addressing these 'facts'. Someone who built up a set of arguments which did not relate to these common construals would be described as naive or unrealistic.

Commonality in respect of arguments is critically concerned with what is taken to be certain and what is not, and the persuasiveness of arguments is linked to an appreciation by arguers of modalities of this kind. Consider the following two statements, which are two very simple arguments:

'You cannot lift a two-ton weight'
'You cannot speak of a fox's tail'

Toulmin proposed that we feel that the first modal qualifier 'cannot' is more persuasively or strongly used because it refers to a physical impossibility whereas with the second argument it is actually possible to talk of a fox's tail rather than the 'brush' even if it is not done at the hunt ball. This follows a rationalist or empiricist view of argument and gives an ascendancy to features of the physical world (Toulmin, 1958). Yet someone who imagined that they could lift a two-ton weight or someone who felt that they could talk of the fox's tail at the hunt ball would be equally unrealistic; in each case they are violating an aspect of common construal and its effect is likely to be similar in each case in destroying the ability of their audience to make sense of them.

CONCLUSION

In marshalling our arguments to devise a good case, if we were to follow the advice of the Sophists, or even of Aristotle, we would perhaps focus upon the needs and wishes (as we saw them) of our intended audience, for:

I have been told, my dear Socrates, that what a budding orator needs to know is not what is really right, but what is likely to seem right in the eyes of the mass of people who are going to pass judgement. (Plato, *Phaedrus*)

Will self-interest necessarily supplant reason? I have argued in this chapter that this dichotomy creates a confusion which is morally enforced between rationality and value, to such an extent that the power of reasoned debate is much neglected in organizational studies. Following some recent work on the use and analysis of argument I have attempted to propose a unified structure for the study of argument which can encompass man as both a reasoning and a valuing animal. I have left on one side much of the discussion on the performance of argument and the devices of rhetoric and many other things which are also part of argument to focus on valuing as a fundamental and dynamic aspect of creating an individual interpretation of the world, and argument as the creation of an explainable and predictable world.

Arguments must be plausible in that they provide a linked set of ideas improving explanatory power; they must be agreeable in that they support or relate to our needs; they must be realistic in that they relate to the taken-for-granted world; they must be usable in that they enable the individual to make better sense of experience. We think we know when we know causes, the world is only explainable rather than discoverable and argument is the process of explanation.

Organization Analysis and Development
Edited by I. L. Mangham
© John Wiley & Sons Ltd.

Improvising Order

CHAPTER 5   *Alistair Preston*

INTRODUCTION

The perspective of this chapter is that an organization is a gathering of people (Silverman, 1970). Yet an organization is in many obvious respects different from a football crowd, which may also be described as a gathering of people. This perspective is chosen to emphasize that organizations are made up of interacting individuals. Therefore, what makes an organization distinct from a football crowd and one organization distinct from another is the way in which members of the organization or setting interact with one another and thereby align their individual courses of action. From this point of view, organizational reality is seen to be constructed by the participating individuals (Berger and Luckmann, 1967) as they gather and interact within the spatial and temporal confines of a particular social setting.

This chapter strives to reinstate individuals as the primary agents in the construction of organizational realities and to rescue them from collective nouns and reifications, such as groups, coalitions, systems and organizations, which have come to dominate the literature of organization theory. This is not to suggest that I am dismissive of such collective nouns and reifications. However, I believe that they should be prefixed with 'people' — people in groups, people in coalitions, people in systems and people in organizations. As Gouldner (1971) notes:

Men are coming back into the picture — trickly little devils, but still men — and the sturdy social structures drift away into the background. (Gouldner, 1971)

In this chapter Burke's (1936) perspective of incongruity is taken seriously, namely:

Planned incongruity should be deliberately cultivated for the purpose of experimentally wrenching apart all those molecular combinations of adjective and noun, substantive and verb which still remain with us. (Burke, 1936)

81

To create incongruity the metaphor of 'jazz' has been chosen. This metaphor may employ a language that is unfamiliar to organizational theorists. In this respect its choice has been deliberate. The unfamiliarity serves to distance the concepts and ideas contained in this chapter from the mainstream of organization theory. By choosing such a metaphor I am attempting to use the unfamiliar to re-view the familiar — to use the incongruous to engender a reconsideration of the traditional perspectives of organizations.

JAZZ AND THE COMPLEXITY OF ORGANIZATIONAL LIFE

Within the perspective of this chapter, jazz is an appropriate metaphor. Jazz is a player's music (Newton, 1959) in which the individual members of the band or jam session interact with one another to construct a musical performance. The music is the collective expression of a group of individuals as they perform, interpret and respond to the performance of the other members of the band. Another attribute of the metaphor is that jazz is a human endeavour and so avoids the dehumanizing, mechanistic or biological metaphors typically employed in organization theory.

Jazz as an entity in itself and each individual jazz performance defies a single or precise definition. The variety of jazz music and its continually changing nature from one performance to another (even with the same musicians playing the same tunes on the same instruments and, though less likely, to the same audience) renders all definitions inadequate or obsolete. Jazz is in a continual state of flux; a continual state of creation and recreation, production and reproduction, development and redevelopment. Jazz is not in a state of being but is in a continual state of becoming.

In this respect jazz is similar to organizations. They too are in a continual state of flux. Organizations are characterized by the creation and recreation of the social order contained within. They are merely arenas, and not very easily defined arenas, in which people act, interact, interpret and make sense of themselves, their actions and their interactions. As one attempts to define them or even one of the myriad of events or situations that take place within them, they move on, change and transform into something else. Organizations may only be precisely defined at the expense of their dynamic and continual transformation.

The use of nouns to define organizations as tangible structures or things in themselves has served to disguise their transitory, ever-changing nature. At best an organization, like jazz, may be defined as an evolving process. As Weick (1979) notes, we must attempt to use verbs, not nouns, to describe organizations as processes rather than concrete structures.

Within this perspective of organizations, situations are seen as a complex of events or an interplay of previous actions and interactions. The course of action chosen in response to a given situation will in turn have consequences for the subsequent actions and interactions of the actors and other related parties. For a given situation there is no beginning or end *per se*. Rather, it is a part 'bracketed out' (Schutz, 1962) and defined from a continuous stream of experience by the individuals involved. Furthermore, the stream of experience is not linear and separate, but meshes with, and has consequences for, other patterns of actions and interactions. In this sense organizations are messy (Mitroff, 1983), and individuals are constantly required to interpret, define and make sense of that mess before constructing a course of action. The precedents and antecedents of a given situation may not be fully known to the acting individuals. Thus, individuals are required to act in situations which are ambiguous to them, and may only make sense of their actions and the situation retrospectively (Weick, 1979).

In addition to the complexity of organizational life, things, situations and events have no inherent, objective meaning, but are subject to interpretation by the acting individuals. Individuals act towards things on the basis of the meaning that things have for them. Moreover, meanings are socially constructed through interaction. Yet meanings may be ambiguous and subject to reinterpretation, either during or after the implemented course of action, by the interacting individuals (Blumer, 1969). It is therefore possible that multiple and even conflicting definitions may be constructed, which further adds to the complex messiness of organizations.

It is the complex and subjective nature of organizational reality that permits or even fosters change. The patterned regularity of organizational life is largely a myth. Beneath the superficial façade is an undercurrent of ambiguous, almost chaotic activity. The uncertainty and irregularity of organizational life, as constructed and experienced by the participants, requires that individuals constantly explore, define and possibly redefine their own reality. Such a process permits individuals, should they choose to, to alter their perspective or frame of reference and construct new and novel courses of action.

Such complexity and ambiguity in organizational life was readily apparent within my own research into the daily activities of the factory managers of a large plastic containers manufacturer. Far from the patterned regularity depicted in their organizational chart, the managers, directly involved in the production process, were often engaged in almost frenetic activity as they went about (in their own terms) 'trying to find out what the hell was going on' and then 'deciding what the hell to do about it'. The managers, directly involved in problematic situations, would gather in each other's offices, on the shopfloor or in the canteen at lunch to discuss the nature of problems. They would discuss possible courses of action which they might undertake in response to situations and the implications and consequences that such courses of action might have for them. In a very real sense the managers were constructing a definition (or definitions) of the situations by deciding what they meant. On the basis of this definition, should one be arrived at, they would then decide on what action to take. These processes of interaction appeared more appropriate as depictions of organizational reality than were the more formalized 'official' depictions. These interactions were the forum in which the managers introduced new or novel courses of behaviour into their daily activities.

The chapter attempts, at least in part, to answer the question posed by Mead (1934) as to how change within a social order may take place without destroying the social order itself. To this end I shall employ the specific and most celebrated characteristic of jazz, which is that of improvisation.

THE ESSENCE OF IMPROVISATION

In essence, jazz improvisation is concerned with change. Improvisation is a process of introducing changes into a musical performance while maintaining the unity or continuity of the performance itself. Improvisation is to be distinguished from rewriting a musical score in that changes are introduced during the performance by the performing individuals and not by a composer before the event.

Improvisation in jazz is a creative process in which variations are worked into a theme. The theme is normally a popular tune, on which the performer improvises by drawing on the melodic fragments and rhythmic patterns contained in his or her memory. In doing this the performer invents new relationships and permutations which bring to the music novel and innovative phrases. The other members of the band are then required to respond to these changes and integrate the improvisations into the performance as a whole.

Improvisation takes on a variety of forms. It may involve the extemporaneous creation of a complete performance (something rarely accomplished) or mere ornamentation around notated parts. Most improvised jazz falls somewhere between these two extremes. The jazz musician improvises by placing new melodic lines over the given harmonies of the tune. On the one hand, improvisation may take the form of ornamentation, in which the musician embellishes or makes slight alterations to the tune, referred to as 'paraphrasing' (Hodeir, 1956). On the other hand, improvisation may take the form of creating entirely new melodic lines over the given harmonies, referred to as 'chorus-phrasing' (Hodeir, 1956).

In part, improvisation is a cognitive process in which the performer imagines (thinks out) how a newly constructed musical phrase will fit into the context of the performance as a whole. However, this is an over-rationalization. Improvisation is also an emotional expression based on an intuitive feel for the music. The emotional content of jazz gives it its characteristic vitality and may also be seen as a source of spontaneous inspiration which cannot be satisfactorily explained in terms of the intellect alone.

Collective Improvisation

Collective improvisation is a common phenomenon in a jazz performance. Such improvisation is to be distinguished from the adjustment made by the rhythm section to integrate the improvised solo of another performer. Collective improvisation is characterized by two or more performers creating and introducing significant new phrases during the performance. This process, therefore, emphasizes the interactive nature of jazz music. In collective improvisation, a soloist performs an improvisation to which another member of the band responds with an equally significant improvisation. It is also possible that collective improvisation may take the form of a duet where individuals perform simultaneously. Improvisations lead therefore directly from one to the other, or are played in unison, without necessarily returning to the basic theme of the tune. Each musician is thus required to listen to the improvised phrases of the other performers while playing the background music and at the same time constructing their own improvised piece. In collective improvisation the potential for chaos is greater but so is the potential for creative excellence.

Improvisation and Arrangements

Although in jazz emphasis is placed on the creative individual, a performance nevertheless takes place within the context of a band. In order to preserve the musical performance as a whole, the improvising soloist must have regard for the other members of the band. Whether the improvisation is of a paraphrased or chorus-phrased variety, the basic thematic and harmonic structures of the tune or musical arrangement must be adhered to. Without these basic constraints, the other members of the band will be unable to integrate the improvised solo into the performance. Even so-called 'free jazz' is constrained by a general framework which serves to preserve the basic harmony and unity of the performance. In free jazz the chorus-phrasing is taken to the extreme, and the performance reaches a crescendo of near chaos only to be pulled back from the brink when some form of harmony is maintained.

In addition to the thematic and harmonic structure of the tune and the chord progression on which the tune is based (Coker, 1964), there usually exists a further framework which includes some indication of the sequence of improvisations and choruses in the performance. This framework constitutes a shared arrangement, either implicitly understood by the members of the band or explicitly laid out in the form of a notated 'lead sheet'. These shared or 'working' arrangements provide an order within the band which permits the individual members to hold the performance together. Arrangements in jazz, particularly in small ensemble performances, typically have loose and simple structures. The basic tunes are simple and the sequence of events flexible. This loose structure may result in the arrangement changing, even during the performance, and thus the arrangement itself may be said to be improvised. The jazz band therefore constitutes an improvised order.

It may seem incongruous to talk of improvisations and arrangements together, yet a shared agreement permits the individual to perform an improvised solo and to know at least roughly what the other members of the band (the rhythm section) will be doing (Cameron, 1954). An arrangement, while constraining improvisation, may also be liberating to the soloist in that he or she may take for granted certain characteristics of the performance and freely improvise within the general framework without fear of the musical structure collapsing.

Before metaphorically linking the key aspects of the above, necessarily brief, introduction to jazz to my perspective on organizations, I shall present an example of improvised behaviour from my research. This example, it is hoped, will breathe life into the following discussion. No single interaction is sufficient to explore the full richness of the jazz metaphor; however, this example, supported with other material, serves to ground the discussion in a real-life context.

AN EXAMPLE OF COLLECTIVE IMPROVISATION

The managers of the plastic containers factory were facing an unfamiliar situation. During the 1980 lorry drivers' strike, the factory was picketed by striking lorry drivers. The in-house drivers were non-union and yet refused to cross the picket lines. Chris Davis, the managing director, convened a meeting of both senior and middle managers to try and decide on a course of action. The following are edited excerpts from that meeting.

> Mike Shilling (department production manager): (as though presenting a *fait accompli*) If they [the pickets] don't let anything in or out we'll just have to shut down.
> Cyril Jenkins (operations manager): OK, I agree, but that must be the last resort. We're here to see if we can avoid closing. We don't want to lose production ... Or orders from our customers.
> David White (financial manager): We're all in the same boat; Jason Plastics and Tin Box (competitors) have pickets at their gates so we're not going to lose any orders.
> Jim Brown (production planner): I know this won't help production, but are the pickets at the warehouse? (The company had a warehouse on the nearby Northwood industrial estate.)
> Sean Davies (distribution manager): (Speaking emphatically) Pickets are everywhere, the whole of Northwood is closed down.
> Martin Keyes (materials buyer): Well, if we can't get the goods to the customer, why don't we build stock? At least the machines will be kept running.
> Charlie Johnson (department production manager): (Somewhat scathingly) What's the use of that? Where the bloody hell will we store them? (Shortage of storage space was a recurring problem in the organization.)

Cyril Jenkins (operations manager): (Apparently approving of Martin Keyes' suggestion) Well there's a little room in the loading bay, but we could fill that in a day. But it's a good idea, though.

Martin Keyes (materials buyer): (Determined not to let the suggestion drop) We could cut back on production, maybe only work one shift or three days a week, then we wouldn't fill up the loading bay so quickly.

Charlie Johnson (department production manager): (With heavy irony) Why should we? We can't get the goods to the customers. All we'd have is more bloody congestion when we started working at full capacity again.

Peter Travers (sales manager): (Interjecting to support Martin Keyes) There's something in what Martin says. It would be good to have some stock we could send out immediately after the strike, otherwise we *could* lose customers. They'll try Jasons or Box if we can't deliver. (There was a murmur of agreement and then the discussion centred around which goods to manufacture and for how many shifts. The managers reached agreement on these issues.)

Chris Davis (managing director): (Who had remained silent until this point, sounded pensive and a little disappointed) OK! That's worth considering, but it's not much of a solution. (The other managers who thought they had already reached a reasonable solution began to mirror the managing director's disappointment. Chris Davis continued, unwilling to close the meeting.) Assuming we close down or cut back, how do our customers stand, what levels of stock have they got?

Mike Shilling (department production manager): (With some satisfaction in his voice) It doesn't matter, they're going to be picketed as well. If they can't get anything out they won't need any pots. (The term 'pots' was a common expression for the plastic containers.)

(Another general murmur of agreement)

Jim Brown (production planner): (Interjecting once more) Ah! but is that right? They're not picketing the food manufacturers. Birds Eye, Van de Berghs, Walls, Cadburys, Express Dairies, Rowntrees; they're all food manufacturers. They're also all of our biggest customers. So they can go on producing until they run out of containers.

Chris Davis (managing director): (Sounding much more enthusiastic) If you look at it that way, I suppose we're in the food processing industry ourselves.

Peter Travers (sales manager): Yes, if they haven't got the pots they can't produce the goods. So maybe we should be exempt from the strike as well.

(All the managers now showed renewed interest in the meeting and gave their support to the new theme.)

Chris Davis (managing director): (Returning to the practicalities of the situation) But will the pickets agree? Sean (distribution manager), you know some of the pickets on the gates, I believe.

Sean Davies (distribution manager): (Somewhat surprised that the managing director knew this about him) It might work, but remember we make other goods. I mean, the seed trays and so forth. Some of these lads have driven for us, so they know that not everything goes to food manufacturers.

Negotiations with the pickets and the union representatives lasted the remainder of the day. Much to the surprise of many managers, the union representatives finally agreed that certain containers, for essential foodstuffs, would be permitted through the picket lines after the loads had been inspected. They would not, however, agree to lift the pickets on the raw material suppliers. In spite of this, the factory could run at reduced capacity for a number of weeks with existing stocks.

The metaphor of improvisation provides a framework for analysing this interaction.*

THE SITUATION

The lorry drivers' strike was a unique situation. The managers had no experience of such a situation before and therefore they had no 'cookbook recipes' (Schutz, 1962) to call upon. The consequence of not taking action was, however, fairly obvious: the plant would have to close. Therefore, to avoid this eventuality, the managers were required to constrcut a new or novel course of action. The nature of this situation has an important bearing on the process of improvisation.

The Familiar and Unfamiliar

A distinction between situations that are familiar and those that are unfamiliar to the individual is important in understanding the process of improvisation and change. First, though, it must be stressed that familiarity and unfamiliarity are a matter of definition by individuals faced with a particular situation. A situation unfamiliar to one person may be familiar to another.

Within their daily activities, people in organizations may be required to respond to new and unfamiliar situations. Such situations may be created by others and introduced into an individual's arena or arise from the interplay of a number of other events, composed in a new manner, hitherto unknown and unfamiliar to the individual concerned. In such scenarios individuals are required to improvise and create new or novel courses of action in response to the situations they are confronted with. (Alternatively, individuals may seek to redefine unfamiliar situations and act towards them as if they were familiar.)

In addition to the lack of precedents in unfamiliar situations, the intended outcome and consequences of the proposed course of action are likely to be ambiguous and uncertain. In a wider sense, 'to improvise' means to cope or ingeniously adapt to a set of circumstances. Improvisation is therefore, to some extent, a process of experimentation. Individuals may embark on a course of action without necessarily knowing where that course of action will lead. As Weick (1979) notes, individuals may have to act in order to know what they are doing.

*Ramos (1978) uses the metaphor of improvisation in conversational analysis. While this intriguing paper is highly illuminating, it is grounded in the analysis of a specific conversation and does not explore the consequences or implications of improvised behaviour within the context of a social order.

The lorry drivers' strike was certainly recognized by all managers as being unfamiliar. However, within the organization the managers were also confronted with regular, routine situations with which they were more or less familiar.

In the case of these familiar situations, the need for improvisation was less imperative and the scope for improvisation more constrained. In familiar situations there are, to some degree, precedents or established practices for action which may be called upon by the acting individuals. Such standard responses are referred to as cookbook recipes by Schutz (1962) or scripted responses by Mangham (1979). Improvisation in such situations is in many respects from choice and is a deliberate intention to change the standard response to a given set of circumstances. As will be discussed more fully, improvisation takes place within a social context. This may serve to reinforce existing or established practices, creating constraints on individuals' performances, which in turn limits improvisation and change.

The unfamiliarity of the lorry drivers' strike created a situation in which creative or chorus-phrased improvisation could take place. Although such creativity was not assured, the unfamiliarity of the situation and the lack of precedents for action could be seen as an ideal forum for improvised behaviour.

THEMES AND IMPROVISATIONS

Throughout the meeting three separate themes for possible courses of action were explored. The first suggestion by Mike Shilling, a departmental manager, of closing the plant was not a course of action *per se*, rather it was a resignation to the situation. Closure was the inevitable outcome of *not* taking action. This suggestion was rejected by the other managers.

The first original theme, proposed by Martin Keyes, the materials buyer, was that production should be continued and stocks built. This solution received support and yet was still rather scathingly criticized by Charlie Johnson, the other department production manager, owing to the shortage of storage space on site.

The second, again introduced by Martin Keyes, was a compromise of the previous one. This theme entailed producing a limited range of products and operating the factory at a much reduced capacity. This suggestion was picked up and improvised upon by the other managers and all but accepted as the most likely course of action. The managers even decided on which production lines should be kept running.

Chris Davis, the managing director, was unwilling to simply accept this solution and kept the discussion alive by asking further questions. The third and final theme then began to emerge. Its origins stemmed from the previous discussion and Chris Davis' questions about the customers' position *vis à vis* the strike. At this point Jim Brown, the production planner, remembered (from a

TV programme, he advised me later) that food manufacturers were exempt from the strike. This point led to the realization by Chris Davis that the factory was part of the food processing industry. In many respects, the managers effectively redefined the company. Previously it had been part of the plastic containers industry; now it was part of the food processing industry.

Each of the themes may be seen as improvisations upon the basic notion of trying to keep the factory running. This was, after all, what the meeting was convened for. Each of these themes was then improvised upon in the ensuing discussion. Furthermore, the themes were interrelated; each one leading from, or having its roots in, the previous discussions. In this respect the process of improvisation was collective.

This example displays the notion of themes within themes and the relationships between each. In many respects the superordinate theme was to keep the factory running. This constituted the base note of the entire interaction. It was the basic issue around which all subsequent improvisation took place. The three themes outlined above emerged from improvisation around this base note and they in turn were improvised upon as the managers explored their feasibility and their consequences. Each of the themes can be seen to have its roots in the previous theme. The second theme was really an adjustment of the first theme. This improvisation was one of ornamentation and therefore could be defined as paraphrasing. The third theme, however, had a more significant, creative or orignal content. This theme could therefore be described as chorus-phrased improvisation.

This example demonstrates that, as in jazz, improvisation and change within an organization may be said to take place around basic themes. The themes, and to some extent the following improvisations, will be drawn from the individual's memory or 'stock of experience' (Schutz, 1962). This stock of experience, however, differs from the popular tunes of jazz. A person's stock of experience is more varied and diverse.

A theme or inspirational idea may emerge from a complex arrangement of fragments of experience, possibly half forgotten by the individuals (Johnson, 1977). In many respects a new theme or idea is surprising even to its originator. Themes may be drawn from the individual's entire lived experience and not simply from experience of like situations in the past. This is particularly applicable for situations, such as the lorry drivers' strike, which are defined as unfamiliar and for which there are seemingly no precedents.

A Fusion of Thought and Feeling

The origins of ideas or themes and indeed the entire creative process itself are problematic (Meehl, 1965). To date, most organizational theory and social psychology has concentrated on the cognitive process and has sought to explain human behaviour solely in these terms. The result of this over-rationalized perspective has been to ignore or at least to disguise the emotional content of human experience. Douglas (1977), however, suggests that human behaviour is a fusion of thought and feeling. Any satisfactory explanation must therefore recognize the emotional as well as the cognitive content of human experience.

In confronting the complexity and changing nature of organizational reality, individuals bring with them complex and changing personal histories, comprised of a fusion of previously experienced thoughts and feelings. This confusion of fragments of half or vividly remembered experiences will be drawn upon by individuals in forming subjective interpretations of the current situation. The resulting interpretation may appear to others as consistent and rational or, on the other hand, it may appear inconsistent or indeed irrational. Nevertheless, as Thomas (1937) notes, 'if something is defined as real, then it is real in its consequences'. The interpretation given to an event or situation, be it primarily determined by the emotional or by the cognitive, will be the basis upon which the subsequent actions are constructed. This interplay of thoughts and feelings (themselves both variable) enhances the possibility of multiple interpretations of a given set of circumstances, and hence the possibility of constructing new and novel courses of action.

The emotional response towards the lorry dirvers' strike is not immediately obvious from the interaction. Yet underneath, the seemingly rational attempt to find a solution had an emotional vein. The managers, and in particular the senior managers, Cyril Jenkins and Chris Davis, felt frustrated and resentful towards the pickets. The meeting was in some senses an attempt to undermine or circumvent the strike. There was a very real emotional commitment not be 'dictated to' by what the managers regarded as unfair secondary picketing and this emotional commitment played a role in the satisfactory outcome of the meeting.

At each stage in the interaction there was the potential for collapse. The momentum of the meeting was only sustained by the commitment of the participating individuals. At any moment and for a number of possible reasons, the contributions could have dried up. Indeed this was very nearly the case. It was only the tenacity of Chris Davis, the managing director, which kept the meeting going and led to the final theme being introduced. There was considerable jubilation amongst the managers when they succeeded in persuading the union representative to allow containers for essential foodstuffs to be shipped out.

Emotions might not only be directed towards situations themselves. Emotional responses to the other members of an interaction may also have a bearing on an interaction's outcome. Put starkly, people harbour likes and dislikes for each other. The emotional reaction to one another may take a variety of forms. Personal animosity, jealousy and grudges, as well as friendship, personal respect and admiration, will influence the degree of collaboration and thus collective improvisation between the interacting individuals. This emotional content again emphasizes the importance of recognizing the whole individual in organizations and highlights the danger of collective nouns and reifications that ignore the human essence.

In the lorry drivers' strike meeting, personal hostilities, albeit tempered by the current setting, were still apparent. Charlie Johnson, one of the department production managers, was known to openly dislike Martin Keyes, the materials buyer. Charlie scathingly dismissed both of Martin's suggestions to continue production by building stocks. Mike Shilling, the other department production manager, made negative comments which reflected his bitterness towards senior management. His aspirations for promotion to operations manager had recently been thwarted when Cyril Jenkins, a young outsider, was promoted to that position. On the other hand, Jim Brown, the production planner, and Peter Travers, the sales manager, who were recently appointed to their positions and were regarded as the 'bright young men' of the company, were basking in their new positions and they contributed appreciably to the improvisation; indeed they were instrumental in developing the final theme. Thus, the various managers brought with them to the meeting their own and related personal histories. They were not cognitive automatons, but responded both with their feelings and their intellect to the situation and to each other. Even in this particular serious situation, the drama of their personal lives was acted out.

The Creative Process*

Improvisation is a creative process. It may be viewed as one of giving form, in a novel way, to the subjective ambiguity and uncertainty of daily life. It is a process of constructing a definable and novel reality out of the ongoing stream of experience. The creative process may be seen as one in which order is brought out of disorder, form out of chaos. The individual brings his creative work out of the chaos of his own subjective life and out of the disorder of the world (which is itself subjectively interpreted). There is, however, order in the world as well as disorder, this being the order that has been created before: the taken-for-granted responses and existing patterns of interactions and interpretations. There is also order in the subjective: the various meanings of things for the individual and the impulse which impels a particular order to emerge. The creative process therefore must transcend, in one degree or another, both forms of order: the order of the world as interpreted by the individual and the more nebulous order of the subjective. The creative process produces something new, something that goes beyond what has been. This is not to say that the fruits of the creative process are better, they are merely different and therefore novel.

The creative process, as Schorer (1968) notes, is often defined as intuitive or inspirational. However, these are only metaphors for a mystery that eludes

*The section on the creative process was inspired by Schorer (1968) and his discussion of creativity in fiction writing.

rational inquiry because the process itself may be 'non-rational'. The impulse that leads to a novel interpretation of the ongoing subjective reality has not been successfully explained or articulated within the social sciences or indeed any other sciences (Meehl, 1965). Nevertheless, creativity, the process of introducing new and novel interpretations and actions, is an observable and hopefully experienced phenomenon. I suggest each individual has the potential, to some degree, to step slightly aside and look at the world from a new angle and interpret what he or she sees differently. Furthermore, this creative process, or the process of formulating 'a new', is derived from a fusion of thought and feeling and is not merely a process of rational or logical analysis.

Not all improvisation is necessarily dramatic or even entails an inspirational idea. Many courses of action within the factory, for example the rescheduling of production to meet customer demands, were really only of a paraphrasing variety. In these situations the managers sought to make minor adjustments to the production plan. In many situations there was a genuine attempt to minimize the repercussions of an intended course of action; an attempt to minimize dramatic or extensive change through introducing the minimum necessary changes.

In the case of the lorry drivers' strike, which was a serious and unfamiliar issue, the final theme was inspirational and creative. Stein (1975) defines creativity as a 'process that results in a novel product or idea which is accepted as useful, tenable, and satisfying by a significant group of others'. Within this definition, the redefinition of the company from a plastic containers manufacturer to being part of the food processing industry was certainly novel. Its usefulness and tenability were borne out when the union representatives accepted the idea and this proved extremely satisfying in a very real emotional sense to the managers.

Improvisation versus Negotiations

Some collective improvisation may be coloured by the strategies and instrumental intent of the interacting individuals. Situations and their solutions are not necessarily neutral but may have a political overlay in which the interacting individuals vie with each other to achieve their own personal desires. Such strategic improvisations may be better defined as a process of negotiation (Strauss, 1978). In such situations the change process is deliberate and intentional rather than experimental. Features such as bargaining and exchange rather than creative improvisation may dominate the interaction. Non-resolution of such situations may not be for lack of ideas, but rather because of a breakdown in negotiations. Whilst in jazz the emphasis is always on preserving the harmony of the performance, in organizations disharmony may result from the intransigence of the interacting individuals. Such strategic interactions were particularly prevalent at meetings to discuss resource allocations for capital purchases. The departmental managers invariably came armed, determined to negotiate for their case, often at the expense of others.

THE ARRANGEMENT

The lorry drivers' strike meeting constituted a newly formed arrangement to meet the requirements of an unfamiliar set of circumstances. No regular meetings of the full spectrum of senior and middle managers were held. Although the meeting was conducted in such a way as to downplay the superior/subordinate relationships within the organization, these relationships were nevertheless apparent. Chris Davis, the managing director, adopted a passive role at first, only entering the discussion when a number of themes had been proposed and explored. However, when he did speak, the other managers were more subdued, indeed were slightly deferent to his status. The structure of the meeting was loosely assembled and this was instrumental to the free flow of ideas. Yet patterns of relationships were still apparent in the interactions. The meeting was orderly, reflecting the presence of the two levels of managers.

This particular meeting, in effect a semiformal arrangement, was not very representative of the shared or working arrangements constructed and maintained by the factory managers in conducting their daily activities. As noted previously, the managers regularly met each other in their offices, on the shopfloor and at lunch to keep one another informed and to discuss possible courses of joint action. These arrangements were not arbitrary. They formed a pattern of relationships, reinforced over time, between particular managers who found it helpful and useful to meet regularly and discuss, in depth, problematic situations or events. The make-up of these arrangements was in part situationally determined, but personal likes and dislikes played an imporant part in their composition and continued existence. Certain managers, for example Charlie Johnson and Martin Keyes, deliberately avoided each other, which could often cause problems in the production departments. On the other hand, Jim Brown, the production planner, Peter Travers, the sales manager, and to a lesser extent Charlie Johnson, a department production manager, formed a fairly consistent working arrangement in which they met regularly to tackle problems. These arrangements constituted a forum for interaction and hence the possibility of collective improvisation.

Arrangements in Organizations

Improvised behaviour in an organization takes place within the context of an existing social order. This social order is composed of the patterns of relationships, meanings and interpretations as constructed and made sense of by the interacting individuals. It is a socially constructed order (Berger and

Luckmann, 1967), or one constructed out of the social milieu and continually reinforced or else modified and changed by the interacting individuals. The construction of the social order may be influenced or constrained by a number of factors such as task, technology and even the architecture or physical layout of the setting. Furthermore, formal and imposed structures of authority and power, inasmuch as they are internalized by the participating individuals and are defined to be a meaningful part of their social reality, will also give form and character to the social order.

A social order may be viewed as a series of intermeshing, shared arrangements, formed by the participants of the setting in order to align their individual courses of action so that they might act in concert. These shared arrangements from the fundamental building blocks of the social order. Weick (1979) suggests that organizations may be viewed as loosely coupled subassemblies and adds that 'relatively small units — such as double interacts, dyads and triads — become eminently sensible as places to understand the major workings of organizations'.

Arrangements, as in the jazz band, permit the individual participants to act and, while doing so, to know at least roughly what the other members of the setting will be doing. These arrangements are constructed within the social milieu and are implicitly recognized by the interacting individuals. They constitute a complex of taken-for-granted rules which improvising individuals must take cognizance of when introducing their new or novel courses of action. These taken-for-granted rules are rules-in-process (Mangham, 1979), continually reinforced by the interacting individuals or modified through the process of improvisation. The structures of shared arrangements are simple and themselves subject to improvisation by the participating individuals. They may be continually adapted to meet the requirements of the current set of circumstances. The make-up of arrangements (the persons involved) may be constructed from scratch in response to unfamiliar situations, as in the case of the lorry drivers' strike, or may take the form of long-established relationships in the case of familiar or routine situations.

Arrangements constitute an improvised order which serves to preserve the social fabric of the organization while still permitting change to take place within it. They are an arena in which improvisation and change may take place and, as a result of improvisation, are themselves subject to change. They are therefore in a continual state of flux, changing as the members invent and respond to the introduction of new or novel courses of action.

Arrangements also act as a constraint on improvisation, requiring the improvising individual to consider the consequence and impact of his or her intended action on the existing patterns of activities and relationships that comprise the current social order. Mead (1934) describes this process in terms of the 'I' and the 'ME'. The 'ME', which represents some generalized or specific other, acts back upon the 'I', which represents the impulsive, inspirational self, setting constraints and giving form to the subsequent acts or resulting in the individuals abandoning their intended actions.

The Familiarity and Experience of the Participants

The familiarity of the members of a working arrangement and the extent of their experience of working together will play a part in the process of collective improvisation. Paradoxically, a high degree of familiarity between the members of a working arrangement may help to facilitate *or* impede the process of collective improvisation. A stable working arrangement may serve to reinforce existing practices through habitual responses to given situations, thus reducing the scope for improvisation and change. Even when the members are then confronted with unfamiliar situations, resistance to change might be experienced. Alternatively, familiarity and experience may serve to encourage improvisation because of the intuitive understanding that may develop between individuals over time.

In jazz, collective improvisation has much to do with rehearsal. Much collective improvisation takes place in small ensembles during jam sessions. The fruits of the collective improvisation are then incorporated into subsequent public performances. Collective improvisation is not merely the product of a certain combination of instruments, but is derived from a group of virtuosi musicians who can interpret and respond, almost intuitively, to each other. In a similar sense, collective improvisation within an organization is not merely the product of a combination of roles, for instance the financial manager, the marketing manager and the production manager, but is a function of how the individuals perform their roles in respect to each other. As in jazz, collective improvisation may benefit from rehearsal, or the continuing joint experience of a group of individuals.

Within the plastic containers factory, managers could be seen to make and maintain arrangements with each other. Two predominant and related types of arrangements were arrangements to inform and arrangements to work together. Within the arrangements to inform (or alternatively the process of informing), managers evolved implicit understandings to keep each other informed of events and situations that they regarded as being significant. Jim Brown, the production planner, commented that he could rely on being informed about machine breakdowns within an hour of them happening. These arrangements to inform were fairly stable ongoing understandings. In contrast, arrangements to work together were more situationally determined. Various managers would be consulted on specific problematic situations if it was considered necessary to involve them in the problem's solution. The managers, in effect, would arrange to work together and the arrangement would last as long as it took to resolve the situation. Such arrangements might then dissolve and be reformed for like situations in the future. Other non-work-specific arrangements also existed.

Arrangements to socialize and to gossip were also prevalent. These gave further form and structure to the patterns of relationships that went to make up the social order of the organization.

More formal arrangements, such as the weekly production meetings, were in evidence. Such imposed arrangements differed in nature from the socially constructed shared arrangements. These meetings were sometimes aggressive and chaotic, where the managers gave full vent to their thoughts and feelings. Rather than a single theme, as in the case of the lorry drivers' strike, in each production meeting a number of themes were addressed, not all of which were resolved. In the production meeting, where the members were thrust together involuntarily, vested interests were more apparent since the managers were more strategic and this often led to recriminations and conflict. Yet these formal arrangements were also instrumental in giving form and substance to the organizational order.

The metaphor of an organizational order as an intermeshing series of shared arrangements is intended as a contrast to the notion of a stable monolithic structure. Shared arrangements emphasize that organizational orders are constructed from within and not imposed from without. Arrangements are emergent rather than designed. In this sense arrangements are not entities in their own right, but are rather mechanisms or processes through which individuals 'arrange' to interact or act together. Arrangements between individuals are formed through a process of improvisation as they invent and respond to new ideas and courses of action. Improvisation is a continuous process and thus shared arrangements must be continually reinforced or else modified to accommodate new relationships and patterns of action.

IMPROVISATIONS, ARRANGEMENTS AND ORGANIZATIONAL DEVELOPMENT

Much of what is written above would be anathema to traditional organizational theorists and designers, indeed to a large section of practising managers. In contrast to the above representation of an almost chaotic improvised order, traditional organizational theorists emphasize the following in their description and prescription of effective organizations. Organizations are portrayed in terms of stable and formalized hierarchical structures with well-delineated lines of authority and responsibility represented as superior/subordinate relationships. The typical model is that of a reified system, composed of interacting subsystems, which as an entity in its own right interacts with an environment through a well-defined boundary. The model of human behaviour in this perspective is deterministic and passive. Human beings are defined as rational and purposive, and are seen as responding to environmental stimuli and problematic situations. Reality is viewed as objectively verifiable, non-problematic and concrete.

The implications of the traditional perspective of organizations and behaviour are twofold. First, this model is thoroughly deficient as a representation of organizational reality as constructed, interpreted and experienced by organizational participants. As such, the model provides a shaky and indeed misguided foundation upon which to base principles for organizational development and design. A second, and interrelated, implication (and one with more ominous consequences) is that the traditional model creates a series of imperatives towards adopting particular structures and processes that may impede creative improvisation and change and which in turn may endanger an organization's survival. The portrayal of improvisation and change in this chapter is both descriptive and prescriptive. It is descriptive in the sense that improvisation and change form an inevitable part of social reality, despite the attempts of organizational designers and practitioners to stem it. It is prescriptive in the sense that I believe that improvisation and change is not only inevitable, it is essential. Individuals in organizations are faced with an ever-changing and complex reality; much of it of their own making. In order to make sense of this reality and to act effectively, individuals must adapt to new and differing situations. As Mangham (1982) notes:

> In every conceivable type of agency, creativity is a premium if these bodies are to respond effectively to challenges which confront them. (Mangham, 1982)

Furthermore, improvisation and change is also necessary in routine and repetitive situations. It is needed to alleviate the suffocating monotony of the routine and to stimulate the individual participants to experiment with new and possibly more effective courses of action.

The characteristics from the traditional perspective of organizations which are most instrumental in suppressing or impeding creative improvisation and change are I believe as follows: (1) formalized structures; (2) standardized procedures; (3) imperatives towards rationality.

It may be argued that these structures and processes create a climate of conformity which in many respects may be defined as the opposite of creativity or improvisation.

In the following sections I shall examine each of these characteristics in turn.

Formalization of Structure

Within a brief historical perspective there was a decline of improvisation in western art music after the Baroque period. This decline was largely due to the introduction of large orchestras with more complex and formalized structures. Thus both size, in terms of the numbers of participants involved in the performance, and formalization, in terms of the structure of the orchestra and the complexity of the task, required that the musicians conformed to a precisely notated score which left no room for improvisation. It is possible to construct a metaphorical relationship between the decline of improvisation in western music and the development of large complex organizations.

Within the growth of large organizations performing complex tasks, management may be seen as attempting to 'orchestrate' the performance of the organization by constructing and imposing formalized structures. These are intended to coordinate the various activities of the individual members to achieve the overall objectives of the organization. Within such a view of the organization, improvisation (which I have argued thrives in situations with little formal structure, whereby the participating individuals are not constrained by formal relationships and rigidly defined patterns of communications), is inevitably impeded by the structural constraints of formalized management hierarchies.

Organization theorists typically view organizations in terms of large interlocking and fairly permanent structures and ignore, or worse attempt to suppress, the smaller working arrangements constructed by the participating individuals, which are the arena for improvisation and change. The perspective of arrangements is not simply advocating that 'small is beautiful' (Shumacher, 1974) but rather, when considering the design and development of organizations, it may be important to recognize the extant arrangements as formed by the participating individuals. These arrangements are flexible and adaptive to new and changing situations and therefore facilitate improvisation and change. Within the metaphor of arrangements, formal structures may be viewed as arrangements imposed from without, rather than being constructed within the social milieu. These imposed arrangements, enforced through formal rather than take-for-granted rules, lock individuals into specific roles, creating rigidity in their working arrangements which effectively impedes improvisation and change.

Standardization of Procedures and Objectives

It has been noted that improvisation takes place around basic themes. Thus, the number and variety of themes available for an individual or group of individuals to improvise upon will in part determine the extent and degree of new ideas and courses of action introduced into an organizational setting. Themes, derived from an individual's stock of experience, may effectively be limited by the imposition of standardized procedures in an organization to control the activities of the participating individuals. Two examples of such procedures are the budgetary control system and the management information system. These are designed to control and evaluate the performance of participants through the comparison of actual performance against some predetermined objectives. Such systems may create a symbolic framework through which the managers of organizations come to interpret situations. By concentrating the managers' focus on a predetermined set of objectives and procedures, creative improvisation and experimentation is constrained if not actually penalized.

Far from developing standardized procedures and predetermined objectives, organizational developers and practitioners should seek to enrich the experience of the members of the organization and encourage experimental approaches to both familiar and unfamiliar situations. Weick (1977) suggests that [people in] organizations are, and I suggest should be, encouraged to be 'garrulous'. People in organizations talk to each other, and in talking may construct new definitions of both familiar and unfamiliar situations. The process of interaction itself is an important aspect of improvisation in which individuals develop and introduce new and previously unthought of themes and courses of action into the setting. Standardized procedures and predetermined objectives reduce the need for interaction and thus the scope for improvisation and change.

Imperatives Towards Rationality

March (1976) describes one of the articles of faith in the theory of organizational choice as the 'primacy of rationality'. This may suggest that certain processes and beliefs in organizations may be seen to create imperatives towards rationality. These imperatives are more abstract than formalized structures and standardized procedures and objectives. They belong to what might be defined as the organizational culture (see Bate, 1984), which serves to reinforce the collective or organizational definition of rational or correct behaviour. Typically, correct behaviour in organizations is bereft of emotion. Correct behaviour is said to be 'calculated' and not 'clouded by emotions'. Thus, the emotional content is largely excluded from the analysis of behaviour in organizations. Indeed, emotions are seen as detrimental to organizational efficiency. Behaviour is judged in terms of rationally and hence efficiently achieving objectives. Human behaviour, however, both in its organizational and wider social context, is a fusion of thought and feeling. Inspiration, which may be seen as the cornerstone of creative improvisation, is derived from an interplay between the cognitive and the emotional. Imperatives towards rationality reinforce the cognitive at the expense of the emotional, which again constrains creative improvisation. Imperatives towards rationality, which are reinforced through formalized structures and standardized procedures, may create a reduction of space and free movement (Argyris, 1971) to construct new and novel courses of behaviour.

With specific reference to information systems, Argyris (1971) poses the following question:

> How would individuals react to increased rationality in their lives? Will they think as many humanists believe, namely that information science rationality can lead to a

mechanistic and rigid world which, because of the narrow concepts of efficiency, will dominate man and eclipse his humanness. (Argyris, 1971)

Inasmuch as the creative process is an integral part of being human, increased rationality in the pursuit of efficiency may indeed dominate man and eclipse his humanness, as well as suffocating improvisation and change.

CONCLUSIONS

In organizations, people are routinely engaged in familiar, repetitive activities. This patterned regularity is reinforced (if not actually created) by constructing formalized hierarchies, imposing standardised objectives and procedures and, less directly, creating imperatives towards rationality. Such a perspective, however, represents only a single and limited dimension of organizational life. In contrast or in addition to the above image, organizations may also be seen as complex socially constructed arrangements of people. Furthermore, these arrangements are subject to continual change as the improvising individuals invent new forms of behaviour in response to the uncertainty and ambiguity of unfamiliar, non-routine situations.

It is this area of almost chaotic uncertainty that fosters creative improvisation which in turn is so important in responding to a changing and dynamic world. In many respects this chaotic, yet flexible and adaptive social order should be preserved. Mechanisms which minimize uncertainty and ambiguity (the objective of many conventional management practices) run the risk of creating a stale, overly rational environment which stifles the creative spirit of the organizational participants and impedes improvisation and change.

This chapter is intended as a celebration of individual creativity and ingenuity. Individuals are seen, at least potentially, to be inspirational improvisators. They are able to adjust their behaviour and working arrangements to meet the dynamic and changing nature of organizational life which they themselves create and form part of.

The organizational order, as subjectively experienced by the participating individuals, is seen as an improvised order in which individuals arrange to align their individual courses of action. These arrangements, born out of improvisation, are themselves subject to change through subsequent improvisations. These arrangements form the arena in which improvisation and change is created.

The conventional wisdom of organization theory and development, far from engendering a spirit of creative improvisation, actually impedes it. The conventional wisdom concentrates on monolithic structures instead of recognizing and encouraging socially constructed shared arrangements. It concentrates on the development of narrow standardized procedures and objectives instead of permitting or providing organizational members with varied and challenging experiences. Finally, it creates imperatives towards rationality instead of recognizing that human behaviour is a fusion of thought and feeling. Each of these strategies may have the effect of constraining creative improvisation, which may in turn endanger the survival of the organization.

Organization Analysis and Development
Edited by I. L. Mangham
© John Wiley & Sons Ltd.

From Harmony to Counterpoint
Reconstructing Problems in an Organization

CHAPTER **6** *David Sims*

INTRODUCTION

In this chapter I shall describe research that I did for my Ph D, and then show how the ideas that I developed in the course of that research were put to work in an intervention that I conducted in a Council for Racial Equality (CRE) in a large city in the southern UK, which I will refer to as Notreading. My plan is:

1. to describe briefly the basis on which I did my original Ph D research;
2. to describe the framework of ideas that arose from that research;
3. to tell the story of my intervention in Notreading CRE, and to show how the framework affected my practice;
4. to draw some conclusions about the interrelationships between research and practice.

THE RESEARCH BASIS

I started my research from the premise that reality is constructed, not given. Human beings are active in the processes of perceiving and understanding their worlds. We actively make sense (or nonsense) of the things and activities around us, and the reality that we live in is the one we construct; we do not live in some 'objective' reality. As Thomas and Thomas put it, 'If men define situations as real, they are real in their consequences' (1928).

Take, for example, somebody who smiles at you. Even the physical difference between a smile and a grimace, which may be very clear from inside the face involved, is not always clear from the outside. A test match cricketer who is hit in the groin by a ball from a fast bowler will usually break out into a smile. This does not necessarily mean that he enjoyed it; it is more likely to be a way of disguising his pain and demonstrating that such things will not disturb his concentration, for the benefit of the opposing players and the television audience. If you tell someone a joke and they smile at it, it is then left for you to interpret whether they are amused, embarrassed or suffering from indigestion. Some people smile when they are about to do something nice to you, some smile when they are about to attack you, and some smile on both occasions and leave you guessing (perhaps they have not made up their minds). A smile can be intended and interpreted as friendly, threatening, ambiguous, or many other possibilities. So there are many interpretations that can be put on a smile, and we behave on the basis of our interpretation. Misinterpretation may have serious consequences. It is said that some early Christian missionaries in South America smiled at the tribespeople they met in the jungle (smiling = friendliness). Their conversion targets, however, had a different set of constructs for interpreting smiles (smiling = baring teeth = aggression), and therefore decided that it would be prudent to attack first. So they killed the missionaries. Our constructions of reality can have serious consequences.

The differences in the realities we inhabit can partly be explained socially and partly individually. The missionaries' mistake with the smile was an example of the social construction of reality (see Berger and Luckmann, 1966). A society, by means of its culture, imparts certain understandings of the world to its members. These understandings may only become visible to us when a visitor from another culture comments on them, or when they are being changed. Concern or lack of concern over pollution, for example, seems almost self-evidently appropriate to those who experience it, but may be incomprehensible to visitors from elsewhere (Crenson, 1971). Japanese conceptions about what constitutes an acceptable living space are quite different from western conceptions. Similarly, the dangers of overeducating people for the jobs they are going to be offered, often discussed in Britain (especially by those who sniff a possible way of reducing public expenditure), are incomprehensible to the Japanese. Their reality is socially constructed in a way which can make no sense of such an idea.

But there is also the individual construction of reality. We might both take a smile to be friendly rather than aggressive, but you might be sensitive enough to know that this particular smile betokens embarrassment rather than joy. We do not all reach the same understandings of events within the same society. Everybody is different, and everybody has different constructs for understanding their own reality (Kelly, 1963). This can be observed when any two people sit down to read newspapers; their eyes alight on different headlines and different stories, they take the pages in different orders, give different amounts of time to their reading, and reach different conclusions. One of them may even put the newspaper down and go and do something different. In a similar way, the same events may be played out in front of different people and be understood by them in different ways. This is one of the reasons why little knots of people gather in corridors and lavatories after meetings; they wish to share and compare their observations and understandings of what was going on. This is distinct from the knots that appear before meetings, where people are more likely to be making deals and fixing events in order to control what is about to go on.

So we all inhabit different realities, but we do not believe them to be separate; if we did, we would not believe we could communicate, and you would not be bothering to read this because you would take my reality to be quite different from yours and therefore incomprehensible to you (Eden *et al.*, 1981). Social skill, as Kelly said, is to do with the extent to which we can understand the constructs with which other people understand events.

In such a view of the world, the place of the individual's definition of the situation (McHugh, 1968) becomes central. The research I did for my PhD asked how, when everybody saw things differently, members of teams could come to some agreed definition of what the problems were that they were facing. So individuals define their situations and construct their realities (with influences from society), and problems are not 'things' with some external provable existence but constructions or definitions made by us in order to make sense of our world.

We are surrounded by a near infinity of situations which could be seen as problems. Even if we do not see a problem, we know that if someone else were to take our place they could see one. Different people see different problems in the same situation (if different people can be said ever to be in 'the same situation'). Problems are the property of individuals. A problem is only a problem because at least one person sees it as such. There is no such thing as a problem which is not owned by anybody (Sims, 1979).

So problems are constructions — partly social and partly individual. This makes sense of a lot of everyday observations about problems. For example, some people seem to construct characteristic problems for themselves. For some people, it seems, if their wife leaves them, their best friend dies, they lose their job and their house starts collapsing, they experience this as a temporary difficulty to surmount. For other people the choice of a new carpet is a long, anxious and worrying problem. For some people servicing their car can be a problem; they want to do it, but are not sure if they will be able to do it properly. For others it is no problem because they know they can do it, and they know that they wil be able to surmount any difficulties they meet along the way. For me it is also no problem because I know I cannot do it.

Different people see problems in different locations. This may be partly because their professional training has equipped them to do so; the training of an accountant equips him or her to see problems of a particular kind, as does that of an engineer. Their training has simultaneosuly equipped them with a blindness to other kinds of problem (a phenomenon which Thorsten Veblen described as 'trained incapacity'). Confront them with the same case study and the chances are that the problems they construct out of it will be in quite different areas. This may be because of their different training, but it may also arise from their roles and responsibilities. Thus the marketing person is charged with constructing marketing problems, and the Midlands director with thinking about how events will impinge on the Midlands.

Different people see different styles of problem. In one of the teams where I did my field work, the chairmanship passed from a physician to a surgeon. Another member of that team explained to me that we could expect to see different problems coming from the team in future because, while physicians saw complicated problems arising from multiple causes, 'surgeons are always the incisive ones, "Right, that's a problem, right, do it booboom" — all problems are like that as far as surgeons are concerned.' The other version of this frequently heard comment is to say that, so far as surgeons are concerned, everything is cut and dried.

Another stylistic variation in problems is that some people tend to construct problems in terms of something which they can act upon, while other people seem more likely to construct a problem in terms of things that are beyond their control. Nobody falls totally into either category. We would not want to give ourselves the responsibility of doing something about all our problems, so we would want to define some of them in terms that can be attributed only to 'the government' or some other conveniently inaccessible root of all evil. However, such definitions never lead to problem-solving, and it might be of practical benefit in some organizations if a high value were placed on a style of problem construction which produces definitions that are capable of leading to action.

These differences may be attributed to individual or social constructions of reality. For example, the people who regard themselves at present as having 'a weight problem' would not be the same as the people who would have so regarded themselves at the time of Botticelli. Social construction means that a particular shape and weight of body is much more likely to be taken as 'excessive' and 'a problem' now than then; individual construction means that some people are more concerned about their physical appearance than others. We are currently seeing an interesting reorientation beginning on the issue of suntan. Vast amounts of money have been spent on solving the problem of how to get a 'healthy suntan'. In recent years, however, public concern has started to grow about the attendant dangers of skin cancer. We can expect to see social and individual problem construction about 'sickly' untanned skin changing.

But people have to agree problem constructions. Somehow, teams of people with different styles, different backgrounds, different roles, different preoccupations and different levels of tolerance of ambiguity manage to come together to produce problem definitions which are clear enough and well enough agreed to form a basis for executive action. That was what my Ph D research was about.

THE EMERGING FRAMEWORK

So what did I find out from my research? My methodology was based on using, as far as possible, the words and the theoretical constructs of the team members I was working with (Glaser and Strauss, 1967). Such 'grounded' method produces findings which are very often useful to others working in similar situations but which are difficult to condense. The findings work by offering those who wish to make use of the research more than they can cope with and leaving them to select the parts which seem to resonate best with their own experience and needs. Even the summary chapter in my thesis, in which I tried to draw the main strands together, is eighteen pages long! The full framework that emerged can be found in Sims (1978; 1986). For the purposes of this chapter, I will describe five themes that emerged and which influenced my intervention practice in Notreading CRE.

First, people working in teams were very conscious of different ways of defining problems. I have already quoted the example of surgeons' and physicians' styles of problem construction. Another person said that problems were actual for them if they could actually go and spend some money on them. I heard several irritated descriptions of people who were uncritical in their problem-finding. For example, '... he's confused and muddled and everything else, and just because something arrives on his desk he thinks he's got to do something with it. ... Something hoves into his ken, he thinks it's his problem, and tries to do something about it.' Someone else described how the training of doctors leads them to be confident and concerned about the patient in bed in front of them and not to be concerned with the 300 or so others who are still on the waiting list, nor much with the last 300 they dealt with.

There was also much awareness that people could construct a particular problem because of their past experiences, or because of something they had been reading recently. People construct problems on different time scales; sometimes people will criticize each other for being concerned only with short-term tactical ways of constructing problems when they think they should be more concerned with longer-term strategic approaches. Another source of problem construction was talking to other people — usually either others in similar positions or people in other parts of the organization whose problems had not been known about before. Some derived problems from what happened to particular cases, either ones that they had dealt with or ones that they had been told about by field workers. Others would be more likely to derive them from looking at a set of norms and statistics. Sometimes a problem was only discovered in the light of a proffered solution.

Secondly, there was much awareness among team members of the political processes by which definitions become dominant. A team may have a particular orientation in problem construction because of the people who hold power within it. One team was described to me by several of its members as having been very hospital-orientated in its approach to problems for the first year of its existence. This, I was told, was because the hospital-based members were the only ones who were accustomed to working in such teams, so they had all the power to start off with. Similarly, people often try to persuade a team of which they are a member to take on a problem for them. They may succeed because of a trading arrangement which often seems to grow up — I'll take your problem seriously if you take my next one seriously. Some people are taken by others to be destructive of good problem construction. They spread a misty confusion which may be accidental but which may also prevent the clear construction of problems whose resolution might be detrimental to them.

There was quite a lot of interest in the way in which some problems were persistently not constructed in teams. Whole areas could be defined as unproblematic because none of the people who could have done anything about them were interested. Thus several individuals, including even a team chairperson, bemoaned their inability to get any team to accept that there was a problem about the treatment of wandering alcoholics in a city centre. None of the specialists were interested in that problem, and the most bizarre red herrings (from my point of view as an observer) were dragged through the meeting whenever discussion lingered dangerously close to the theme of wandering alcoholics. One powerful team member had a range of problem destruction devices of which his colleagues were well aware but about which they could do little. He would push his chair steadily back from the table (they measured it as being six feet from the table by the end of one meeting) or would fall demonstratively asleep if he did not like the direction that problems were taking. As he was a key person in the implementation of any solutions, he always won.

One of the classics of the politics of problem construction is the power of the secretary. The more diffuse the discussion the greater is the opportunity for the secretary and the chairperson to produce minutes of what they think the meeting ought to have concluded.

Quite a lot of team members take the view that a team can only handle so many problems at a time. To stop the solving of non-problems may then be an important step towards enabling the definition of new problems. Similarly, a solution for one problem may ease another problem sufficiently for there to be too little pressure to deal with this other problem, but without actually solving it. This may make problem owners very cautious about giving support to other people's problem constructions.

Thirdly, the effects of problem construction were acknowledged to be significant by everyone. Many of those who participated in the research had never thought in terms of problem construction before. If they had thought at all about where problems came from, it had probably been in terms of trying to be correct in their understanding of problems. I was asking them to do something new when I invited them to tell me about problem construction in their teams. In almost all cases they were willing to tell me what I wanted to know, and this entailed their thinking about the ideas and making them their own. So I am not arguing that team members were already thinking in these terms, but they did find it very easy to do so, and they claimed a lot of new insights into their teams as a result.

Fourthly, there is a considerable body of rules, both formal and informal, about what is permissible in problem construction. The terms of reference of a committee may be part of this. They are a statement of what kinds of problems that committee is allowed to construct. Along with the rules, there are various sanctions, more or less clear to the members, which are applied in the event of the rules being broken. The sanctions depend on the seriousness of the transgression, the power of the transgressor and whether the error is seen as deliberate.

A rule may be broken accidentally, often where the rule-breaker is not party to some piece of information. So someone may make a proposal which is against a policy which has been set by a higher body but not yet communicated to them. This is then brushed aside by those in the know. The proposal is not worth making, and some powerful individuals know that, but they are unwilling or unable to explain why to the person concerned. Most of us who are familiar with being in meetings as a relatively junior member will be acquainted with this sense that the people who know consider what you are saying worthless in the context of what they know in the higher-level games in which they are playing.

Rule-breaking may be regarded as excusable. The words the participants in my research used to describe this mostly derived from children whose charm led to their naughtiness being condoned. People would talk about their teams being used wrongly, but would say that they could understand that the person who had done it had tried everything else to achieve some laudable end, and had had no choice. Alternatively, rule-breaking may be excusable because you see the person who broke the rule as being another participant in a game which you are all enjoying and in which judicious use of the professional foul is all part of the game. You may actually like them for the (semi-)innocent merriment they find in their virtuoso performance of breaking the rules.

Rule-breaking may be regarded as inexcusable. This was most dramatically illustrated in one of the teams in my research study, where a member contravened the rules. He argued that health care planning teams should be about health in the 'narrow' sense, that is, about diagnosable sickness, and not about well-being. This was utterly against the rules of the teams, and he was vilified, both to his face and behind his back, marginalized and embarrassed in every way that the powerful and central members of the team could find. One of them pointed out to me on one occasion and on a different issue that 'The trouble is, of course, that Dr X is right, but there is no way I can say that. I shall just have to wait until everybody forgets that this idea came from him, and then bring it back myself.' The transgressor told me that he knew that nobody would listen to him directly, but 'they are wandering along, and somebody has got to say these things'. He was aware of the price that he paid for transgressing, but felt that he had no moral alternative. He also consoled himself by noticing that other people picked up some of his points later.

Fifthly, the game of constructing problems in teams is played at two levels. When it is your turn, you may use that turn either to start some problem that you regard as important on its way, or you may use it to try and affect the rules.

In the short term, members often feel that they can achieve what they want best by staying within the rules. In the longer term, they may think that the rules need changing if they are ever to achieve what they want. This is a constant dilemma for many team members, and was one of the major issues which arose in my intervention in Notreading CRE, to which we will turn next.

THE INTERVENTION

At this point, I come to the story of my intervention in Notreading CRE, and how it was affected by my research. Because of the way I handled the intervention, I have divided the story into the following five sections:

> The initial approach
> The approval
> The study
> The crunch
> The aftermath

The Initial Approach

I was approached to help with a review that had already started in the Notreading CRE. The members of the Review Group who invited me in were clear from the outset that what they wanted was not someone to come in and run a change programme as an outsider, but a someone to play a 'hands-off' role and to comment, guide, and maybe occasionally cajole. I was to work not on behalf of them or with them, but through them. The Review Group members were individually more sophisticated in their understanding of their organization and of organizational change than most steering groups in manufacturing industry would be. So the question I kept repeating during my early contacts with them was: 'Why do you need an outsider to help you with the change plans that you have? Surely you could do this yourselves?' There seemed to be six main answers:

1. Because of the complexity of trying to develop such an organization. While the members might be more sophisticated than their counterparts in the private sector, the tasks and pressures they were dealing with were far more complex. The number of different constituents and pressure groups trying to act on a CRE makes life in some multinational companies look like a holiday.
2. To pass on some extra skills and ideas to do with organizational change to those who were involved. They accepted that they already had some ideas, but thought this was a good opportunity to learn more.
3. To suggest skills and approaches that had been used elsewhere, and to make some comments on proposals for new organizational structures. I was to use

the breadth rather than the depth of my experience to help them anticipate the effect of proposed changes.
4. To take a 'fairer', more detached view than was possible for those who knew the situation and the personalities well.
5. To provide legitimacy for the Review Group by being seen as an 'objective outsider'. If I were to lend my support to a particular suggestion, it would not be seen as flowing from the interests and preoccupations of the members of the Review Group.
6. As I was not a permanent member of the Notreading community, to be the person who could be blamed if it all went horribly wrong.

It seems likely to me that these last two answers are always part of the reason why an external consultant is called in (see McLean *et al.*, 1982). What was unusual in this case was that members of the Review Group were prepared to acknowledge that these were among their reasons for wanting me. The list of reasons did not emerge in one clear session. It was the usual process of consultant and client investigating each other, which has been likened to the way two dogs sniff each other on meeting (Mangham, 1978).

As usual in the quasi-voluntary sector, the money to pay me with was problematic. It seems that if an activity is called 'training' it is relatively easy to find the money, but problems arise if it is called 'consultancy'. Training rarely changes anything without some other intervention coinciding with it, and so I am reluctant to go along with the assumption that training is a good use of time and money but consultancy is a luxury.

I cannot afford to work for nothing, at least not for very long, and I do not think that it makes for effective interventions. I thought of a figure which seemed to me the minimum they could pay me and still take the exercise seriously. As I sat in their office talking to them about the arrangements, and absorbed the state of the walls and the furniture, I knocked off a further 20 per cent. The amount I then quoted, in the words of one commentator, 'seemed like Everest' to some members of the group. It was actually quite low compared with the full cost of employment of some of their full-time staff, but that was irrelevant to them because there was central government funding for full-time staff and not for consultants. Budget headings have an important influence on problem construction.

The Approval

The Review Group had been set up before my first involvement with the project, by the Executive Committee of Notreading CRE. So once the Review Group had accepted me, the Executive had to be asked to approve my involvement.

They were asked to give such approval on the basis of the Review Group's recommendation, but they deferred on the grounds that 'they would like to meet me first'. That is an eminently plausible argument which only begins to sound suspicious if you ask exactly what sort of information the members were hoping to gain from such a meeting. What could emerge from such a meeting which would give the Executive better data for making a decision about whether to employ me than the Review Group had?

I went along to meet the Executive as asked. The part of the meeting for which I was present mirrored the problems that I had heard about from the Review Group. The Executive members seemed to be committed, articulate, intelligent, concerned, and totally immobilized by each other. My suspicions about why they had asked to meet me seemed paranoid once I was there; there clearly could be no common purpose behind asking me to come along to meet them, or indeed behind anything else they did. One member would ask me some fairly detailed questions about how my style of intervention related to some of the range of different styles that are available and of which he appeared to have some knowledge. The simplest answer I could manage to that question prompted another member to say 'I am afraid all this is going straight over my head. What are you actually going to do?' This sort of thing happened several times during my three-quarters of an hour with the Executive. Questions came from different angles, betokening radically different understandings of the problems being faced by the Council and by the Executive. Each of those understandings was held firmly and with conviction, and with the belief that those who claimed to understand things differently were probably bent on sabotage.

For people in teams to have such different understandings of problems is quite normal, I think. What was different here from many teams I have worked with was:

1. Members of the Executive spent most of their time in other organizations (with the exception of the community relations officers, who were full-time officials), and had more conflicting views of the world as a result.
2. The issues around race relations are probably more complicated, less understood and less easy to discuss than are the issues which most teams and committees deal with.
3. Race relations is a topic very close to the values of members of the Executive Committee of a Council for Racial Equality. Conflicts are very often conflicts of values, which means (as Bailey, 1969, p. xii, pointed out) that they matter so much to the combatants that they will fight as hard and as fiercely as they can for them.

The upshot of the meeting was a unanimous vote in favour of asking me to help the Review Group. According to some of those who were there, this was despite the fact that several of those present (probably a majority) did not want me; this was in most cases for the very good reason that they thought any intervention would not be likely to serve their particular interest. However, that is not the sort of reason that people can go public on, so when it came to a vote they apparently felt they could find no legitimate reason for voting against.

The Study

One of the original ideas of the Review Group had been to get members of the Executive to talk to members of various ethnic minorities about their needs and about the extent to which the CRE was or was not meeting them. The Executive as a body had agreed to do this, but the individual members had not actually done anything, which was symptomatic of one of the problems that was worrying the Review Group. To them it typified the vicious circle of frustration leading to inactivity leading to more frustration which some Executive members found. So instead the members of the Review Group went round to members of the Executive, and to some recent ex-members, to talk to them in some depth about what they thought should be different in the conduct of the Notreading CRE, and what they thought were the important issues in local race relations.

The interviewers wrote up the interviews they had conducted and we then discussed them in the Review Group. I then put them together in a report. This was an occasion on which I was using my expertise and experience in grounded research in order to put ideas together in a reasonably balanced and coherent way to reflect the views held in the community which I was researching.

This first report aimed not to go much beyond the interview material and not to be noticeably evaluative. It ranged over six main areas of emergent findings. *Firstly*, there were comments on education, where the word was used in two senses. The less important sense (for the participants in the study) was the question of ensuring adequate access to the educational system for members of ethnic minorities. The more important and more frequent sense was to do with educating the community, particularly the white community, through the whole spectrum from school students to senior management, about race and racism.

Secondly, there were issues about employment. These were both directly concerned with enabling more members of ethnic minorities to gain employment and also with pressuring employers such as local authorities to employ members of minority groups. The latter was important partly for employment, partly for encouraging other employers and partly because it was thought likely that it would lead to greater trust of the authorities and more expertise in the local authority about race problems, and hence a reduced caseload for the CRE.

Thirdly, was the CRE trying to tackle racism or to increase racial harmony? There could clearly be a conflict between focusing on fostering harmonious relations within the community and attempting to tackle racism, including the almost invisible phenomenon of institutional racism.

Fourthly, there were comments on the functioning of the Executive Committee, about the endless reports it requested from its officers, its lengthy decision-making about detailed matters, the mutually conflicting expectations of members about their roles (particularly whether they were primarily responsible to the organization or minority that put them on to the Executive or whether they should exercise a wider-ranging responsibility). It was suggested that destructive personality rifts among the four most powerful members were being indulged at the expense of the CRE.

Fifthly, there were comments on the role of the CRE. What was the CRE for? Was it there to raise the confidence of the ethnic minorities, or to try to promote respect for all cultures, or to give support to ethnic groups? Should the CRE be a campaigning body rather than a welfare body? How independent should it be of political parties, or should it work with them? Should it be more of a referral agency and less of a casework agency? Should it handle specialist casework? Should it be carrying out grass roots work with self-help groups? Should it be spending more time combatting racism and fighting discrimination? Should it be trying to influence policy-makers, acting as an information centre for ethnic minority groups, engaging in more campaigning? Should it be undertaking more community projects, encouraging self-help among ethnic minority groups and visiting such projects to find out how they were doing? Should it be attacking the National Front? Should it be undertaking more 'organizational casework', helping groups to find premises?

Sixthly, there were a lot of issues about the CRE as employers, particularly to do with how the Executive and the officers could discover what criteria the others were using for judging the importance and urgency of the different issues they faced.

The Community Relations Officer and I also compiled a second, shorter report, which highlighted major points from the fuller report and suggested options for action. These were divided up under the headings 'Objectives', 'Structure' and 'Work Plan'. This laid out some ideas, founded in the six areas above, and attempted to face Executive Committee members with dilemmas about what objectives they wanted to see the CRE pursue (given that it could not simply solve all problems experienced by black people), what structure would be needed to enable those objectives to be met, and then in detail what the work plan would be for whom over the next twelve months to start meeting those objectives with that structure.

The Executive agreed to spend a whole day on discussing the reports and the issues that were raised in them and attempting to make decisions about future directions for work.

The Crunch

The meeting took place one Saturday in a community centre, which enabled us to spend some of the time all together and some of the time split up into smaller groups. The great majority of Executive Committee members attended, as did all the Review Group and I. Different members of the Review Group chaired different parts of the session, and there was always one person responsible for taking running notes of the meeting on a flipchart. The two people with the least obvious roles in this event were the Community Relations Officer and me. In his case, the unclarity arose from the fact that many of the items for discussion involved him as an employee, and therefore under the direction of the Executive. At the same time, he was acknowledged by almost everybody concerned to be the most authoritative source of ideas and the most important repository of wisdom on most of the topics, by virtue of working on them full time. This meant that both parties, the Community Relations Officer and the Executive, acknowledged that he should be answerable to the Executive, while at the same time recognizing that the Executive members did not know enough, and probably could not know enough, to act as informed managers for him and his staff. Thus his role would inevitably be confused at any policy-making meeting.

So far as my role was concerned, I had agreed to help the Review Group with their review; I had not been asked to run my own review. It was therefore not appropriate for me to have a very high profile in this meeting. I was spared the usual problem of feeling that I had to put on an impressive song and dance act in order to appear to have been worth hiring. Consultants sometimes feel that they need to put on such an act, while knowing that it will ultimately only increase the problem for those left behind who have to try to maintain the momentum in the absence of the performer.

But if my role was not to be the leader in making things happen, what was it? We resolved this by giving me the roles of court jester and commentator. In the first of these roles, I was licensed to say the things that nobody else felt themselves to have the right to say; for example, if there seemed to be too much cosy collusion around some idea, I would be able as an outsider to draw attention to it. This was not very significant, however, because whatever else the CRE might have suffered from, it was not cosy collusion! A more useful feature of this role was that I could throw ideas around using what McLean *et al.* (1982) call a 'grapeshot' approach; I could suggest a range of different ideas, and leave other people to see which ones seemed to resonate for them and which they would therefore take up and think more about.

In the commentator role, I was seen by all present, I think, as not having any axe to grind. If two members of the Executive started an argument which seemed to have more to do with long-standing quarrels between them than with the substantive issues of debate, then I could comment on that, and suggest a way of stopping it without the need for anyone to win or lose, in a manner which would not be possible for anyone who had been more involved in the relationships and the interpersonal politics over time.

The meeting consisted of four sections:

1. the aims and objectives of the CRE
2. the structure of the CRE
3. the next year's work plan
4. a final session, which excluded those of us who were not members of the Executive, for them to make formal decisions to ratify what they had informally decided earlier on in the day.

This structure worked exceptionally well; it proved impossible to control the earlier sessions enough, and so the discussion about work plan had to be postponed to a later meeting, but the idea of concluding with a formal committee meeting at which nearly all of the people who had been present during the day would still be present had two beneficial effects. Firstly, it meant that the decisions made were approved officially while members could still remember the reasons for them. It meant that those who had spent the day thinking through the issues had control over the political process. Secondly, it meant that earlier on in the day, when the discussions were taking place, there was a continuous incentive to make sure that decisions reached were real ones, which could be stated in such clear and simple terms that they could be written down for ratification at the Executive meeting later. This helped to prevent quantities of false consensus, of illusory agreement and of foggy argument.

The Aftermath

After the executive had made its decisions at the end of the all-day meeting, those decisions still had to go before the Annual General Meeting of the CRE to be approved. As the changes proposed included changes to the Aims and Objects of the Council, to the number of members on the Executive, and other similarly sensitive issues, it was important that the members of the Executive should be prepared to support their decisions for the full Annual General Meeting. This in the end turned out to be no problem, and nor was there any problem with acceptance of the Executive recommendations at the AGM. This may have been partly because of some preparatory work done by members of the Review Group, both in reminding the Executive why they had come to their decisions and also in talking to other members of the Council about the proposals that were to be put and the reasons that lay behind them. In addition, the Executive had prepared a set of fallback proposals to implement the same changes more slowly if the immediate changes proposed ran into difficulties.

The members of the Review Group believed it would be important for them to maintain an active role in monitoring the changes as they took place, both to see that what had been intended was what happened and also to ensure that these 'solutions' actually turned out to help with the problems they were intended to help with. Thus they took their process and their dealings with each other to have continuing importance beyond the end of the AGM. We therefore agreed to keep in touch for a few months after the meeting to monitor the fruits of our efforts.

I was very concerned in my work with the Review Group to see that our attention was concentrated on the effects we were trying to have in the CRE, and on the Executive, rather than looking at the functioning of our own Review Group. Not long before this intervention, some colleagues and I had discovered, in the course of a research project, several 'steering groups' which had become predominantly concerned with their own functioning (McLean *et al.*, 1982). Using some such argument as 'We can't go about doing things in this organization until we have got our own process right', they had then spent months or even years trying to get those processes right, while losing all interest in the organizational change which they were initially set up to steer. We had even discovered one steering group who had been running for two years and had done lots of interesting things, including making a film of their own group processes. They had steered nothing.

On this occasion I think I encouraged the Review Group to go too far in looking away from themselves and towards the situation they wanted to influence. The Review Group was immensely successful. It examined the issues, developed solutions, got those solutions accepted by the Executive, and was then able to take them on with the Executive's support for acceptance by the Council. However, the members of the Review Group were not of one mind on some issues of both value and style. For example, the Community Relations Officer was thoroughly abrasive in style. At times he seemed almost paranoid in his belief that other people were out to defeat him, and his tendency to mount preemptive strikes caused great anxiety among his friends. About a month after the AGM he got into such fierce and public conflict with the leader of the local authority that two of the less confronting members of the Review Group decided that he was deliberately sabotaging the whole Review. I was able to suggest ways in which they could test out (a) whether he had intended sabotage and (b) whether he had achieved it (both negative), and to retrieve the situation. But the coalition which had lasted long enough for the Review did not last long enough to monitor the implementation of their changes.

RESEARCH AND PRACTICE

The whole of this intervention was illuminated and influenced by using a problem construction framework. Essentially, the Review Group was trying to change the problems which the CRE handled. The members of the Review Group wanted to turn away from the issues of racial harmony which had seemed to be paramount when the CRE had been set up, ten years earlier. These were issues about how the different ethnic minorities and the majority white community could all live in peace together. They saw this as potentially exploitative; if you happen to be doing very nicely out of a particular social order, it will be in your interests for that order to be maintained peacefully. If ethnic minorities are being oppressed by a social system, it is not in the interests of those minorities that the system should be made to run harmoniously.

For these reasons, they wanted the focus of their problem construction to turn towards racial equality, which can be a conflicting goal and lead to a quite different set of problems. This would mean that the CRE's work was no longer to try and prevent or minimize conflict, but was instead to try and develop an equality for small minorities with the majority community, an object most likely to increase conflict.

The members of the Review Group did not need me to tell them that they wanted to influence the way problems were constructed in their organization. My initial research with health care planning teams, however, had led me to focus on the processes within the team and the structure of the organization as major factors in looking at problem construction. The work with Notreading CRE introduced me to two other areas of problem construction which were clearly important to the Review Group, namely legal factors and work programmes. I shall therefore divide this section as follows:

1. Process
2. Structure
3. Legal factors
4. Work programme

Process

Most of the things I have said above about the framework that emerged from my research were to do with processes of problem construction. For example, when people talk about their consciousness of different ways of defining problems, they almost always talk in terms of the processes that occur in their groups when such different definitions are offered. As was said above, when people talk about different construction styles this is often accompanied by discussion of the political processes which can be seen when the styles are operated. So when a member of the Review Group told me that one member of the Executive had been employed as secretary to the Community Relations Officer but had had to leave because 'she could not see things the same way', I explored this not only from the point of view of learning about residual bitterness, but also to find out what it could tell me about problem construction style.

When team members talk about problem-solving in their organizations, I have claimed that they often talk about problem construction as the crucial element of this. This was how the Review Group in Notreading CRE defined their project — as being about changing the kind of problems which were defined in that organization. This part of my research framework enabled me to understand what the Review Group were asking for. In particular, apart from wanting to give more attention to problems about racial equality and less to problems about racial harmony, they also felt that the problem construction in their organization was 'insufficiently focused'. They thought that their handling of problems was impaired by a lack of clarity about what problems they should be handling in which order, and by the guilt which could be felt about any problem that had not been solved — regardless of how many other problems had been competing with it at the critical moment. It was suggested to me in one of the early meetings that problems for solution were selected largely defensively; who was likely to make you feel most awful if you did not give priority to their problem. Through all this, there was scarcely a mention of problem-solving except as something which you just went away and did after you had got the definitions and priorities sorted.

The body of formal and informal rules which governed problem construction in Notreading CRE was both very important and fairly visible. It is an organization in which anger is freely expressed, and much of the anger around was directed at other people's infringements of the rules, or their insistence on the rules, or their attempts to change the rules. For example, one trade union representative wanted to see much more concentration by the CRE on employment issues. He kept arguing that any other focus for the CRE was an abdication of their responsibility; that everything hinged on being able to participate in paid employment; and that other topics such as police harassment, racial abuse and education would all fall into place once employment was dealt with. He attempted to argue that the constitution of the CRE, together with custom and practice, supported his case. In a meeting of the executive, three black members in turn told him that this was a very 'white' view of society and of work, and not one which the CRE should have any sympathy with. I was told afterwards by one of the three black opponents of the employment emphasis that probably most of the people there had started the meeting agreeing with the trade union representative in what this member referred to, rather engagingly, as the 'Marxist–Calvinist view of work'. However, he said, it was against the rules for white people to hold out against any position that was taken up by more than one black person.

Much emphasis was placed by those interviewed during the survey by the Review Group on the poor relationships between some of the more powerful members of the Executive. One of the protagonists in those poor relationships argued that this was the sort of thing which was no doubt regrettable but which should not play any part in the discussion of the future of the CRE; after all, she said, 'grown-up people should be able to sort this sort of thing out, shouldn't they?' She was answered with total silence, which I did not time but which seemed endless. Then discussion about the poor relationships resumed as if she had said nothing. She had attempted to suggest that a particular line of discussion was against the rules. One of the others present said to me afterwards,

'She would say that, wouldn't she? And she's one of the guilty parties.' So it was against another set of rules for her to attempt to change that rule, because it involved her too personally. She subsequently did not seek election to the new Executive, and withdrew from all activity connected with the CRE.

Structure

While my previous research has made me familiar with the processes of problem construction, the preoccupation which some members of the Review Group had with structure was new to me. The structural arguments were about the structure and membership of the Executive Committee and the membership of the CRE. On the membership of the committee, it was felt that there were too many members (19) for most of them to feel that they were committed to actually doing anything. The Review Group wanted a new structure with a smaller Executive, who would be expected to take executive action and to engage themselves with all issues which fell within an agreed definition of the functions of the CRE. This meant that there would be no place for some of the existing members of the Executive, who took their role as being to represent a particular racial (e.g. Bengali) or interest (e.g. education) group. It was felt by the Review Group that without such a change in structure, there was little prospect of problem definition becoming sharper within the Executive; equally importantly, they thought that the realism of the problems defined could be improved no end if the members of the Executive knew that they would have to find and implement the solutions to whatever problems they constructed.

The membership of the CRE was a more complicated problem. In most cases, the tradition has been that any individual or group can join their local CRE for a modest subscription, and can then have access to the papers and information about meetings as well as voting rights at the Annual General Meeting. This has led, in some places, to the leaders of some racial minority persuading most of the other members of their races in their city to join the CRE and then to vote members of their minority into all the powerful posts within it. This has had devastating effects on members of other minorities, who may then find their local CRE speaking against their interests. It also leads other public and private bodies not to take the CRE seriously. Notreading CRE wished to prevent this happening.

They also had a more immediate problem with membership. They knew that one of their members was supplying information about their activities to the National Front, because they repeatedly went along to CRE meetings which had only been publicized to the membership and found that the meeting hall was freshly daubed with swastikas or faeces. Even when the police caught the culprit, there was no way that their constitution permitted them to expel him.

The harsh realities of race relations work, in which threats of death are not uncommon even for fairly low-level community relations officers, where broken windows, daubing and abusive letters are commonplace, mean that structural changes are much more crucial to people working in a CRE than they seem to be in the more genteel world of private industry. The alternative emphases on structure or process also seem to associate with political stances; liberals and liberal socialists concentrate more on process, while Marxists seem to live out their belief that structure determines behaviour. It was the Marxists within the Review Group who insisted on the importance of structural change and the liberals who believed that new structures would achieve nothing without some work on the process. It suited my intuitions and my experience very well to consider that we needed both if either were to be effective.

Legal Factors

Members and officers of a Community Relations Council operate in a much more contested field, legally and politically, than most. Quite apart from the political differences that I was talking about in the preceding section, they could not afford to change the emphasis of their organizational activities without changing their constitution and articles of association, for fear of being taken to task (or court) by some highly skilled and well-motivated lawyers and local politicians. There are costs involved in the generally high level of articulateness and political awareness in the race relations industry.

The constitution of most organizations, with its aims and objects, is usually a document of so little interest that its members have not read it and have probably never heard of it. I have never before, when acting as an external consultant, been invited to take an interest in the 'Aims and Objects' of the organization. However, when you are beset by pressure groups who can threaten you with bad publicity in the local and national press, legal action, street demonstrations, the Member of Parliament, the local authority, the Home Office, obstruction in everything you try to do, the Ombudsman, the National Audit Office, the local Labour Party Executive, the local Communist Party Executive, physical violence towards you and your family, and even eternal damnation, under these conditions you may wish to be clear that you are acting in accordance with your constitution.

Aims and Objects can be beguilingly short statements. All that the Review Group wanted was to replace a few sentences about racial harmony and peace within the community with the following:

(a) To work within the Notreading area for the elimination of racial discrimination and disadvantage within a multiracial, multicultural, multifaith society, and to encourage cooperation between different ethnic groups.

(b) To promote equality of opportunity between people of different race and colour within the Notreading area.

(c)   In furtherance of the above purposes to take appropriate actions and to cooperate with statutory authorities and other bodies undertaking activities compatible with those of the Council.

The adoption of these meant, in my terms, that the Community Relations Officer and his staff could feel relatively secure so long as the problems they were giving their time and attention to could be related to these Aims and Objects. Similarly, the Executive Committee of the CRE could address problems within those areas without the risk of being pilloried or dismissed for being out of order. It redefined the whole area within which problem construction was permissible.

But would these aims and objects be acceptable to the Charity Commissioners? If the CRE wished to retain charitable status, with the tax advantages involved, their aims and objects must be accepted by the Charity Commissioners as 'non-political' — which is probably the one single factor which makes people working for charities in the UK more frustrated than any other. Even the most venerable of household name charities have to be continuously on their guard to see that none of their actions can be construed as 'political'. In race relations it is not easy to see that anyone could do anything without being political. The Executive faced this in their whole-day meeting, and concluded that it was worth asking their solicitor to try the new Aims and Objects with the Charity Commissioners, but that it was not worth making any non-trivial changes in order to retain charitable status. Thus they decided that it was more important to work on the problems they thought they should be working on than to have the maximum resources to work on other problems. Fuller solutions to less important problems were not what they wanted.

Work Programme

If the constitutional aims and objects were important in signalling to the outside world what Notreading CRE was doing, and in legitimating their actions, there was still a need for a more detailed mechanism within the CRE for determining which problems should be constructed and then with what urgency they should be attended to. This was provided by the work programme.

As it happened, Notreading and all the other local Councils for Racial Equality and Community Relations Councils were required to produce a work programme, because the Commission for Racial Equality, the national body which is responsible for funding their staff, had decided that it would help them to sort out their priorities (or, as I would say, to be more deliberate in their problem construction).

It seemed to the Review Group that this gave a new opportunity to demand that the Executive thought about priorities at greater length than ever before, and that the work programme would also be an effective way to prevent the debates and recriminations which otherwise took place between the Executive and the Community Relations Officer about the relative importances of tasks. Having sorted out their work programme, it could then form a reference point for mutual guidance between the Executive as employers and the Community Relations Officer and his staff as employees. Then if there was a discrepancy between what the employers were asking and what the employees were doing, they could refer back and see which fitted best with the agreed work programme. Thus they could solve some of the problems of an elected body of inexperts trying to control and manage expert officers. They also operated a ground rule that nothing should go into the work programme without identifying members of the Executive who were willing to help with the work on it.

Thus the major areas for problem-finding were identified and put into an order of priorities by the Executive with the officers. The task of formulating the problems and constructing them in detail was then performed by the officers, as the people with the technical expertise in race relations. Implementation of solutions was to involve members of the Executive, as they had more time and more detailed local knowledge than the Community Relations Officer could have.

CONCLUSION

In my PhD research I had the luxury of developing at length a framework to help me understand something that had been puzzling me for a long time. I had a framework before I started the research, of course, and the research changed and developed that. The resulting revised framework seemed to help me in many different ways with the intervention in Notreading, and at the same time, as I have described above, it led me to expand the framework and give it more detail. This suggests further research which could be done, for example to consider how a work programme influences problem construction, on the pattern of Figure 1.

I think the research loop and the intervention loop are different, even though the research might be action research and the intervention might generate a lot of learning. The problem construction for the researcher/interventionist is

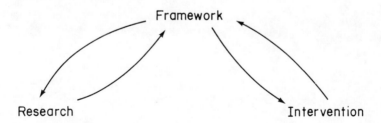

Figure 1

different in the two cases. I could not have developed my problem construction framework within an intervention; the risks of no suitable action resulting from it would have been too high, and because my main problem would have been to help the people I was working with, I would not have been motivated to take those risks. I could not have worked on these issues with Notreading CRE because they could not have afforded to let someone trying to do innovative research stumble around in their local minefield. Research, intervention and the development of usable frameworks are interdependent.

Organization Analysis and Development
Edited by I. L. Mangham
© John Wiley & Sons Ltd.

The Role of Strategy in Technological Innovation:
A Re-assessment

CHAPTER 7   *Michael Saren*

INTRODUCTION

Recently there has been a considerable amount of emphasis on the role of 'strategy' in determining the nature and direction of technological innovation.
A number of different business strategies for innovation have been identified. Essentially these contrast two strategic choices, variously described as 'offensive' or 'defensive' (Freeman, 1974), 'proactive' or 'reactive' (Urban and Hauser, 1980), 'entrepreneurial' or 'positional' (Ansoff, 1979), 'leaders' or 'followers' (Johne, 1982). While there are suboptions within each of these categories, these authors all argue that successful leadership in technological innovation is primarily a consequence of strategy decisions and actions. As Johne (1982) concludes: 'This article has stressed the overriding importance of strategy in determining the pace and type of technological innovation'. In more general terms, Nadler and Tushman (1980) argue that:

> Strategy may be the most important single input for the organisation. On the one hand strategic decisions implicitly determine the nature of the work the organisation should be doing or the tasks it should perform. On the other hand, strategic decisions, and particularly decisions about objectives, determine the systems' desired outputs. (in Tushman and Moore, 1982)

In business organizations technological innovation is normally aimed at the development of new products and processes. A company's innovation strategy, then, has its roots in the corporate strategic planning. This is illustrated by Booz Allen and Hamilton (1981) in Figure 1. Mintzberg (1979) sees business strategy as a 'mediating force' linking the organization and its environment and Crawford (1983) defines it as:

> The set of goals that the organisation's management has decided to achieve and the bundle of policies and programs that serve as the general guidelines for achieving those goals. The overall goal is to achieve the optimum interface between an organisation and its environment.

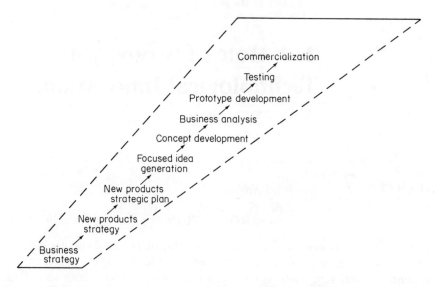

Figure 1 The role of new products strategy. Source: Booz *et al.* (1981)

One problem with viewing technological innovation in strategic terms as a subset of overall corporate strategy is the inherent difficulty of planning for technological advance. There are many examples of new innovation possibilities which arose unexpectedly and which were exploited opportunistically by the organization. Penicillin and Xerox developed from unanticipated discoveries and were therefore, it might be argued, 'unplannable' innovations. To managers strategy formulation is based on an attitudinal approach of predictability in overall corporate operations. Technological change is not easy to encompass within this approach and often an organization's research and development activities are regarded as a purely technical domain, a 'black box' producing technological possibilities for commercial exploitation.

However, it is more generally accepted nowadays that technological change cannot be regarded as autonomous, determined only by technology itself. There has been considerable debate as to the causal relationship which exists between technology supply and technology demand. On the one hand the 'demand-pull' theory (Langrish *et al.*, 1972) holds that the primary determinant of the extent and direction of progress in technology is 'demand' – including economic, social and political forces. Against this the 'technology-push' explanation proposes that developments take place independently through discoveries, theories, ideas and R&D activities which may or may not be subsequently translated into marketable innovations.

Although the latter hypothesis might be regarded *prima facie* as rendering any business strategy for technological innovation redundant because of the 'unplannability' of the process, it does not necessarily lead to this conclusion in principle because the R&D and inventive activities are nevertheless conducted within or under the direction of the business organization itself. The objectives, resources and operations of the scientists and technologists pursuing technological advances can be and are controlled at the strategic level by top management of the organization. Indeed, in a sense the supply of technology is more within the managers' control than the external demand (market, social, economic) from the environment. As Freeman observed, the act of innovation is fundamentally a 'matching' of these supply and demand forces:

> The fascination of invention and innovation lies in the fact that both the marketplace and the frontiers of technology are continually changing. This creates a kaleidoscopic succession of new possibilities and combinations .... Innovation is a coupling process which first takes place in the minds of imaginative people somewhere in the everchanging interface between science, technology and the market. (Freeman, 1974)

From top management's point of view, this relationship between technology supply and demand components which determine the route which technological advance takes is manageable and plannable in principle because technology does not drive itself but is deliberately driven in one of a number of alternative directions by external forces. People in the organization can control some of these forces such as R&D resources and activities and therefore an appropriate innovation strategy can be developed to produce the nature and direction of technological changes which will be required.

This argument provides a rationale for the view that strategy has the most important role in determining technological innovation in the business organization. The central concern of strategic management is making and implementing strategic choices which match the organization's capabilities with opportunities present in the environment to achieve long-term objectives. Empirical research by Johne (1982) based on 16 firms in the UK test instrument industry showed that the nature and pace of technological innovation was closely related to the choice of a 'leader' and 'follower' innovation strategy. Firms pursuing the former placed more emphasis on product innovation, whilst the latter group emphasized process innovation.

However, other research studies of innovating firms have indicated that a large number of factors other than the choice of strategy are related to the rate and success of their technological innovations. These factors can be categorized into four groups:

(1) Economic factors
(2) Social and behavioural factors
(3) Information and communication factors
(4) Organizational and managerial factors

These raise important questions as to how they can be reconciled with the role of strategy. Before addressing these questions a review of the historical research findings associated with this topic follows, based on the above taxonomy.

FACTORS ASSOCIATED WITH TECHNICAL INNOVATIVENESS IN BUSINESS ORGANIZATIONS

Economic Factors

The relationship between the innovation performance of a firm and its size has been the subject of many empirical and theoretical publications. Schumpeter (1928) and Galbraith (1967) have asserted that modern innovations have been created primarily by large firms. Big companies have advantages due to:

1. the high R&D and launch costs of modern innovation;
2. their large-scale production and product diversification which enables them to 'balance' success and failure in innovation;
3. their greater market control.

Evidence indicates that industrial R&D is concentrated in large companies. The National Science Foundation (1966) estimated that 471 firms with over 5000 employees were responsible for 88 per cent of all R&D spending in the USA in 1966. An international survey, conducted by the OECD (1971), found that in the 'small industrialized countries' — Austria, Norway and Belgium —and also in Spain, small and medium-sized firms (less than 1000 employees) accounted for 75, 87, 64 and 68 per cent respectively of the total R&D expenditure in the private sector. In such countries the role played by large firms is relatively limited, OECD conclude, but in USA, Japan and France large companies' (more than 1000 employees) contribution is much more significant, representing 87, 65 and 65 per cent of R&D spending respectively. Other studies (Freeman, 1971; Mansfield, 1963) have produced similar results indicating the predominance of large over small firms (particularly in technically advanced sectors) in terms of R&D expenditures.

However, OECD point out that large firms may use more expensive equipment and facilities and pay higher costs and salaries. Therefore, they provide an alternative measure of 'research intensity', i.e. the ratio between the number of R&D staff and total employees. Using this indicator they find that smaller companies '. . . in general furnish a relatively greater research effort in terms of manpower' (OECD, 1971).

One problem with using R&D spending as a measure of innovativeness or inventiveness is that it is a measure of input, not of output. Although less is spent on research, innovation 'productivity' may be higher. Comanor's (1967) study of the pharmaceutical industry produces some evidence of substantial diseconomies of scale in R&D in large companies, compared to smaller ones. Jewkes *et al.* (1958) found that out of the 61 important inventions and innovations during the twentieth century which they selected, over half stemmed from independent inventors or small firms. Other investigations have reported that the largest US firms have made a relatively small contribution to innovation in the steel industry (Mansfield, 1963; Hamberg, 1964), the aluminium industry (Peck 1962) and the petroleum industry (Enos, 1962).

Mansfield (1963) shows that the largest firms in the US petroleum refining and coal industries account for a greater proportional share of innovation where one of the following conditions exists:

1. the investment cost is large;
2. the minimum size of firm which will use the innovation is large;
3. the average size of the four largest firms is much greater than the average size of the potential user.

One conclusion from Mansfield's results might be that the optimal size of firm will differ according to the nature of the innovation. Indeed, the apparently contradictory evidence concerning this question of firm size might be reconciled if only specific conclusions were attempted. Even studies which have analysed several industries have found significant differences between them in this respect. For example, Grabowski's (1968) report found '... quite different behaviour in the two industries'. He indicates that larger firms contribute relatively more drug and chemical innovations in areas requiring a large-scale input of technological, production and market resources, whereas smaller firms play a more important innovative role in areas that are more specialized and require sophisticated technology without large-scale production and marketing requirements.

The role of large and small firms cannot be expected to be constant over time. As technology matures in an industry, scale factors tend to become more important. But, as new technical opportunities appear so these will open new areas of contribution for the small, innovative firm which may be able to adapt more quickly. Therefore, the balance of size of the innovating firm is likely to vary according to industries, technologies and time.

Grabowski (1968) has shown that in two technologically sophisticated industries research intensity is associated, not with firm size *per se*, but with an index of variables which he constructs and shows to be significant for the pharmaceutical and chemical industries (though not for petroleum-refining). These explanatory variables of firms' research intensity are:

(a) past research productivity (measured by the number of patents);
(b) diversification (product mix; range of Standard Industrial classifications;

(c)   internal funds (sum of the post-tax profit and depreciation charges, deflated
      by sales).

These were found to be positively correlated with research intensity in the
sixteen chemicals and ten drug companies, but no correlation was shown for the
fifteen petroleum-refining firms. The last variable above, internal funds, is
similar to one proposed explanatory variable for the rate of investment in the
firm (see Eisner and Strotz, 1963). Indeed, the relationship between investment
in general and R&D investment may not be limited to the sharing of a common
determinant. The output of R&D is produced in the form of potential
innovations which may be brought to commercial realization by the firm. Since
new capital equipment may itself embody new technical advances, it has been
suggested that gross investment expenditure is one factor influencing the speed
of adoption of innovations. Salter (1960) has shown how increased investment
can be expected to decrease the lag of the average to the best techniques.
However, unless there are existing innovations which have yet to be exploited
increased investment will not necessarily lead to innovation. Indeed, the use of
capital-saving innovations may result in a lower investment rate for the
innovating firm compared to a conservative replacement policy of the less
innovative company. Investment rates need not, therefore, be higher in
innovating firms.

Nor does it appear that innovators necessarily have higher profits. Mansfield
(1963) finds '. . . no close relationship between a firm's profit rate and the rate at
which it adopts a new technique'. Although this conclusion relates to adoption
of innovation as opposed to its generation, there is no reason to assume that
early innovation will necessarily be more profitable than defensive or later
innovation because, despite the potentially higher returns, the risks are also
greater. There are no indications from the economic analyses of variations in
profitability.

Furthermore, the economic studies provide only nebulous implications for
the factors affecting technological innovation in the firm. Various aspects
associated with firm size, investment and profit have been related to innovation,
but only in specific circumstances, if at all, has any relationship been shown to
exist.

Social and Behavioural Factors

American sociologists and economists have conducted surveys of the
adoption and diffusion of innovation processes among farmers in rurual
communities. These may provide an analogy between the innovating farmer and
the innovating firm.

The factors which have been found to be associated with the farmer's
propensity to adopt a new product or process early are:

(a) higher level of production, more utilization of the mass media, higher prestige (Griliches, 1957);
(b) more contact with scientists, more venturesome attitudes;
(c) belonging to more formal organizations, higher acreage (Ryan and Gross, 1943);
(d) lower age, higher income, more education, more cosmopolitan, reading more bulletins (Katz, 1961; Ryan and Gross, 1943).

The results from this research indicate that the most important attributes associated with early adoption are:

1. more communication with others;
2. less traditional/fixed values.

Observations of the diffusion of new techniques among doctors have produced evidence of interpersonal networks independent of external change agents (Coleman *et al.*, 1957). Brooks (1957) postulates that the steeper part of the S-shaped diffusion curve is caused by the snowball effect of these networks increasing the rate of adoption over time. It has been demonstrated that the strength of these effects of interpersonal channels may be dependent on the size of the community (Winick, 1961).

There is difficulty in evaluating the relevance of these sociological case studies for the characteristics of innovative firms because most do not examine large organizations, but farms, schools and doctors. Therefore the features of early innovators cannot readily be translated into organizational or industrial terms. However, a 'two-step' flow of diffusion is indicated, with early innovators relying to a greater extent on contacts outside their peer communities for information (Katz, 1961). The innovative firm might similarly be expected to exhibit more external contact — particularly relating to new technological developments — than the late-innovating firm.

Katz (1961) has found that differences in wealth or financial profitability do not appear to be determinants of the response to an innovation. Neither price nor profitability influences the rate of adoption of innovation in Ryan and Gross's (1943) study. These results confirm the findings from economic studies of industrial organizations (above), that innovativeness need not be associated with the level of profit or investment.

Information and Communication Factors

The Sources of New Ideas

There is a distinction between the activities of basic research and development and those of technological innovation — the output of basic R&D is not an innovation until a commercial product has been launched on the market. US case studies of innovation have been examined by Price and Bass (1969) with reference to the interrelationships between these two types of activities in the innovation process. They conclude that:

1. Innovation typically depends on information for which the requirement cannot be anticipated in definitive terms and therefore cannot be programmed in advance; instead, key information is often provided through unrelated research. The process is facilitated by a great deal of freedom and flexibility in communication across organizational, geographical and disciplinary lines.
2. The function of basic research in the innovation process can often be described as meaningful dialogue between the scientific and the technological communities. The entrepreneurs for the innovation process usually belong to the latter sector, while the persons intimately familiar with the necessary scientific understanding are often part of the former. (Price and Bass (1969) — quoted in OECD (1971))

This dichotomy of functions within the innovation process might therefore have implications for the communications network and channels of the innovating firm. Rothwell and Robertson (1973) argue that: 'The transference of ideas throughout the scientific and technological communities is of prime importance to the stimulation of new scientific and technological endeavours.' As Price and Bass (1969) point out, the scientific and technological communities are not necessarily the same where industrial innovation is concerned. Basic scientific research and technological development may be carried out separately by different types of organizations. The innovating firm does not necessarily conduct basic research itself, but may utilize scientific knowledge generated in other organizations in order to develop new technological innovations. Evidence suggests that most basic research performed in industrial countries is not carried out within commercial firms (OECD, 1970). The OECD study shows that government and higher education organizations perform more basic research than business enterprises in several industrialized countries. Also, they found that in most countries basic research represents a small proportion (generally 4–7 per cent) of the total R&D activities in the business enterprise sector.

Since many firms apparently rely for most of the basic research input to technological innovation on information from other organizations, it might be expected that the source of new ideas for innovations will often lie outside the firm. A summary of the findings from several empirical studies of the sources of ideas for innovation lends considerable support for this view (see Table 1). This shows that external sources have generated the idea for

Table 1 Sources of Ideas for Innovation: A Summary of Findings

A. Myers and Marquis (1969): study of 567 innovations

Source of ideas	Percentage of cases
Vendor or supplier	16.3
Private organizations	59.5
Government agencies	3.3
Unknown	20.9
	100.0

B. Project Sappho (SPRU 1972): 86 innovations

Source of Ideas	Percentage of cases
Internal — 40 innovations	
External — 46 innovations:	
of which	
Universities	22.0
Government agencies	28.0
Other industrial companies	39.0
Outside individuals	11.0
Research associations	0.0
	100.0

C. Freeman (1971): 1667 innovations

Source of ideas	Percentage of cases
In house	53.74
Universities	2.52
Government, defence	1.25
Government, civil	5.63
Research associations	4.20
Related industry	1.14
Unrelated industry	6.00
Individuals	1.25
Parent company abroad	10.50
Abroad	12.66
Under licence from abroad	1.08
	100.0

continued overleaf

D. Jones and Wilemon (1972): 'venture groups' in 24 large US companies

Source of ideas	(Rounded) percentage of cases
External consultants, inventors and brokers	30.0
R&D engineering	24.0
Marketing and market research	14.0
The chairman or president	11.0
Line or staff operating managers	7.0
The venture group	5.0
Literature	4.0
Customers	3.0
Competitors	1.0
Corporate planning departments	1.0
	100.0

E. Langrish *et al.* (1972): 158 'key technical ideas' — in 51 innovations

Source of ideas		Number of ideas
Within the firm	56	
Outwith the firm	102	
External: of which		
Person joining the firm		20.05[a]
Industrial experience		15.00
Educational experience		9.00
Commercial agreement (e.g. takeover)		10.05[a]
Literature (technical, scientific and patent)		9.05[a]
Personal contact in the country (UK)		8.05[a]
Collaboration with supplier		7.00
Collaboration with customer		5.00
Visit overseas		6.05[a]
Government organizations		6.00
Conferences in the country (UK)		2.05[a]
Consultancy		2.00
		102.00

[a]In some cases the sources are not mutually exclusive.

innovation in many cases. The innovating firm may therefore engage in more external communication and possess many outside contacts enabling it to utilize information and ideas from these sources.

Personal contact is reported to be the most important type of communication for the transfer of scientific information from outwith innovating firms by OECD (1971).

The close links observed between national strength in fundamental research and national performances in technological innovation exist because knowledge flows and definition of needs between science and technology are largely 'person embodied': that is, they happen through people talking together frequently or through people moving from one institution to another.... The successful coupling between them (i.e. recognition of opportunities, definition of needs and flow of information) ultimately requires continuing personal and pluralistic collaboration between the Universities and industry. (OECD (1971))

Differentiating between sources of ideas generation and sources of problem-solving in the innovation process, Myers and Marquis (1969) found personal contact to be the single most important channel, transferring 43 per cent of the information for 'evolving basic idea' and 50 per cent in 'expediting the solution'. Work by Langrish *et al.* (see Table 1) shows that new personnel joining firms studied accounted for more than a fifth of the innovative ideas from outside. Other studies (for example Utterback, 1971; Allen 1966; Rothwell and Robertson, 1973) have produced similar results, indicating the roles of personal contacts and experience as idea sources and channels of communication, particularly externally.

On the basis of these findings it may be concluded that two important features of innovative companies may be strong outside personal contacts and a broad range of external communication channels.

The Role of Individuals

Several writers have discussed the role of the individual — particularly the creative individual — in the process of invention, and also innovation. They emphasize the individual's creative, idea-forming abilities in relation to these activities. It has also been proposed that individuals within an organization can play other vital roles in the innovation process. As has been shown above, they may fulfil the role of personal external communication — 'the technological gatekeeper' Allen (1971) labels them. In several organizations, Holland (1972) identifies personnel with 'high information potential' who perform this role.

Another role which has been identified is that of the 'product champion' in a company who is responsible for the promotion of an innovation and challenges resistance to change. He may fulfil an intra-organizational communication function between departmental groups — particularly between R&D staff and management decision-makers — as Gruber *et al.* (1973) have shown. There can also be a formidable gap in contact between R&D teams themselves. An investigation of patents granted during the 1950s in the USA reveals that 40–60 per cent of the patentees worked outside the organized research teams of industrial laboratories (Schmookler, 1957).

In Schon's (1967) view, innovators are often working primarily against organizational resistance. 'It is clear, then, that in recent times individuals working without organizational support have been responsible for an extraordinarily high percentage of important, radical commercial developments.' The innovative organization, as seen by Sheppard (1967), is staffed by individuals with strong 'self-actualizing' personalities, generating more ideas and pushing for their adoption.

However, the role of the individual in the organization as a force towards innovation cannot be divorced from the organizational structure within which he operates, despite the common theme in the literature of the individual inventor's or innovator's responsibility for new ideas and products. Sayles (1974) points out that the employee in a large firm is not simply an individual operating in isolation from his colleagues, nor is he a member of a single group within a larger structure. Rather, the employee interacts in a variety of settings within the organization. He is likely to have a proliferation of memberships of several groups of various types, such as a task group, friendship clique and interest group. In Likert's (1967) theory of organizational behaviour this network of overlapping group memberships, which comprises a large organization, constitutes the main channel of influence within the organization.

The individual champion of an innovation, therefore, must work within the communication networks, formal and informal, of the organization in promoting change. Indeed, the influence of 'groups' on organizational behaviour in general, including the promotion and resistance of innovation, has been challenged by Smith (1973) insofar as a group can be defined by the existence of continuing relationships between its members. In terms of this definition, he argues that many laboratory experiments are not studies of 'groups' at all. They should be described instead as 'collectivities' in order to highlight the contrast between meetings of initial strangers and meetings of persons with interpersonal relationships already established.

The balance of attention by researchers on the roles of individuals in the innovation process has been rather one-sided. The response of individuals to change within the firm may be as equally important as their function of promoting innovation. The fewer the individuals resisting change the less need for a product champion. Bennis' model of a person's response to change (1965) illustrates the factors which can influence this response (e.g. ambiguity of the meaning of change, information about the change, participation in the change, etc.)

Therefore, while recognizing the important role that the individual has played in creating innovations in the past, the organizational and managerial conditions existing within modern firms may also reflect a distinguishing feature of companies with varying performance in technological innovation.

Organizational and Managerial Factors

Success and Failure in Innovation – the Eclectic Studies

Many salient characteristics associated with the success or failure of innovations have been identified by researchers. Carter and Williams (1957) discerned a relationship between technical progressiveness and 24 out of 29 'general quality' characteristics in nearly 200 firms. Companies were awarded a technical progressiveness rating on a scale ranging 0–10 and each characteristic was rated on a 0–8 scale based on questionnaire and interview returns. These results are illustrated in Table 2. They conclude that:

> Technical progressiveness is related to the general quality of the firm; and attention to other aspects of its general quality — for instance, to management efficiency or to salesmanship and market-research — helps to create the conditions for technical progress.

'Technical progressiveness' might be expected to be associated with 'innovativeness' as it has been defined here. This Carter and Williams (1975) survey represents, in that case, a pioneering attempt to identify a range of factors which are common to innovators.

Five hundred and sixty-seven innovations from five US industries were examined by Myers and Marquis (1969). The aspect which was their subject was idea generation and problem-solving and information sources and inputs in the innovation process. Results suggest that R&D management is only one small aspect of the management of technological innovation. Only 21 per cent of successful innovations were based primarily on the recognition of a technical possibility and in even fewer cases did the major information input for idea generation or problem-solving emanate from laboratories. The management of innovation was viewed as a corporate-wide task.

Globe *et al.* (1973) document the case histories of ten outstanding innovations. In each they identified 'decisive events' providing a major and essential impetus to the innovation and compared these to 21 factors which, they consider, might have influenced each event. The results show that no single factor was judged important for every event. Table 3 lists the percentage of all decisive events for which each factor was 'judged moderately or highly important'.

The Globe case studies conclude that the high ranking of such factors as recognition of technical opportunity or need and actions of technical enterprise which involve 'inventive or creative activities' supports the view that innovation cannot be totally planned. They do suggest two '... ways in which management can help it along'. These are:

Table 2 Relation of ratings for technical progressiveness of firms and for 29 other
characteristics (Marks out of 80 — three groups of firms)

Characteristics	Technical progressiveness rating			
	0–4	5–7	8–10	Ratio of 8–10 marks to 0–4 marks (%)
Good information sources	20	42	74	370
Outside standards of performance	10	51	76	760
No secretiveness	21	60	77	367
Readiness to cooperate	22	52	77	350
Good coordination	14	51	73	521
Ideas surveyed	22	47	79	359
Cost consciousness in research	18	41	69	383
Quantified investment decisions	1	46	74	7400
Good management techniques	17	57	76	447
High status of science	9	44	78	867
Scientists on the board	20	46	71	355
Good chief executive	13	58	79	608
Attractive to talent	19	42	70	368
Good recruitment policy	29	50	76	262
Good training policy	11	43	68	618
Enough intermediate managers	10	33	68	680
Managers stimulated	4	37	75	1875
Effective selling	16	45	72	450
Good technical service	23	53	79	344
Good intermediate managers	19	32	76	400
Ingenuity with shortages	6	55	76	1267
Forward-looking tendency	11	54	67	609
High expansion rate	23	68	78	339
Rapid machine replacement	16	37	71	444
Industry scientific	23	19	55	239
Good buildings	23	31	49	213
Top manager a scientist	8	32	54	675
Shopfloor resistance to innovation	64	70	75	117
Adequate finance	48	53	75	156

Source: Carter and Williams (1957).

1. High funding — of all innovation functions; especially R&D. This will
stimulate the innovation process by increasing R&D team confidence.
2. 'Confluence of technology' — by promoting interdisciplinary R&D teams.

Another study was conducted by Langrish (1969) of 84 innovations in
companies winning the 66 Queen's Awards for Technological Innovation in
1966 and 1967 for the chemicals, mechanical engineering, electrical and 'craft'

Table 3 Percentage of decisive events rated moderately or highly important for each factor in the innovation process

Factors	Percentage of decisive events
Recognition of technical opportunity	87
Recognition of the need	69
Internal R&D management	66
Management lecture decision	62
Availability of funding	62
Technical entrepreneur	56
In-house colleagues	51
Prior demonstration of feasibility	49
Patent/licence considerations	47
Recognition of scientific opportunity	43
Technology confluence	36
Technological gatekeeper	30
Technology interest group	29
Competitive pressures	25
External direction to R&D personnel	16
General economic factors	16
Health and environmental factors	15
Serendipity	12
Formal market analysis	7
Political factors	5
Social factors	4

Source: Globe *et al.* (1973, p. 12).

Table 4 Factors in success of innovation

Factors of importance in success of firm	Relative occurrence of factors (%)				
	Chemical $n = 12$	Mech.eng $n = 40$	Electc'l $n = 23$	'Craft' $n = 9$	All $n = 84$
Top person	22.2	27.1	25.7	18.5	25.1
Other person	5.6	14.4	21.4	11.1	14.7
Clear identification of a need	19.4	18.8	14.5	9.3	16.7
Realization of potential usefulness of a discovery	2.8	7.5	6.5	3.7	6.2
Good cooperation	8.3	3.1	5.1	7.4	4.9
Availability of resources	8.3	12.1	2.5	5.6	8.2
Help from government sources	8.3	4.6	2.5	11.1	5.3
Not classified	25.0	12.5	21.7	33.3	19.0

Source: Langrish (1969).

industries. Table 4 shows the important factors associated with the innovations and indicates their frequency of occurrence. The individual is again apparently the single most important factor (especially if one combines the top two factors).

Project SAPPHO (SPRU, 1972) attempts a more quantitative methodological approach to the analysis of success and failure in innovation. Fifty-eight attempted innovations were examined from the chemicals and scientific instruments industries. They were grouped in 29 pairs each containing one successful innovation and one failure. Failure was defined by an innovation which did not establish a satisfactory market and/or failed to make a profit. Successful innovations attained significant market penetration and/or made a profit. Observed variations in characteristics between each innovation in the pairs provided empirical evidence on which to test the relevance of that factor. Around 200 measures were employed with 120 interview questions illustrated in Table 5. Previous studies had tended to concentrate on 'single factor explanations', it was contended, such as size of firms. SAPPHO concludes from the results that five groups of variables emerge as most discriminating between innovation success and failure. These factors are:

1. Successful innovators show a much better practical understanding of users' needs. The innovation fulfils user expectations.
2. Successful innovators pay more attention to marketing and make greater efforts to sell their innovation.
3. Successful innovators perform the development work more thoroughly and more speedily.
4. They make more use of technological advice from outside the firm.
5. The business innovator, who carries executive responsibility for the innovation project, is more senior, has greater authority and a higher personal commitment.

A different approach was taken by another team of investigators who concentrated their attention on innovations that failed ('Centre for the Study of Industrial Inovation, 1971). They attempted to discover the reasons for the abandonment of technically satisfactory developments before market launch. 'Failure' was therefore not a market criterion as in SAPPHO, but a judgement adopted by the firm itself. Table 6 summarizes the reasons for the abandonment of projects which were cited by respondents from the companies concerned. In relation to the innovating firm, the organizational causes are particularly interesting. The internal causes of failure provided some confirmation of the SAPPHO results (although it should be noted that the definitions of failure differ).

A number of factors were included in a detailed investigation by Saren (1979) of the distinctive characteristics of firms with an early and successful record of

Table 5 Characteristics differentiating between success and failure in innovation
Part 1. Some measures which did not differentiate between success and failure

Question	Chemicals			Instruments			Both industries			Binomial test
	S>F	S=F	S<F[a]	S>F	S=F	S<F[a]	S>F	S=F	S<F[a]	
Was the innovation more or less radical for the firms concerned?	5	7	5	4	3	5	9	10	10	0.5
At what level was the decision to proceed with the innovation made?	2	11	4	1	10	3	3	21	5	0.363
Was a time limit set?	4	12	1	1	8	3	5	20	4	0.5
Were patents taken out for this innovation by the organization?	—	17	—	3	8	1	3	25	1	0.313
Did one organization accept the innovation as being more in its natural business than the other?	5	8	4	6	1	5	11	9	9	0.412
Did one organization have a more serious approach to planning than the other?	6	7	4	2	7	3	8	14	7	0.5
Was there a systematic and periodically reconsidered R&D programme?	6	7	4	—	10	2	6	17	6	0.613
What was the company's publishing policy?	5	7	5	1	11	—	6	18	5	0.623
Were there any incentive schemes to encourage innovative effort?	2	15	—	—	12	—	2	27	—	0.25
What outcome was the project expected to have on the careers of members of the project team in the event of success?	3	11	3	1	11	—	4	22	2	0.5

Question	Chemicals			Instruments			Both industries			Binomial test
	S>F	S=F	S<F[a]	S>F	S=F	S<F[a]	S>F	S=F	S<F[a]	
Was the innovation part of a general marketing policy?	5	8	4	2	9	1	7	17	5	0.387
What was the degree of coupling with the outside scientific and technological community in general?	2	12	3	2	8	2	4	20	5	0.5
Would the firm have recruited more QSEs if it could have done so at the time of the innovation?	—	17	—	1	10	1	1	27	1	0.75
In each case, when was the decision to innovate formalized on paper?	5	5	7	1	10	1	6	15	8	0.395
How many months elapsed from prototype or pilot plant to first commercial sale?	7	3	7	5	3	4	12	6	11	0.5
Was there a formal R&D department in the organization?	1	16	—	2	8	2	3	24	2	0.5
What was the scale of growth of the organisation up to the time of marketing (measured by annual growth of turnover in the five years prior to the marketing of the innovation?	1	13	3	4	4	4	5	17	7	0.387
How many years did the business innovator spend in the educational system?	5	7	5	2	5	5	7	12	10	0.315
Was the R & D department regarded as a profit centre?	6	8	3	1	10	1	7	18	4	0.274
Was there any need to find or use new materials?	—	17b	—	—	10	1	—	27	1	0.5

Part 2. Some measures which differentiate between success and failure

Question	Chemicals			Instruments			Both industries			Binomial test
	S>F	S=F	S<F	S>F	S=F	S<F	S>F	S=F	S<F	
Was the innovation more or less radical for world technology?	10	6	1	2	9	1	12	15	2	0.0065
How deliberately was the innovation sought, comparatively?	7	8	2	6	6	—	13	14	2	0.0037
Was there opposition to the project within the total organization on commercial grounds?	1	9	7	1	7	4	2	16	11	0.0112
Was more use made of development engineers in planning and costing for production in one case than in the other?	5	9	3	4	8	—	9	17	3	0.073
Did one organization have a more satisfactory communication network than the other externally?	5	10	2	5	7	—	10	17	2	0.0193
Was the R&D chief more senior by accepted status in one case than the other?	9	5	3	2	8	2	11	13	5	0.105
Was the sales effort a major factor in the success or failure of the innovation?	7	10	—	9	3	—	16	13	—	0.000015
Were any modifications introduced after commercial sales as a result of user experience?	1	8	8	2	6	4	3	14	12	0.0176
Were there any aftersales problems?	—	4	13	1	2	9	1	6	22	0.000005

Question	Chemicals			Instruments			Both industries			Binomial test
	S>F	S=F	S<F	S>F	S=F	S<F	S>F	S=F	S₇F	
Were any steps taken to educate users?	8	9	—	6	5	1	14	14	1	0.00049
If tools or equipment were needed for commercial production were any ordered before the decision to launch full-scale production?	8	7	2	2	10	—	10	17	2	0.227
What was the degree of coupling with the outside scientific and technological community in the specialized field involved?	8	9	—	5	6	1	13	15	1	0.00092
How much attention was given to publicity and advertising?	6	10	1	4	7	1	10	17	2	0.0193
Did the innovation have to be adopted by users?	—	10	7	—	7	5	—	17	12	0.00024
Was there unexpected production adjustments?	1	7	9	1	7	4	2	14	13	0.00636
Did any 'bugs' have to be dealt with in the early production stage?	1	6	10	1	5	6	2	11	16	0.00049

Was any systematic forecasting by the marketing (or sales) department involved in the decision to add the innovation to product lines or to existing processes?	5	7	5	6	5	1	11	12	6	0.166
Were user needs more fully understood by the innovators in one case than in the other?	15	2	—	9	3	—	24	5	—	0.0000001
Did the business innovator have a more diverse experience in one case than in the other?	8	8	1	8	2	2	16	10	3	0.00377
Did the business innovator have a higher status in one case than the other?	8	8	1	5	4	3	13	12	4	0.0245
Did the business innovator have more or less authority (power) in one case than in the other?	9	7	1	6	4	2	15	11	3	0.000656
To what extent was dependence on outside technology a help or a hindrance in production?	10	6	1	6	4	2	16	10	3	0.00221
How large a team was put to work on the innovation at the beginning of the project?	12	2	3	4	4	4	16	6	7	0.0466

Question	Chemicals			Instruments			Both industries			Binomial test
	S>F	S=F	S<F	S>F	S=F	S<F	S>F	S=F	S<F	
How large a team was put to work on the innovation at the peak of the project?	9	4	4	7	4	1	16	8	5	0.0133
How many years had the business innovator spent in industry?	9	7	1	3	4	5	12	11	6	0.119
Had the business innovator had any overseas experience?	3	14	—	5	6	1	8	20	1	0.0352
Did the business innovator have a greater degree of management responsibility in one case than in the other?	10	7	—	4	5	3	14	12	3	0.00636

[a] S>F   Success more than failure, greater than failure, etc., or in success but not in failure.
S=F   No measurable difference between success and failure.
S<F   Success less than failure, smaller than failure, etc., or in failure but not in success.
[b]   Data not available in one case.
Source: Science Policy Research Unit (1972).

TABLE 6   Stated Causes of Project-Shelving

	No.
Environmental	
Unattractively small market	19
Uncertainty with monopsonistic buyers	12
Unattractive level of competition	11
Uncertainty with suppliers	6
Obsolescence	3
	51
Internal	
Lack of market capacity or expertise	14
Lack of production capacity or expertise	13
Poor communication with associates	7
R&D cost escalation	6
Shortage of R&D resources	4
	44
Total	95

Source: On the Shelf, Centre for the Study of Industrial Innovation (1971).

technological innovation. This was based on an in-depth case study and historical analysis of a structured sample of ten firms in the electronics and pharmaceuticals industries. Because the purpose of the empirical element of the study was to highlight and explore the salient differences between early and late innovating companies, the selection of the sample of firms was of crucial importance. The objective of selecting cases was to include pairs of firms which were comparable in as many respects as possible apart from their innovativeness. Other studies indicate that there are several features of a firm which may account for the existence or importance of particular characteristics for innovation. These major features are:

(a) firm size
(b) industrial environment (e.g. competitiveness)
(c) technology/production system.

This means, for example, that a factor which is important to innovation in a large firm may not be an important factor for a small firm. Or, hypothetically, a characteristic which distinguishes between early and late innovators in a highly concentrated, less competitive industry might not distinguish these groups of firms in a highly competitive, less concentrated industry.

It was for this methodological reason that the sample of case studies selected was carefully chosen to include at least one pair of early/late innovators in each industry/size category, as shown in Table 7. For each firm a list of new products

TABLE 7   Sample Design (for each industry)

Firm Category	Innovation Performance	Size of firm
A	Early	Small
B	Early	Large
C	Late	Small
D	Late	Large

Early Innovation: a firm with a record of first or early introduction in its industry of new products —i.e. 'offensive innovation strategy'.
Late innovation: a firm with a history of late introduction of new products in the industry — i.e. defensive innovation.
Small firm: less than the median size for that industry.
Large firm: larger than the median size for that industry.

Sample for each industry to include at least one firm with each group of characteristics, A, B, C and D.

they had introduced onto the market over the previous ten years was obtained by questionnaire, prior to visiting. Factors which might potentially differentiate early from late innovators were sought and measured in each company.

The factors which were found to differentiate early innovators from late innovators are shown in Table 8. These results indicate that certain factors are more strongly associated with the early innovation category in only one industry or size group. For example, differences in the nature and composition of project teams are found to be associated with innovative performance only in large firms (defined as larger than the median for that industry). The same is true for the number of external communications channels and the influence of the marketing department on innovation decisions.

Other factors appear to differentiate early from late innovators only in small firms, i.e. the flexibility of the innovation budget and the extent to which hierarchical levels in the organization are omitted in communicating proposals for innovations. In addition, there were found to be certain characteristics of early vs late innovators which were industry-specific, for example pharmaceutical firms' innovativeness did not differ according to the range of departments involved in the network of communications for the proposal of innovations, whereas electronics firms' did.

The conclusion from this evidence was that while eclectic studies of innovating firms may seek generalized factors with which innovativeness is associated, there also appear to be certain other factors which are important for technological innovation only in specific circumstances. Therefore, the search for generalized explanatory factors should be tempered with the recognition that there may be also be factors with a greater degree of situation specificity

TABLE 8   Measures and Characteristics Differentiating Early and Late Innovators.

Early innovators	Late innovators
More contact with the scientific community	Less contact with the scientific community
More information on market needs (E)	Less information on market needs (E)
More external communications channels (1)	Fewer external communications channels (1)
High-level and reciprocal interest groups	No reciprocal interest groups
Innovation champions in a broader range of organizational locations	Innovation champions in concentrated locus in the organization
Adaptive and interdisciplinary project team system (1)	No adaptive and interdisciplinary project teams (1)
More delegation of responsibility within R&D department[a]	Less delegation of responsibility within R&D department[a]
Earlier consultation with production/marketing departments about innovation	Later consultation with production/marketing departments about innovation
More skipping of hierarchy levels in communication of innovation proposals (2)	Less skipping of hierarchy levels in communication of innovation proposals (2)
Wider range of departments involved in the proposal communication network (E)	Smaller range of departments involved in proposal communications (E)
Higher proportion of resources allocated to R&D activities	Lower proportion of resources spent on R&D
Higher 'rejection rate' of innovation proposals	Lower 'rejection rate' of innovation proposals
Greater influence of marketing department on innovation decisions (1)	Smaller influence of marketing department of innovation decisions (1)
More flexible innovation budget (2)	Less flexible innovation budget (2)
More perceived financial[b] constraint on innovation	Less perceived financial[b] constraint on innovation

These factors differentiate early from late innovators in all categories except where indicated:
(1)   Applies to *large* firms *only*.
(2)   Applies to *small* firms *only*.
(E)   Applies to *electronics* firms *only*.
[a]   Applies to *all electronics* firms, but *only* to *small pharmaceutical* firms.
[b]   Applies to *all electronics* firms, but *only* to *large pharmaceutical* firms.

Source: Saren (1979).

which without sufficient conceptual and methodological safeguards can be mistaken for the former.

The empirical studies which have been referred to in this section suggest that there are a large variety of factors associated with innovation — not one single explanation. There is also a general consensus from their results concerning the importance of the following factors in this respect:

1. Identification of user needs
2. Marketing
3. External and internal communications
4. Efficiency of technical development
5. Top management involvement

These cross-sectional studies have been fairly conclusive, when taken together, in indicating the type of organizational and managerial factors that influence innovation in the firm.

The R&D/Marketing Interface

The nature of the interaction between the marketing function and the R&D function within a firm essential element in technical innovation, according to Schon (1967). SAPPHO and other empirical studies identified the requirement for effective market research in order to ascertain user needs. This information must be channelled to those responsible for the technological development of innovations if customer wants are to be met.

Market research can act as a gate-keeper, Schon suggests, providing a description of relevant product variables which are associated with customer response. However, in the real world many such variables do not appear relevant until the product violates them. He argues that it is impossible to provide an 'exhaustive description of the characteristics of a thing which determine its success or failure, its approval or disapproval, its popularity or unpopularity'. Often, customers do not become aware of a feature of a product which is essential to their approval until that feature changes or disappears.

Because of this, Schon concludes that technologists must make decisions which will invariably affect customer response without the benefit of all relevant market information. He proposes that one of two 'states' characterize the innovation process in many companies. Either:

1. Marketing staff produce requirements for new technology and the technical problem-solving is left to the technologists; no account is taken of the number of covert marketing inventions and decisions that have still to be made; or
2. Technologists produce a new product, developed without information on

potential consumer response and marketing, then develop a suitable sales strategy; any technical changes that might be desirable, discovered by marketing in this process, are identified too late.

Schon comments that in each case there is a 'given' from one department which is 'made the basis of the task of the other'. Each is confined to its 'professional territory'. In the first case 'uncertainty' exists in the technical department, and in the latter case uncertainty is located in the marketing area. This distinction between two hypothetical states in the innovation process of the firm corresponds closely to the 'demand-pull' and 'technology-push' models of the primary stimulus to innovation (states 1 and 2 respectively) which were referred to earlier.

Many problems in innovation are caused by this division between the professional marketing staff and professional technologists. Schon concludes that the process of innovation becomes a series of 'propose-dispose' relationships across vertical and horizontal barriers in the firm. For successful innovation companies must develop effective communication between technologists and marketing managers.

This dichotomy was explained by Moore and Renek (1955) by the fact that the values of business are rejected by many technologists and the entrepreneurial objectives of marketing can conflict with the broader fields of interest of research staff. The orientation of their outside interests differs. The marketing manager tends to maintain close connections with the 'commercial world', whereas the R&D manager has closer association with the 'world' of science and technology. These writers argued that differences in personal values and outlook further hinder effective coordination between marketing and R&D departments.

Transcending values, Summer (1972) sees a 'philosophic' conflict between the perceived roles of marketing and research and development. The view that if something radically innovative and useful is developed then consumers will purchase it conflicts with the marketing attitude that the desires and needs of the customer must be identified and analysed as an input to commercial innovation. Summer's corporate planning experience in industry leads him to recommend not only the encouragement of better communications between R&D and marketing staff, but also more fundamental organizational changes, including the division of marketing and R&D functions into units corresponding to 'national product groupings'. Of course this is of practical application only in large, diversified orgaizations. Venture teams and task forces should be established to develop new products and analyse the existing range. The advantage is in the combining of staff with different skills in one unit.

Gruber *et al.* (1973) also detect a lack of integration between R&D and other corporate functions within 158 firms they survey. Successful R&D efforts are shown to possess '... better communication with each of the other corporate groups' (see Table 9). Their index of R&D performance is calculated on the basis of the perceived satisfaction of company executives from all departments with R&D. They conclude that when the level of R&D performance is unsatisfactory '... the source of failure will frequently be inadequacy of communications and planning at the R&D interface'; the reluctance of non-R&D management to become involved with R&D functions, preferring R&D to operate in isolation, may represent, the Gruber study contends, the greatest barrier to improving R&D, and thereby corporate, performance.

The results of these studies of the R&D/Marketing interface indicate that innovating firms may contain more effective intra-organizational communications between functional departments within the firm in general and between company decision-makers and marketers and staff responsible for the technological development of new products.

Management Techniques

The large company in particular is likely to be confronted with problems of management in encouraging the development of new products. Layton (1972) considers that as a firm grows larger: '... the right management system becomes indispensable for an effective innovation strategy'. On the basis of ten case studies of industrial innovation he proposes six management principles which he claims emerge from this work. These are:

TABLE 9   Quality of Planning and Communication

Percentage of respondents reporting high scores on:	High performance groups	Low performance groups
Index of quality of R&D communication with:		
Top management	71	39
Marketing	63	34
Manufacturing	50	21
Finance	20	6
Engineering	71	49
Index of groups present at reviews of R&D projects	72	59
Planting and goals index	38	16
Index of emphasis on long run: contribution of R&D to company goals	63	35

Source: Gruber *et al.* (1973, p. 31).

1. Explicit overall objectives and strategies.
2. Creation of 'small-firm conditions' within separate divisional enterprises — decentralization plus finance.
3. Organized, systematic movement of people between development and marketing.
4. Clearly defined procedures for innovation assessment and appraisal.
5. Organizational structure and goals 'must be widely known and easily understood by everyone'.
6. Emphasis on system and understanding in company operations.

The importance of aspects such as departmental integration, suitable decentralization and clarity of objectives and firm strategy is stressed.

King (1973) considers that in order to be operationally meaningful objectives should be set in terms of market, products and people. The only purpose of adding financial criteria, he argues, is to specify top management's attitudes to risk and the amount and length of the pay-off period for investment that are acceptable. The results of a survey by Hayhurst *et al.* (1972) of 553 UK companies with over £750k turnover are cited as indicative of the lack of long-term innovation strategies on the part of managements. This showed that only 25 per cent of firms in the sample planned further ahead than three years. Since the technological product innovation process can span a considerably longer time period, new product objectives may therefore be stipulated only in short-term goals.

A similar survey by Bruno (1973) examined new product development activities in 35 high technology US firms in order to provide some empirical data relating to the suggestion that the level of management sophistication in new product evaluation is low. The objectives of the new product introductions were not explicitly stated in eleven of these cases (see Table 10). He finds the most salient feature of these responses to be the '... relative absence of a reference to profitability, return on investment or market share...' as a measure of success/failure for companies' new products. King concludes from the Hayhurst (1972) results that management style should:

(a) make risk-taking on innovation rewarding; and
(b) create an environment in which project groups will operate effectively.

He provides little advice on how management can achieve these effects and conditions.

Booz, Allen and Hamilton (1968) reported that 81 per cent of companies with successful new products in their US survey experienced organizational problems with new product development. The 'new product staff department' was the most common form of organization in the firms. These were located outside the normal hierarchy and management structure, enabling the development of

TABLE 10   New Product Objectives

Explicit Objectives	No. of times specified
Dollar sales volume/growth	6
Profit	4
Profit margin	3
Payback	3
Return on investment	2
Earnings per share growth	1
Market share expansion (percentage)	2
Product price	2
Value added	1
No explicit objectives	11

Source: Bruno (1973, p. 28).

closer contact with top decision-makers and freedom from short-term problems and departmental vested interests. Disadvantages of this type of department are that staff can lose touch with the rest of the company and resulting innovations can create transfer problems when sales or marketing personnel become involved — the staff department is likely to have developed a stronger commitment.

An index of sophistication of new product decision-making has been constructed by Bruno (1973) on the basis of firms' product-planning characteristics such as objectives, budgets, financial anlysis, etc. The results of applying this index to real firms led him to report that:

1. the degree of sophistication in new product decision-making (NPDM) was generally independent of the age of the firm;
2. larger firms, in terms of both sales value and employees, contained more sophisticated NPDM;
3 firms with a lower index of NPDM sophistication had lower average profitability than those with a higher index.

The use of more 'sophisticated' product evaluation techniques in large firms is largely to be expected. The fact that profitability is associated with their use does suggest that these techniques are at least effective in screening out potential failures before the investment in the project is large.

Empirical information indicates that the management techniques used for innovation themselves require considerable development.

The Management of R&D

It was pointed out above by Rothwell and Robertson (1973) that a company's innovation performance depends, in part, on its technical performance — i.e. its research and development activities. In most large enterprises these functions are performed in an R&D department. In the same way that techniques of management and organizational structure of the firm can affect the results of innovation, it has been suggested that the management and organization of research and development itself will influence the rate and success of new product output.

Across UK industry in general five types of organizational structure for the research and development functions within firms have been identified (in a survey by NEDO, 1972).

(a) Subject/discipline structure: consists of a number of permanent departments, each staffed with particular scientific or technical specialists (e.g. bio-physicists, chemists). The head of each major department normally reports to the research director. This type of structure is common in the science-based industries.

(b) Stage/phase structure: composed of a number of separate departments each of which is concerned with a separate phase of a research and development programme — e.g. fundamental research, applied research, technical development.

(c) Product-type structure: several permanent teams are each responsible for R&D work on a particular class or group of products, e.g. cosmetics, deodorants, etc.

(d) Process-type structure: similar to product type with a number of multidisciplinary teams each concerned with separate types of processes as opposed to products.

(e) Project/problem structure: multidisciplinary teams are created to conduct a particular research project or to solve a particular problem. These are temporary groups (in contrast to teams in process-and product-type structures) which on completion, or abandonment, of a problem task or project are dismantled and staff reassigned to other project teams.

These different structures are not naturally exclusive. An R&D division, for example, may be divided into departments along stage/phase lines with each department sub divided into sections according to subject disciplines. This is illustrated in Figure 2 (a). Another example combines a permanent sub-ject/discipline structure with a number of *ad hoc* project teams formed along project/problem lines by pursuing a specific aspect of the programme (e.g. Figure 2(b)).

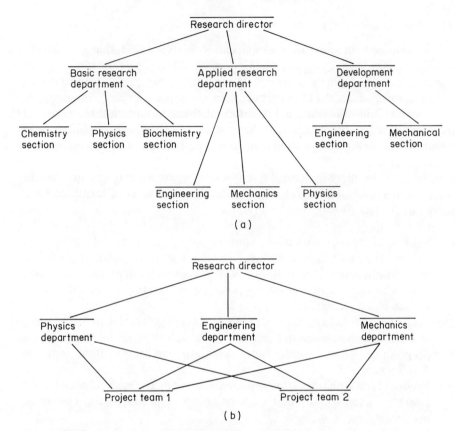

Figure 2 Examples of alternative research organizational structures.
(a) Subject/discipline structure along stage/phase basis. (b) Subject/discipline structure combined with project/problem structure

A firm should adopt the type of R&D structure which is considered to be most suited to the technology and timespan of its projects and which creates the most conducive environment for creativity, communication and coordination, NEDO concludes.

Based on his experience as a director of applied research laboratories, Gibson (1964) proposes a number of principles of R&D management:

(a) Departmental authority should rest with scientifically and technologically creative individuals, the 'nucleus' of an R&D organization.
(b) The objectives of the department should be well formulated in technical and operational terms and staff at all levels should understand how their activities contribute to their achievement.

(c) Task responsibility should be delegated: 'complete responsibility' for specific areas of the laboratory programme should be assigned to supervisors.
(d) Leadership qualities should be encouraged: training and opportunities for staff to develop the skills of communication initiation and coordination must be developed.
(e) Further education and development of technical and scientific skills.
(f) Success feedback: 'corporate pride' in laboratory achievement and recognition of individual contribution to success should be emphasized at all levels.

Although these aspects of R&D organization can improve a laboratory's performance in invention, Gibson suggests that certain 'by-products' of the operation of an R&D laboratory can reduce its efficiency. First, administrative practices can develop too quickly and become institutionalized, resulting in a waste of effort. Also administrative and technical structures which are created for specific tasks can become obsolete or unsuitable as technical conditions and product goals change. 'Accepted' management doctrines can be applied indiscrimately to R&D organizations. Newly established laboratories often produce a high quality and quantity of inventive output initially, but subsequently performance drops significantly to the level of 'the routine'. This may be caused by a 'fatigue of objectives' (as Gibson describes it) which affects both staff and their performance. Changes in both staff and goals/tasks are the means proposed to counteract this phenonmena.

Another cause of reduced R&D performance, suggested by Collier (1970), is the size of firm itself. Large corporations, he argues, tend to be 'anti-innovative'. As an organization grows in terms of staff, geographical dispersion and product diversity, intra-organizational communications become less frequent and more complex, the uncertainties and risks of innovation become less attractive to managers, and the administrative growth tends to relegate innovation to the low-level priority of the company. (This latter effect is debatable, as stated by Collier. There may be less innovation, but no evidence of a reduction in prioritization.)

The solution to this dilemma that he proposes is the establishment of a corporate R&D laboratory which will cover all the major technologies which are incorporate within the company's various activities and products. Any new developments should be made the responsibility of a 'product champion'. When the development does not fit into the technology or product ranges of the existing divisions, a new 'venture company' can be established to conduct the commercial development of the new product or process. These venture companies should be headed by the product champion, or others who are personally committed to the development, and given entrepreneurial freedom by the corporation in terms of the use of marketing, manufacturing and financial staff drawn from the rest of the corporation. (This is similar to how a group like Racal has developed, with separate companies each based on new developments in specific market areas.)

In a subsequent article (1974) Collier argues for a more broadly defined R&D function in a company, encompassing innovation in addition to inventive activities. The R&D department should develop a business orientation. Developments created within it should be 'transferred', as above, to the appropriate manufacturing, technical or sales departments, or venture companies created to develop them commercially.

This external venture company formation is a more radical alternative for the large organization than that preferred by Bujake (1972). He proposes that 'venture teams' led by product champions can be formed within the corporation, concentrating on the development of new business on the basis of particular new products produced by the R&D department(s). These provide flexibility, spontaneity and motivation behind the project, which he considers '... bigness tends to obliviate'.

R&D laboratories' organization, he continues, should be a combination of subject discipline and project team forms. 'Matrix teams' composed of a project manager and a number of various disciplinary departments would play dual hierarchical roles. Research staff report to their discipline department head for technical support and professional advice and to their project manager for project direction and leadership. This is a flexible system which encourages the development of future managers (thus satisfying Gibson's principle (d) above) and it can be installed without disruption or destroying existing line departments.

However, Peters (1974) considers that rather than attempt to short-circuit the communication gaps inherent in the hierarchical subject discipline structure by compensating for this defect with a dual structure (such as that proposed by Bujake), a more appropriate action is to adopt a different concept of organization altogether. The R&D organization could consist of a cell structure such as that proposed by Jay (1967) illustrated in Figure 3. The central cell lays down general guidelines of policy and budget and each cell manager is free to build as creative and innovative a section as he needs. This system eliminates several levels of command. There is no pretence of equality between cell leaders and cells will vary in size, although in Peters' view smaller cells tend to foster more creativity.

Peter's model induces incentives on project teams by objectives and needs from the research committee and competition between teams. Research products are subject to preliminary testing in a 'pilot facility' prior to review by the research committee which is 'subject to management interest'. (It is unclear whether this means a general management member on the committee or its responsibility to them.)

Green (1965) feared that the image has developed that organization charts, themselves, inhibit creativity and that creative research can only be achieved

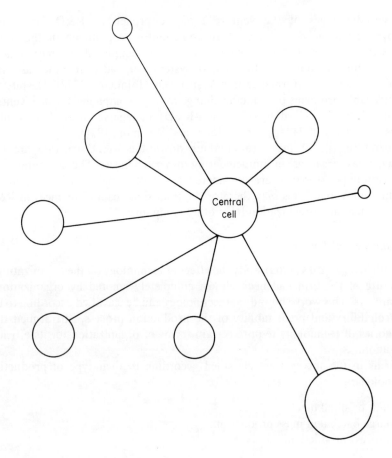

Figure 3 Cell structure organization. Source: Jay (1967), cited in Peters (1974)

through an 'unorganized, individual approach'. His experience (Green is ex-Vice-President of Bell Telephone Laboratories) led him to the conclusion that 'orderliness in relations among people is as important as it is in tackling scientific problems'. Furthermore, groups can be at least as creative as individuals in commercial R&D and the small project team approach he saw as an over-reaction against the previously dominant functional, subject-division approach. Similarly, Weisblat and Stucki (1974) emphasize the advantages of a 'goal-orientated' (i.e. product/type) structure only to a limited degree. A total breakdown of the subject/discipline structures and reallocation of resources between each separate product research unit would require, in their view, an enormous investment (because of duplication and loss of scale economies) on which '... the return would be completely inadequate'.

The advantages of the venture group approach to R&D (and other innovation) management have been consistently propounded in theoretical terms in the research management literature and empirical evidence suggests that the implementation of this type of system can lead to real increases in a firm's innovative performance (see Vesper and Holmdahl, 1973). Despite the considerable problems of inducing change in large companies the new venture group was 'well received' by other (non-R&D) managers in over 60 per cent of cases in a survey of 24 large firms (Jones and Wilemon, 1972).

Therefore, the obstacles to breaking down the R&D structure are not, perhaps, as great as in implementing other changes. The advantages to innovation performance are considered by most authors to be conclusive. Highly innovative firms may therefore contain significant differences in R&D management and organization from other companies.

Organizational Factors

Until Woodward's (1965) study the effect of technology on the organizational structure of the firm had been almost completely ignored by organizational researchers. This work showed that technology can be classified according to the controllability and predictability of the production process. She argued that categories of technology require certain forms of organization for its efficient operation.

Firms in the survey were classified according to their type of production technology:

(a) unit or small batch;
(b) large batch and mass production;
(c) process production.

The organizational characteristics varying directly with technical advance were:

(a) the length of line command;
(b) the span of control of the chief executive;
(c) the percentage of total turnover allocated to wages and salaries;
(d) the number of managers: total personnel ratio;
(e) the number of clerical and administrative staff: manual workers ratio;
(f) the direct: indirect labour ratio;
(g) the graduate: non-graduate supervisors in production department ratio.

Woodward did not conclude from this that technology was the only determinant of organizational structure. 'It is not suggested that the research proved technology to be the only important variable in determining organizational structure ....' There was clearly a close relationship, however.

Another study of organization and technology in industry led Burns and Stalker (1961) to conclude that a flexible, organic form of management is appropriate to the firm in conditions of rapidly changing objectives and technology, whereas a formal, mechanical structure is more suitable where objectives and technology are well established and not subject to rapid change.

Lawrence and Lorsch (1967) conceived of commercial organizations as possessing environments which can be divided into a market segment, a technological segment and an R&D segment. Each of these environments is likely to exhibit different rates of change and feedback times for decision-making and response. The conditions confronting the innovating firm in this model exhibit a high growth rate, fast transmission of knowledge, an uncertain environment and a longer timespan for feedback. In these circumstances, Lawrence and Lorsch suggest that a loosely structured organization, with an 'egalitarian, democratic ethos' and a high degree of personal discretion, is better able to perform — and survive. They further propose that this environment will necessitate procedures for coordination between organization 'segments' that will differ from those required where all components of the organization have the same rate of change and timespan of feedback.

Cyert and March (1963) refer to these type of conditions in their examination of the multiple objectives of the organization and the expedients used to avoid the worst consequences of environmental and organizational segmentation. Lawrence and Lorsch are primarily concerned with the structural prerequisites for adaptive integration necessitated by the nature of the firm's activities. They emphasize the importance of effective integration mechanisms for the innovating firm, which will require several characteristics — flexibile structures, collegiate relations and longer time horizons.

There is a distinction between technical innovations and administrative innovations. Evan and Black's (1967) survey of 50 firms indicates that different organizational characteristics will affect the type of innovations that are proposed (as opposed to adopted). Firms with higher formalization and centralization, more communication between line and staff and higher management receptivity to change are more likely to receive administrative innovation proposals. Those with more professionalization of management and a larger number of proposals per manager are more likely to receive technical proposals.

It is agreed that growth in the size of a firm is associated with organizational changes that affect its ability to innovate. An increase in firm size may result in more administrative levels. Blau (1974) considers that this will increase the amount of structural differentiation within the organization, and Porter and Applewhite (1966) found that 'flat' structures produce greater feelings of 'self-actualization' in managers whereas 'tall' administrative forms result in an emphasis on their value of security.

On the other hand, the model of organizational development constructed by Lippitt (Lippitt *et al.*, 1958) implies that the organization will have a higher propensity to innovate not only at its 'birth' stage but also during its early maturity, when it will be concerned with the major issue of whether and how to change. Therefore, size *per se* may not lead to tall organizational structures; rather this may be determined by the stage of the organization's development.

The proposition inherent in many of the arguments and hypotheses reviewed here that the manipulation of certain structural characteristics of the organization can alter individuals' attitudes and behaviour (e.g. concerning speed of work, industrial relations, creativity) clashes with a view held by several psychologists that the personality characteristics of individual members are more important in determining the innovative performance of the organization. Galbraith (1967) drew attention to the fact that the modern corporation can hope to manipulate and even create the demand for its goods and services. The existence of this phenomenon would provide an important element of qualification to the suggestion of environmental determination of firm behaviour in general and its innovative performance in particular. However, although there are many theories and theorists in this debate, there is a serious lack of reliable empirical evidence concerning both the environment and the structure of the innovating firm.

The Burns and Stalker (1961) hypothesis that an organic form of organization will be common in firms with high innovation rates receives little support from the results of Project SAPPHO, which sought to identify the causes of success and failure in industrial innovation. This concludes that: '... there appears no support for the theory that firms with "organic" rather than "mechanistic" structures are more successful innovators; that a general familiarity with the technology involved accounts for the difference between success and failure; or that successful innovation comes from firms facing greater competitive pressure than their counterparts.'

These findings do not necessarily refute the hypothesis that an adaptive/flexible organization will be more innovative than an authoritarian/formal structure. The SAPPHO results are based on the characteristics of two groups of firms: in one group each had introduced a successful innovation; the others had each produced a failure. Each company may have produced and launched many other innovations during the period of existence of that particular organizational structure. Some are likely to have been successful, others failures (particularly on the SAPPHO market criterion). All innovations from that organization over a period should be examined in order to determine first the firm's 'innovativeness' and secondly the effect of the organizational structure on the market success of innovations.

Taken together, the empirical studies reviewed here indicate that there are a large number of factors — both general and situation-specific — which are associated with firms' performance in technological innovation. The economic environment, the creativity of individuals, communication and information process, the size and structural characteristics of the organization, management and decision-making methods and even the nature of the technology itself have all been found to have some relationship with the pace and efficiency of firms' innovation activities. Given the potential multitude of determinants, the role of strategy requires considerable explanation if its primacy as a determinant of technological innovation is to be established.

THE ROLE OF INNOVATION STRATEGY

In the previous section only the studies by King (1973), Bruno (1973) and Layton (1972) provide any empirical results directly related to innovative management at the strategic level. All conclude that the setting of clear overall strategic objectives by top management is important for successful innovation. Unless all the other factors which have also been found to be related to firms' innovativeness can be demonstrated to be themselves determined by the innovation strategy which is chosen by top management, then it must be regarded as doubtful that the development and selection of the strategy itself is the prime determinant of the pace and direction of technological innovation, as it has been agreed.

However, a formidable case can be made that strategy should be regarded as the starting point of the innovation process. While there a number of alternative conceptual approaches to modelling the intra-firm innovation process that have been proposed (see Saren, 1984), most encompass at some point (although not necessarily at the start) the role of overall business objectives or strategy as one element or 'stage' in the process. Referring back to the diagrammatic representation constructed by Booz Allen and Hamilton (1981) (Figure 1), it can be seen that the innovation process stems from the overall business strategy as the first stage, followed by the new products or 'innovation strategy'. The subsequent steps of idea generation, concept development, business analysis, prototype development, testing and commercialization can be regarded as the implementation of the innovation strategy.

If viewed in this fashion, most of the other explanatory factors emanating from the empirical studies which have been discussed are associated with the later stages in the innovation process and therefore affect the successful implementation of the chosen strategy. For example, the structures of R&D and project teams have their impact on the innovation process during the concept development, prototype development and testing stages; conditions for 'creativity' affect idea generation and concept development; size and organizational structure perhaps affect the implementation of the whole process.

Strategy formulation may therefore determine the initial direction and pace of innovation activities but during the process of implementing that strategy a large number of other factors can alter or hinder its successful outcome.

These other elements which determine the operationalization of the innovation strategy have also been shown to determine subsequently the pace and direction of innovation. Particularly for 'leading' or 'early' innovating firms, the empirical evidence suggests that there do appear to be at least several *sine qua non* factors for success, one of which may be the formulation of innovation strategy.

There are also further complications in understanding the role of strategy in the innovation process. The most problematic is the possible interconnectedness between the various determinating factors. For instance, as Lawrence and Lorsch (1967) *inter alia* have shown, organizational structure itself can be determined by the environment, and the different subenvironments faced by the various departments in the firm can result in a number of matching substructures leading to greater organizational differentiation. These are likely to affect the behaviour of groups and individuals in different ways. Indeed, the technology itself may affect the structure as Woodward (1965) proposed. Technological innovation changes the technology itself and therefore the outcome of the innovation process may impact on the structure of the organization. Yet, organizational structure itself has been found to affect the innovation process. Hence the multiple direction of causality in this case opens up the possibility of a symbiotic relationship between the organizational structure, technology and the direction of the innovative process.

If strategy does not determine all of these elements, how then can it be regarded as the primary determinant of innovation?

Of course, it can be argued that strategy does in fact have a relationship to organizational structure. Miles and Snow (1978) found that in different types of business organizations strategic type, structure and managerial process tended to be related. They distinguished four strategic types of firms — 'domain defenders', 'reluctant reactors', 'anxious analysers' and 'enthusiastic prospectors'. (These are remarkably similar to reactive/proactive, leader/follower and offensive/defensive innovator categories of the business strategy literature cited earlier.) Pfeffer (1982) comments on their results that:

> Whether strategy preceded structure or *vice-versa* was not critical and in fact reciprocal relationships probably occurred.

Thus, even if a close association between strategy and structure can be demonstrated the same problems of interconnectedness and direction of causality occur here too. For strategy to be the primary determinant of innovation it must be shown that strategic choice determines structure if the latter is itself associated with innovativeness.

However, this is not to argue that strategic choice in innovation is itself determined by the environment, technology, size, structure, etc. Even within the same business/market environment firms can be seen to adopt substantially different strategies. All small firms do not choose the same innovation strategy. Companies employing the same technology do not have a uniform strategy. The differences in strategy which the empirical st dies have identified and categorized often occur amongst similar sized firms operating in the same product/market environment with the same technologies.

Managerial discretion for strategic choice in innovation does not appear to be totally limited by and contingent on these other factors which have also been found to be associated with technological innovation. However, the interconnectedness between all of these determining elements and the inherent uncertainty of the innovation process itself do provide strong grounds for reservations as to the primacy of strategy in determining the nature and direction of technological innovation.

Organization Analysis and Development
Edited by I. L. Mangham
© John Wiley & Sons Ltd.

Social Criticism:
A Social Critical Practice Applied to a Discourse on Participation

CHAPTER 8   *Robert Westwood*

INTRODUCTION

This chapter is based upon a substantive piece of research[1] undertaken in England around the turn of the decade concerned with the attempt by a manufacturing division of a multinational pharmaceutical corporation to introduce a 'worker-participation'[2] scheme at one of their manufacturing sites. The study involved the maintenance of close contact with the company over a two-year period, frequently on a weekly basis, but never less than once a month and with occasional extended periods of engagement. Multiple methods of data collection were pursued that gave rise to a rather daunting quantity of qualitative material. This research activity and the continuing confrontation with the emergent data provided a site of productivity within which, and through which, certain theoretical and methodological notions could work.

It is not the intention of this chapter, however, to provide a descriptive case-study account of a participation exercise. It is more concerned to address itself to a research practice that developed in the attempt to find a way to sensibly talk about what apparently took place within the company and to answer certain questions that posed themselves. In that sense the topic of participation and the events relating to the research project are not the focus of interest here and will hereafter be largely backgrounded and employed primarily as illustrative material to illuminate the research practice with which they were engaged.

That research practice emerged in the effort to locate a methodological and theoretical approach that provided some satisfying scope for tackling phenomena at the level of meaning: a common enough, but rarely seriously pursued injunction from much recent sociological commentary. Rather than accept the notion of participation as a given, contained by received definitions, or attempt a purely structural analysis of the development of a participation scheme, it came to seem important to consider what 'participation' itself could possibly mean, and what meanings were being played out in the arena of this particular setting. It rapidly became abundantly clear that there was no unitary

167

definition of participation, no stable, shared meaning present. There immediately began to emerge a kaleidoscope of diverse meanings, constructed at different times in different contexts and apparently being made to serve a range of different purposes. Basic questions of the potentiality of meaning: of possibilities, alternatives and realizations of the meanings(s) of participation, and later, of the struggle for the control of the meaning of participation, began to form themselves. What meanings of participation were emerging, and why? How were various meaning relations being constructed and presented? Why did particular relationships emerge and not others? Why was it that certain meaning relations entered the discourse, and obtained a relative coherence and fixity, whereas others faded almost as soon as they were uttered?

These questions proved resistant to sensible answers. This chapter, then, treats of the potential of what is termed a social critical practice for addressing such questions of meaning. Such a practice inevitably operates primarily at the level of language and language use but does not exclude other forms of signification. Such a level of engagement projects the analytic into a treatment of the place of language in the structuring, power and control processes of organizations (although it offers prospects in other spheres of social activity also) and thus ultimately is required to examine the relationship of language and ideology and the connections between arenas of discourse and the broader social formation. It thus offers returns by providing something of a bridge between the micro and macro, a niggling problematic in much organizational analysis. Before turning to some of these considerations more fully, the generation and lineage of the proposed research practice requires some exposure.

ACCOUNTING FOR MEANING:
FROM DEFINING SITUATIONS TO
TEXT

The attempt to come to terms with and provide an understanding of the events taking place in this company (let us call it Tridy Drugs Inc) led to the research practice undergoing a series of perspectival shifts. The trajectory of theoretic and methodological interests described a passage that began with an orientation that Burrell and Morgan (1979) refer to as the interpretist paradigm and Morris (1977) collects under the label of 'creative sociology'; on through ethnomethodology to a series of perspectives derived from recent developments in linguistics and the philosophy of language. Within the former a handle was originally sought on the phenomena in that realm of social psychological theorizing that loosely fits under the rubric of symbolic interactionism.[3] Time was also spent within approximately adjacent areas of sociological discourse, viz. the social constructivist perspective;[4] the sociology of the absurd;[5] the dramaturgical perspective;[6] and ethogenics.[7]

Underlying these broader perspectival movements remained a continued interest in a more specific conceptualization, but one which largely remains embedded in the interpretist paradigm. This conceptualization acted as a sounding-board and an orienting frame for both theoretic perambulations and reflections on the data. It was taken up quite early on and retained quite doggedly. It was constantly held up to both data and theoretic development in a mutual testing out, a dynamic in which each draws on the other. The conceptualization was the old 'sociological story'[8] of the definition of the situation.[9] That 'story' was held to have an initial value and continued to provide a fairly powerful instrument with which to engage the phenomena emerging in the research data. However, it came itself to be viewed as being limited and flawed for the purposes of providing an adequate analytic for the emerging data. It was this inadequacy and the search for an alternative that also prompted a significant shift away from the interpretist paradigm generally.

The starting point for this further excursion was the statement by McHugh (1968) that 'the definition of the situation is the sociological notion analogous to the more general one of "meaning"', but that the theoretical perspectives engaged thus far proved flawed in this regard. That is, there was a perceived failure to provide an adequate and encompassing theory of meaning with which to underpin the more pragmatic statements. And 'flawed' particularly because the perspective fails to tackle at sufficient depth the contribution of language and language use to the definitional process.

The posed questions about the emergence of different meanings of participation, about how these meanings were constructed and how some became socially accredited whilst others faded, were not being readily answered by the existing frames of reference. The lack of a developed theory of language and meaning became troublesome. The interpretist paradigm, with its assumptions about intentionality and the subjective conscious, became an increasingly uncomfortable analytic to accommodate.

There has been a pressing injunction from a variety of sources throughout the recent history of sociology and social psychology to investigate phenomena at the level of meanings; an injunction shared by the theories of definition of the situation. But, in deciding to take that injunction seriously, one encounters a proliferation of philosophical and methodological dilemmas. Quite simply, the question of accounting for the meaning of any social phenomenon has proved highly problematical. Indeed, from the point of view of the 'definition of the situation', the problems remain largely unresolved, or at best equivocal.

At root the problem is one of providing the grounds for an adequate formulation of the events(s) under consideration. How can the meaning of an event be determined, and how are we, as researchers, able to demonstrate that the account we offer is a correct, accurate, appropriate or even plausible and sensible one?

A rather depressing theoretical cul-de-sac seemed to have been entered. However, progress became possible by shifting to an entirely different academic discourse that appeared to address some of the same issues.[10] Recasting the dilemma within the realms of an entirely different discourse offered new positions of intelligibility and opened up new analytic possibilities. A potentially analogous analytic practice began to be realized in the discourses of literary criticism and linguistics.

If we talk about a piece of (verbal) behaviour in terms of the construction and attempted presentation of meanings, then we could ask the question: how do we extract an adequate 'reading' of that phenomenon? This interpolation of 'reading' draws attention to a different critical practice. The practice of literary criticism specifically has continued to confront the issue of how to provide an adequate formulation of the meaning(s) that are assumed to be present in some textual material.

What then became a possibility was that the efforts of contemporary critics to come to terms with the problem of providing sensible formulations of texts (and other areas of signification) might prove highly illuminating for the sociological enterprise. And indeed, examining the various grapplings of contemporary criticism with this issue reveals movements that in some senses prefigure efforts in sociology.

The conceptions of what, by the same aberration and arrogance that spawned 'Modernism', came to be called New Criticism[11] represent one such movement. That movement involves a significant reaction against what we, by their tyranny, must now call 'old criticism'. Their work critiqued the search for the meaning of literary works in things beyond the text, usually by reference to the author's biography, the author's psychology, the positioning of the work within a (literary) history or, more importantly, by reference to the author's intention.[12] I take this to have a certain echo in some contemporary sociological practices, particularly so in aspects of the ethnomethodological programme and amongst those other theorists who value an approach that treats members' accounts as something other than epiphenomena (e.g. Harré and Secord, 1976; Harré, 1977; Lyman and Scott, 1968; Silverman and Jones, 1973; 1976).

The New Critics formulated a corruscating attack against a critical practice that asserted:

(a) the authority of the author over the text: its content and meanings(s);
(b) a conception of meaning as existing prior to material expression;
(c) which tended to imply the presence of a single, unitary, immutable meaning confined to some location (usually the author's intending consciousness) other than the text itself.

The attack on intentionality and the rest of the old paradigm has profound implications for the reader-writer relationship and the grounds for providing a warrantable formulation of the text.

New Criticism offered new critical possibilities, but it too came under attack and represents a way-station on the track to a more radical conception developed out of Saussurean[13] linguistics and early semiology leading into post-structuralist criticism.[14] From the post-structuralist conception New Criticism's exclusive focus on the internal machinery of the text ended up by imposing new constraints upon language and meaning. It proposed a new formalism, a new metalanguage that presumed to reveal the deep structures of narrative and text. It came to speak of the 'structure of the text'; a foundational and formalized patterning that constrained a text in the possibilities of its meaning and offered yet another totalizing origin, a new source for the guarantee of meaning. It proposed a structured, preformed system and set of rules that when made available to a self-conscious presence ensure the generation and comprehension of meaning.

The same imposition can also be witnessed in the efforts of structuralism[15] itself and in early attempts to construct a fully scientific and stable semiology.[16] It was criticized equally in that realm by the post-structuralists. From their perspective such efforts merely perpetuate the 'logocentric fallacy' (Derrida, 1976; 1981) by holding the 'false' hope of a formalizing system that once again provides the means for locating the irreducible, mandatory meaning of a verbalization. Structure freezes meaning and shackles the free play of differences. It holds meaning artificially still, gives us perhaps a panoramic view, a totalizing, but at the expense of the 'force' (Derrida, 1978). We lose the process; we lose the movement in the frame. Saussure's crucial statement on the nature of language as a series of relations without positive terms (Saussure, 1974) is bastardized by the attempt to provide an explanation that goes beyond the weave of relations. Or as Derrida (1978, p. 5) has it, there is a 'neutralization of meaning by form'. Structuralism becomes yet another 'method', another metalanguage that offers to arbitrarily close the text: the potential proliferation and deferment of meaning are harnessed.

In Barthes' (e.g. Barthes, 1976; 1977; 1981) and others' reinvestigation of the sign,[17] there is a return to a re-stressing of the importance of the signifier in the signifier-signified relationship. Meaning can be said to exist only in the 'moving play of signifiers'. Meaning is wholly constituted in the syntagmatic and paradigmatic relationships between signifiers that extends, as the common metaphor has it, in a 'seamless web', ever changing and in a constant process of coalescence and disintegration. Meaning consists of these shifting patterns of signifying relations. It is constantly in process, always emerging; not anchored to a permanent signified itself rooted in a stable, essential reality.

With the post-structuralists, then, we arrive at a radical materialist conception of language and meaning.[18] There can be no meaning at all independent of the signifying system. The reversion to the original conflation of the signifier and signified means that each sign is meaningful only by reference to its articulated or potential distance: its 'play'.[19] The articulated difference between signs is not formal and static, but forever shifting, emerging and fading. There is no real possibility of obtaining a fixity of form or structure, either prior to its realization in particular articulations or by hermeneutical interpretation subsequently. Most radically, in relation to the latter, Foucault asserts that 'If interpretation can never accomplish itself, it is simply because there is nothing to interpret' (cited by Donato, 1970). Nothing is offered for interpretation since nothing is referenced but other signifiers, the meaning of each constituted only by that and other possible relations.[20]

With his (anti-) concept of 'writing', Derrida (1976; 1978) further breaks down the logocentric bifurcation of 'writing–reading' (and by extension 'language–speech') and introduces the full nature of the free play and undecidability of language. Meaning is endlessly dispersed and deferred. Not least it is dispersed across what becomes for the post-structuralists an extended sense of text.[21] As Barthes puts it, 'The Text (is) experienced only as an activity, a production' and, 'The Text ... practises the infinite deferral of the signified ... the Text is dilatory; its field is that of the signifier' (Barthes, 1977, p. 75).

'Text', then, becomes an important point of analytic focus. We arrive at a juncture where the productivity of language is emphasized; where meaning has the tendency to proliferate and has a fundamental undecidability; were meaning has a radical and irrevocable plurality. Text has no inherent structure, no centre or origin; it cannot be captured as a totality.

MEANING IN CONTEXT

The post-structuralists thus offer a highly developed and sophisticated conception of language and meaning, something that held analytic promise in the present research context. A serious difficulty remained, however. Much of the post-structuralist analytic is developed only in relation to literary, or certainly written, significations. But, if we consider the speaker–hearer relationship, if we move off the printed page and look at speech acts, does it move us beyond the scope of the offered analytic? If we include the social context in the contextual determination of meaning, are we required to abandon or make crucial adjustments to the theory?[22]

The contextual determination of meaning is, of course, perhaps the central problematic of the ethnomethodological programme.[23] When we consider the details of that problematic in terms of the triad of *reflexity* (see Mehan and Wood, 1978; Attewell, 1974,) *indexicality* (see Garfinkel, 1967; Abercrombie, 1974; Attewell, 1974; Barnes and Law, 1976; Phillips, 1976; Heritage, 1977; Coulter, 1979; O'Keefe, 1979) and *literal description* (see Sacks, 1963; Goldthorpe, 1973), then certain difficulties in the straightforward application of post-structuralist conceptions to the social realm become apparent. However, there are certain continuities between the two and when we put the ethnomethodological concept of the contextualization of social meanings together with the post-structuralist conception of linguistic meaning in a constructive tension rather than as mutually destructive criticism, we reach a distinctive point in this excursis.

From a consideration of the post-structuralist position[24] it can be seen how they posit a 'textual', 'written' conception of language and meaning — a view that proposes the productivity, plurality and deferment of meaning and the 'in principle' impossibility of providing a closure on meaning. They deny:

1. the possibility of locating a fixed, final and absolute meaning;
2. that there is a locus (or logos) that can act as a point of origin and as guarantor of meaning — neither in an essential signified reality, or the intentional consciousness of a subject or any other more or less metaphysical source;
3. that meaning can be fixed and held by an imposed metalanguage.

Metalanguages are antithetical to the notion of language's productivity, its plurality and its tendency to proliferate meaning. They do violence to the textual. The post-structuralists emphasize process. Meaning is process — is emergent. Structuration is preferred to structure.[25] They direct our attention to the movement of meaning.

From the other direction, although there is much that is confusing and diverse in the ethnomethodological programme, what they have consistently achieved by a rigorous focusing on and problematizing of everyday language use, is to make it abundantly clear that part of everyday interactional activities *are* movements to control meaning: to close meaning. From their perspective this need not be conceived of as a manipulative, strategic or even intentional matter, but rather as the inevitable result of the use of indexical expressions, accomplished by mundane interactional work. The more general point, though, is that normal social interaction *is* characterized by movements to provide a closure on meaning — interactional work that poses utterances as final, absolute, transparent, or at least adequate and passable for the practical purposes at hand. In practical social affairs meanings are not pursued to a presupposed originatory point, but such a point is indexed in such a way that it can be taken for granted. The indexical expression is taken, at least tacitly, by all present as being as far as one can go, or needs to go, and as adequate to validate meaning.

TEXT AND THE SOCIAL CRITIC

The analysis of the events at Tridy Drugs Inc was able, then, to develop around a dialectic engendered by the relation between these ways of theorizing and the emerging data. At the heart of that dynamic is a creative and irresolvable tension between the theoretic notions of the productivity of language, deferment and the proliferation of meaning, and that pragmatic process of the closure of meaning encountered as persons engage in their routine interactions and practical activities. That tension drove the analysis. It led ultimately, via the consideration of closure as a practice, to an examination of the place of rhetoric and ideology in those processes and a necessary passing on to a conception of the act of signification and the definition of situations as an exercise of power.

Adopting the post structuralist conception of language, and particularly the notion of text, has important implications for research practice. Such a practice, when applied to the social realm and mindful of the process of closure revealed by the ethnomethodologists, I want to refer to as social criticism and the person engaged in that activity as a social critic.

Part of the implication of this practice is that any attempt to unearth the meaning of, in this case, 'participation', even within the confines of this study, is doomed to failure. There is no single, unitary, identifiable meaning that can be gleaned from the events at Tridy. There aren't even meanings in the sense of a coherently categorizable grouping arrangeable in taxonomic form. Traditional sociological research practices, especially attitude surveys, frequently aspire to divulge to a waiting audience what 'such and such' means to a group of people under scrutiny. I too possessed such aspirations initially. However, such a meaning or set of meanings is a veritable philosopher's stone: much sought after, but forever elusive.

It is not incidental that the alchemist's philosopher's stone is an instrument of transformation: transmogrification even. To assert the discovery of *a* meaning, to create a mould to fix the phenomenon in a stable, coherent, unified form, is to transform the phenomenon. Like a photograph, a fixed structured meaning is something other than that which it pretends to represent.[26]

The practice also excludes the possibility of divulging meaning by any interpretist strategy that proposes to reveal the speaker's intention. So, a mere collection of individual speakers' declarations of what participation means to them will not do either.

A social critical practice engendered by the adoption of text and discourse as the appropriate level of analysis[27] does not seek to discover *the* meaning of a phenomenon. Such a strategy is covertly hermeneutical; it assumes that such a meaning exists and that the meaning has always been there, a secret hidden thing awaiting the illumination of the archaeologist's torch. But, as the poststructuralists demonstrate, meanings are not complete, static phenomena, approachable by the analyst, to be stared at, of a piece from a distance, and then transposed intact onto the page of a report to be received, untrammelled, by the reader.

However, it can scarcely be said that there are not certain meanings apparent in the context of participation at Tridy; indeed, there are a bewildering number. What then is the nature of those meanings and how are they to be tackled? I would assert that their nature is primarily textual and that they must be analysed from that point of view. Intending to locate and lay before the reader a meaning of participation, or a structure of meanings — static, total, enclosed —I instead engaged a text.

The focus of interest, then, is not so much the divulgence of a meaning or series of meanings as the process of signification, the signifying work taking place within the research context. There is an interest in the how of meaning; in the activity and productivity of text, its movement; in text as production and not as product. The text of participation is a process; meanings remain emergent, deferred and dispersed.

A social critical practice has no need to invent a source and locate it in or outside the text as a means of guaranteeing the veridicality of the meanings, as an auditor of the origin and veracity of meanings. Nor will it engage in remedial work that seeks to paper over the inconsistencies, omissions and contradictions in the articulation of members;[28] rather the opposite — it should take them as the exclusive and rightful property of the text. But in so doing a corollary would be that the participants' actual attempts to elide those features of the text, their own attempts to provide a smooth surface, would be exposed. Mundane attempts to close off meaning — to present coherence, order, unitary meaning, reason(ableness) and naturalness — should be drawn attention to, and the ultimate failure in principle, and partial success in practice, of such attempts highlighted.

Part of the social critical practice is to confront this process of closure; to locate those points to which meaning is pursued in members' talk, points that are accepted as final or adequate to secure and guarantee meaning for present purposes. Its job is to locate the contradictions and omissions in those processes and the points where the positing or indexing of a source, a logos, undercuts itself and reveals the ideological/metaphysical nature of the search and the supposed guarantee. Its task is to re-reveal that which is repressed; what in the closure of meaning is being cast off-limits; what alternatives have been bypassed, not noticed or repressed: and how all that is achieved.

Much of the traditional sociological method, like traditional literary criticism, seeks unity, coherence — it seeks to iron out, repair and explain deficiencies in the phenomena or in the data. It smoothes out contradictions, offers a 'perfect' explanatory account; it itself seeks closure on meaning. It transcodes the data into its own discourse — into its own preformed code or metalanguage. It becomes an accomplice of an ideological practice.

It recognizing the naturalness of contradiction and the rhetorical in narrative and everyday discourse, social criticism seeks to display it. Partly, for what it reveals about the ideological underpinning of such discourse. The point at which a discourse contradicts itself, or the point to which it takes its search for a guarantee of meaning, displays what is allowed to pass and what is accepted in that discourse as the root and source of meaning. It reveals a discourse's inclusive-exclusive practice. It is at that point that the discourse is seen to rely upon some presupposed and presumed shared ideology or episteme that is taken as natural and immutable (at least in that instance).

Members' talk aspires to an acceptable coherence and internal consistency, to incorporate itself into a habitual mode of discourse in intelligible and consistent ways. A social critic might expect to find that, in spite of these efforts, incoherences, absences and transgressions will be exposed. They, and the attempt to mask them in the rhetorical, reveal the partiality of any discourse and the inability of an ideologically informed language to create total coherence. The constructed and emergent discourse can be expected to provide not a unity of meaning but a multiplicity — a bodged assemblage of incompatible elements, unfinished runs and contradictions hastily papered over. The multiplicity of meanings, if fully released, interrupts the alleged coherence in the espoused discourse.

Within each discourse, and talk that situates itself within a discourse, are implicit points where the reliance on ideology surfaces and where its facility to mask its own enterprise fails. Traditional and familiar values, epistemes and other assumptives embodied in the ideology are made to surface and are, at points, shown to be in collision with the espoused project of the talk and the indexed discourse. The social critic is in the position of highlighting these lesions and displaying how the discourse contains within itself an implicit critique of its own values and ideological practice.[29]

The conception of ideology emerging here owes something to Althusser (1971). Ideology is that which makes (linguistic) relations appear natural and obvious, and certain ways of ordering as taken-for-granted. A viewpoint that remains present but not explicit in Garfinkel. Barthes' notion that ideology is that which makes the arbitrary and conventional appear as natural, is also clearly relevant here,[30] as would be Foucault's useful linking of discourse to the struggle for power and the mechanisms of inclusion and exclusion.

So, a social critical practice should work to display the plurality of meanings inherent in the discourse. With the acceptance of notions like 'writing', 'textuality' and 'dissemination', the idea of deciphering a text, of submitting it to a hermeneutic interpretation, becomes somewhat redundant. It is, rather, more like a process of the multiplicity being 'disentangled', and also, as Derrida (1978) has it a 'desedimentation' of elided and repressed meanings.

The social critic is not, like the purely linguistic critic, interested solely in splitting apart or unearthing latent meanings, but, with the ethnomethodologists, he is interested in showing *how* something means; with the way particular meanings are constructed and put forward as *the* meaning. Meanings *are* closed off and the processes by which this is accomplished or attempted are also important to the social critic.

A simple sense of plurality is realized from the assumption that the meaning of a linguistic item varies from one discourse to another. To the extent that the speaker/hearer participates in these discourses or is familiar with them, he will be able to locate one or more possible readings.

Utterances are intelligible within specific discourses — discourses offering a more or less self-enclosed system of relations of differences. Words within specific discourses accrue meaning by entering habitual relations of difference. Those habitual relations are ideologically informed. Words, sentences and utterances are locatable within specific discourses and in particular relations which thereby provide positions of intelligibility.

A social critical practice should recognize the realization and imposition of 'obvious' positions of intelligibility in actual everyday discourse — and, of course, be aware of the ideological practice and other means by which that is achieved. Speakers' talk will attempt to create fixed positions of intelligibility for its audiences. What these positions are and how they are achieved/imposed should again be of interest to the social critic. Speakers' talk offers itself as an authoritative transmitter of unambiguous sense. It attempts to position the audience to accept the purveyed message passively, as real and correct — as *the* meaning — masking out alternative readings.

Such positioning practices are clearly associated with, and a reflection of, existing ideological and power arrangements apparent in the language community. Such positioning serves to encamp the hearer in specific positions of intelligibility and to accept those positions as natural and obvious. The strategy operates reflexively since the given/adopted position offers the possibility of renewed recognition (misrecognition) of that which the person already 'knows'. The positioning of the subject allows/forces an acceptance of and a perspective on the spoken in ways that are wholly familiar and known. The positioning of the subject caters for the means of intelligibility and the obvious achievement of intelligibility reinforces the correctness of the positioning. The position given/adopted provides access to a discourse in which the myths and signifying systems are able to represent experience in the ways that it is conventionally articulated in that language community.

A social critic should explore these positioning practices. The 'obvious' positions of intelligibility presented should be scrutinized. A social critical practice should actively seek out the processes of production of the text; the organization of its various discourses; the rhetorical and figural strategies by which it smoothes over the incoherences and contradictions and reveals the ideological practice inscribed within it.

Two final points.

The plurality of language — when recognized and accepted — offers the possibility of change — or, at least, a way beyond the tyranny of closed and unitary meanings. The effect of rejecting consigned positions and of being aware of alternative positions of intelligibility is potentially liberatory.

The social critic needs to remain constantly reflexive. A truly critical practice is an activity — it is a productive process itself. It will, we should recognize, transform what it critiques by releasing 'more' than was said. It is not, then, merely a process of recognition, of 'pointing out', but the creation of a relationship with its audience that again produces a site of productivity, that allows the reader to actively and interrogatively engage the critic's text and release further meaning(s). There is a ceaseless flow of productive activity resulting from the ineluctable and unconstrainable (even by the critic) play of language. Any text, even a critical commentary, remains defeasible.

THE MOVEMENT OF PARTICIPATION

A more comfortable analytic practice had, then, been located and began to work against the emerging data. The first obvious realization is that, as text, participation and its meanings are not entirely demonstrable, to be laid clearly before the reader. 'Participation' exists in the emergent text at Tridy, not in any stable, objective structure or social formation. There is no structural form or set of social practices that can sensibly be indicated and said to adequately represent participation — or if there is, then only insofar as that structure or set of practices are conceived of themselves as discursive constructs. The text of participation is non-static; it consists of a shifting arrangement of signifiers loosely networked around the item 'participation' itself. This fabric of relations is in a constant state of flux, ever shifting and changing. Certain relations become temporarily foregrounded whilst others fall away or remain in potentiality. There are periods of relative cohesion when a particular series of relations features strongly and with some regularity; there are other times when there is very little unity.

If we accede to Barthes' (1979) dictum that a text is a 'methodological field', then we are committed to the inevitable incompleteness of the text. The meanings of participation are never, in principle, complete. The arrangement of signifiers that gives participation a meaningfulness can only be halted by an imposed and authoritarian movement to close off the 'play' of the signifiers. However, in any arena of practical interactional activity there *is* an inevitability about such a movement. In my own critical practice it occurs, for instance, because of the finitude of my own discursive possibilities and because my own writing does not posses the quality of innocence.

In the talk and practices of those involved at Tridy such a practice also occurs. The accomplishment of practical interactional activity invariably involves an exercise of power in which the act of signification is critical. 'Participation' is insinuated into an existing discourse involving political and ideological relations. Its involvement in such a sociolinguistic context entails that there is a movement to foreclose on the possibilities of meaning around participation. Such efforts, however, struggle against the nature of text. So we again have the tension. The insinuation of 'participation' sets in motion a ceaseless chain of signifiers, and the commencement of signifying work immediately creates a site of productivity where meanings are plural and can proliferate. These relations of signifiers are not halted, and are always incomplete. But mundane activity requires a process of closure. It requires that some apparent halt be called to thus unruly movement.

'Participation', then, is released, or rather is introduced (by the talk of certain members) into exisiting company discourse as an interpolated 'newness'. It was not previously a linguistic element of much significance within that discourse. Upon release it possesses a powerful meaning potential; a capacity to enter into new relations of difference within the extant discourse. The relations into which it could form and the meanings it could accrue are potentially boundless. And it is not simply the theoretically proposed overflowing and excess of meaning already referred to — it is also the fact that meanings become uncontainable by individuals or groups. The particular relations realized and their potential can be said, however, to become located in particular positions of intelligibility, positions in particular discourses. Each of us is partially locked into a varying but finite range of discourses that are reflexively enabling of these positions and the consequent possibilities of meaning. Thus at least some of the tensions at Tridy are engendered by these varying positions of intelligibility that further create possibilities of meaning variation.

These potentialities mean that fresh associations and relationships emerging will impinge upon existing relations in the extant discourse with the consequent possibility that the original discourse is altered. The form that these relationships will take cannot be predicted or fully controlled; there exists, then, a possible disruptiveness and transformational capacity in this potentiality of participation — the newness may subvert and disrupt existing relations. Change and radicalness, for instance, are possible extended relations in such a situation.

The tensions outlined above can only be indexed here by recourse to a very partial disclosure of the text that emerged at Tridy. The text of participation could be partly characterized as the realization of a series of meaning potentials through the selection of options from a networked system of linguistic levels (but primarily the semantic). The selection of options in the development of the discourse around participation is part of what provides the basis for meaning. Participation exists firstly as a syntagm of present relations. But fundamentally, it is not only on the basis of what *is* selected or constructed that meaning is determined, but also on the basis of what *is not* selected — the absent is as much determining of meaning as the present. Thus the paradigmatic relations are also vitally constitutive of meaning.

So, then, to take a fragment of the text. In the early stages of the scheme shopfloor members tended to locate participation within an existing discourse that spoke about company matters. Participation became a possible contrastive newness in relation to that discourse. It came to be spoken of in terms of the possible amelioration of grievances as embodied by that discourse which became a kind of relevancy nexus *vis-à-vis* participation. Amongst the shopfloor, as well as this positioning in an existing discourse, participation appeared in syntagmatic relation to a range of other signifiers such as: '(sharing of) information'; '(improving) communication'; 'consultation'; 'recognition'; and so on. At other points it formed a relation with a texture of signifiers around the item 'meetings', thus: 'veto', 'committee', 'elections', 'minutes', 'representation', 'chairman', etc. The meaning of participation for sections of the shopfloor (at that time, and in the context in which those terms were used) is derived, at least in part, from these relations in the syntagm. There is, of course, already a complexity of arrangement where the various textures themselves interrelate, for instance some of the relations around 'meetings' are in association with the relation between 'participation' and 'a proper airing of views' or 'having one's voice heard'.

There is a second level of complexity when one considers the paradigmatic — one might say the likely/possible connotations relating to each item-in-use that are not articulated. But then that connotational force is part of the (nearly) limitless play of the signifiers. Some of that is revealed diachronically as an item, such as 'consultation', comes to form and reform into fresh relations that alter its meaning, and its meaning in relation to participation, as the discourse develops.

A good example is provided by the early relations of 'participation-action'. A number of the shopfloor (although a minority) made reference to that relation in preliminary discussions. At that time it indexed a conception of the need for issues raised by the shopfloor to be acted upon (and not 'squashed', as was the common conception in the existing discourse). However, it became apparent that 'action' was conceived of in terms of the issue being presented to management (preferably at a relatively high level) and them initiating action. The responsibility for action was given over, by the workforce, to management. (This itself indexing a further aspect of early shopfloor discourse in which the rights, obligations and responsibilities of management were conceived of in traditional, even conservative ways, such that the shopfloor expected and obligated management to take control over issues and to act upon them — 'that is what they are there for; that is what they are paid do'.) As the scheme and the discourse around participation developed, the relation 'participation-action' became associated with a different arrangement of relations. It came into contact with the developed notion of group solidarity and the perception by the representatives of the shopfloor that they must take responsibility for action themselves or in meaningful partnership with management. It linked in with the developed relation that participation was concerned with a 'mutual resolution of problems for the benefit of all'. One might simplify the relations thus: a shift from 'participation-action-unilateralism' to 'participation-action-mutuality'.

One could imagine that one could begin to build up a supposed network of relationships in this manner, hoping to map out the system of meaning relationships arranged around participation. There was, for instance, another series of relationships apparent in the talk of middle management in these early stages. For example, 'participation' was put in syntagmatic relationship to 'fairness', 'equity', 'democracy', 'improvement', 'confrontation', 'self-protection', etc. But quite apart from the enormous and debilitating complexity that one would encounter, such a schematization would provide an imposed structure that wasn't there in the phenomena and which would halt and detract from the processual and emergent qualities of the signifiance of the text.

A further consideration is that such relations are not attributable to specific individuals. Each enters the public discourse and features in the text of participation freed from the constraints of intending individuals. To scrupulously delineate each participant's particular set of relations would tell us little about the overall nature of the discourse. It would further denature the productive and interactive process of meaning. Each contribution is released into the sociality of the situation and also releases the meaning potential in that relation. The possibilities of meaning become available in the public domain by their entry into the discourse and by their textual nature. The meanings are not fixed in those relations at the point of utterance. Their utterance is an issuance in which the possibilities of meaning — of change, and transformation, of new relations — begin, and not where they end. The source of meaning is not located in the intending consciousness of the utterer but in the relations of difference of those spoken items and others entering the discourse at that point, in that situation; and elsewhere and at other times. To continue to ask what a person meant when a particular utterance was made is a tiresome and ultimately reductivist task. Garfinkel (1967) has repeatedly pointed to the problem of the indefinite elaboration of accounts and Cicourel (1967) made reference to the problem of indefinite triangulation. Meaning is not located prior to occasions of its use; neither in the mind of the individual nor in some prefigured structural prescription of the meaning of words nor upon grammatical or situational rules of legitimate use.

As these relations with participation enter the discourse, some only remain in the discourse very briefly, others enter more fully in the sense that they are used in other contexts of the situation and by other people. There is a relative cohesion in such longevity. However, it is a spurious cohesion for the entry of the relation into the discourse invariably entails that it becomes dispersed in the text. It immediately becomes ensnared in a new and ever-shifting fabric of other relations. Thus, the relation 'participation–power' generated in the discourse of the shopfloor in the early meetings has initially a relatively discrete set of syntagmatic relations and works off an apparently constrained arrangement of paradigmatic relations. Initially it was associated with committee ratios of shopfloor representatives to management representatives and the progression of unresolved issues out of the matrix of the department. It belonged almost exclusively in that texture of meanings around the notion of meetings. However, as the discourse developed the item 'power' (or like terms) became engaged in numerous other relations that added to the complexity of its meaning potential. It became related to textures around the legitimacy and warrant of supervisory power; it became involved in the set of relations generally about the issue of decision-making; and so on. Its meaning potential magnified and proliferated to a degree.

Other items held an initially strong potential in this way, but then faded, dropping out of the discourse or becoming confined to a restricted or habituated set of relations. The paradox is that the fleeting relations often had more coherence and unity than those items that had a prolonged life, entered the discourse more fully and thus came to be more widely dispersed in the text.

A text has no beginning and no end — this is a feature of its inevitable indeterminacy. Thus at Tridy, although rigorous investigations could pinpoint the first time that the word 'participation' was employed (in other than a purely 'casual' way), that would not do as the starting point for the text. That would be to suggest that there was a definite origin for the text. It would be to assume that the entrance of the discourse of participation was the result of an invention of the grounds of that discourse by some determinate force. It would ignore the *intertextuality*[31] of all texts. And it is clear that even in the talk of senior managers, who could be said to have presented the notion to the company, there are already 'resayings' — a tapping of an already developed intertext. Indeed, explicit reference is made to that by these managers. The personnel manager, for example, makes direct reference to the wider debate on participation in academic, business, political and journalistic circles. The text, then, slips off into the intertext and the origin and beginning is lost.

But I have been diverted from my course. I have not yet made clear the full contribution of the paradigmatic relations to the determination of meaning. It is quite clear that any single item from the lexicon derives a significant portion of its meaning from other items in the lexicon, and not only from those items that are present in the syntagm synchronically. The meaning of present items can be considered as a meaning potential against a background of paradigmatic possibilities. The presence of an item has significance in relation to other items that were not said, but *could have been*. In the context of the preliminary meanings of the shop-floor then, each item present can be considered in relation to what could have been there instead but was not. In very general terms the item 'good' is drastically diminished without the possibility of presence of the item 'bad' in its place. More subtly, the occurrence of 'good' in the syntagm has meaning in relation to other items that could sensibly take its place, such as 'pleasant', 'average' etc. In this way what is not present in the participation discourse tells us as much about the meaning of those items that are present in the syntagm as those items and their relationships themselves. Again in the very broadest terms, the item 'participation' has a meaning potential in relation to those paradigmatic relations that provide options of selection. The existence in the lexicon of items such as 'totalitarianism', 'autocracy', 'unilateralism' and so on, creates the necessary meaning potential that forms the paradigmatic environment for the occasions of the use of 'participation'.

There are, of course, relatively clear lexicogrammatical, syntactical and phonological constraints on the sensible nature of that paradigmatic environment. But there are also constraints of tradition and convention that would appear to put limits on the feasibility of the range of items that might stand in the paradigmatic environment. There is also a sense in which the paradigmatic environment is itself a contextual construct, related to the context of the situation in which the syntagm is being acted out. The contextual determination of the situation of the utterance will at least partially determine the feasibility of the elements in the paradigmatic relations. I believe it is important to consider the context of the situation itself as a semiological construction. The context of the situation is more than minimally created by the nature of the discourse developing within it. The items in the syntagm and their relations help to define the context of the situation, which in turn has a determining effect on the possibilities of the relevant and sensible components of the paradigmatic environment (which contributes to the meaning of the item in the syntagm). Thus the context of the situation is at least partially a discursive construct too. However, not all the signs present in the situation will be linguistic. There will be signs that exist in other forms. There might be emblematic signs, signs embodied in pictures, architecture, style of dress, and so on. A full-blown semiological practice would want to take note of those other sign systems.

There is a sense in which the items in a syntagm under consideration at a particular point in time are an index of items appearing diachronically at previous points in time. It might be said that those prior items appearing in the discourse are in paradigmatic relation to those appearing in the current syntagm. Thus at time A a relation between 'participation' and 'communication' may appear; whilst at time B a relation between 'participation' and 'consultation' is present. The meaning of the relation at time B could be said to be given further value by the replacement of 'communication' by 'consultation'. The value of 'consultation' is added to by the fact that in that context 'communication' could have been used but was not.

A good example of this type of relation is provided by the series of terms by which the scheme at Tridy was referred to at different points in time by senior management. Thus at different stages and in different contexts of situation there appears: 'participation' (scheme) as 'project'; 'participation' as 'experiment'; as 'trial'; as 'exercise'; and so on. The meaning potential of each item is in part derived from the sense of options and a realization that alternatives have appeared previously. The selection of the different options can be seen in terms of their rhetorical function.

However, in considering the dynamic between the syntagmatic and the paradigmatic there remains an element of speculation as to the content of the paradigmatic environment. Any analysis from a negativity, from an absence, is fraught with difficulties.

So, as 'participation' enters the arena in the context of Tridy a whole kaleidoscope of relations begins to form. Participation consists of that text in which relations such as 'participation–communication', 'communication–

influence', 'meetings–power' and so on build up and become a shifting fabric of signifying activity. This is the movement of participation as text. But further, this fabric of present relations and their paradigmatic relations offers a site of productivity in which the contests for the control of meaning at Tridy are enacted. The very textuality creates the potentialities that allow for the possibility of alternative definitions and the seeds of negotiation and challenge.

However, under the pressure of movements to provide closure, some series of relations do appear to form themselves into a relatively discrete and cohesive 'texture' from time to time and in certain contexts of use. The relations around 'participation–representational democracy', involving a type of subtext of 'meetings' and associated terms, are an example of an area of relative cohesion. The rhetoric and the ideological underpinning of that central relation is supportive of the structuration of the scheme. It allows the discourse to develop in terms of programmed meetings, elections and representative committees on a departmental basis, and so on. It ultimately permits the managing director to employ a rhetoric that allows participation to be discursively structured in ways that perfectly map the supposed existing hierarchical structure of the company; as we will see.

The text of participation, characterized by this activity of the signifier, should not be thought of as a growing process moving towards a final and resolving point. Participation is not finally there when the site-wide scheme is made manifest. The movement of signifiers is not a linear one towards this finishing. There is no resolution, no final revelation and convergence of meaning at a point of maturity. Nor is there a sense in which the movement of the signifiers is one that necessarily brings a sophistication or an enrichment. The textual activity does not necessarily move towards a greater profundity. There is no sense of the text moving towards a more significant and highly developed meaning of participation. It simply moves. One would not excavate the layers of text and reveal an increasingly civilized construction of meaning as one went 'deeper'. There is not, then, a hermeneutic delving for the true heart of the text with a promise of the delivery of a revelatory understanding of what the text 'really' means. There are no neat thematics that can be captured and shown to relate to, and lead one to, a meaningful core that gives up the secret of the text. Participation is not developing towards some teleological point of completeness. Rather there is pure activity, ceaseless and unending. Text is the site of the activity, and, as has been made clear, it has no origin, centre or end. It is a movement of shifting relations and not necessarily of positive cumulations and deliberate and satisfying building. There is no coherence provided by the supposed ordering of an end in sight. There are dyings and witherings aways. There are births, rebirths and abortions. There are omissions and contradictions. There are small movements of a deranged nature constructed for particular contextual contingencies that would not fit comfortably into a presumed overall grand design. There are movements that dislocate other relations; that draw in; that cast out.

A social critical practice, then, seeks to display the textuality (of participation); to reveal the plurality of meanings and their dispersal through the text. But also to show how that textuality is both the site of, and the means by which there is an active productivity that offers the liberty of the language, and also the means of control; of exclusion and inclusion. There needs to be a concern, then, with the process of meaning, the how of meaning; with the relation of text to rhetoric and the tropological features of the text. What processes are involved in the presentation, the control and attempted closure of meaning? How do certain meanings attain a kind of ascendancy and relative cohesion? It is suggested that this is largely a rhetorical and ideological movement. But also that the very textuality of participation — its proliferation and its ineluctably metaphorical and ideological nature — is likely to undo the espoused project, the attempted control and closure, and will reveal the pragmatic and rhetorical attempts to provide closure on meanings in particular ways. It is to these issues that we must now turn.

CLOSURE AND REHABILITATION

There is a recurrent dynamic in the text of participation between the entry and seeming usefulness of the term 'participation' and its full strangeness, newness and potential disruptiveness (witness the initial avoidance of the term in the early discourse of management).[32] That dynamic creates a tension that engenders a movement to rehabilitate the term to habitual and familiar discourse(s). There are numerous points in the text where participation is returned to domains of discursive familiarity — movements that operate an attempted closure; that work an exclusive–inclusive practice; that seek to deny alternative, potentially interrogative, even radical interpretations; that posit the espoused presentations, definitions and relations as natural, obvious and right. It is an essentially ideological movement that retrieves participation for the dominant social formation — for established and accredited ways of ordering things.

Ideology serves to disguise the limits of particular arenas of discourse. The inevitable and necessary partiality of discourse, and its inconsistencies and incoherences, are circumvented by an ideological practice that establishes traditional and/or legitimized points of adequate finiteness and recirculates the language tautologously back into the domain of the discourse. Ideology might be said to disguise what may be referred to as *doubt* in the text. It makes those arbitrary points of finitenes, those stops to productivity in the text that are accepted as the extent of the search for a warrant and guarantee for the meaning/origin of the text, seem as natural end-points in the discourse.

The definitions offered by management talk at Tridy will aspire to a naturalness — will present themselves as the 'right' and appropriate definitions (as will other groups' attempted definitions). The textures of meaning constructed by the given relations will be supposed adequately to map out the boundaries of the term, to stand up as an ordered, complete, cohesive and final coverage of the possible meanings of participation in that context. The result presents itself as an interpretation devoid of muddling inconsistencies, gaps and contradictions. It must appear as such if it is to completely fill the space it has created in the discourse of the shopfloor. Any omissions or contradictions — any free play allowed to remain — are in danger of being exploited and widened and used to introduce other, unwanted and unplanned interpretations that could disrupt the aspired-to definition. The talk will try to convey to the audience a natural, obvious and transparent 'message' with which they can readily concur and accept as 'right' and 'correct'. It is the task of the style of presentation and the employed rhetoric to achieve that. The constructed textures attempt to transparently convey to the audience an obvious relationship to features in the supposed reality of company affairs and activities.

The task is at least partially aided by the management presentations and talk being, by fiat, part of an official discourse (official in the obvious sense and in the sense implied by Burton and Carlen, 1977). 'Company' discourse, as a version of 'business' discourse, say, aspires to a status of neutrality — a right and objective way of speaking about and ordering things within the context of the company. Participation is located within that discourse and accrues the concomitant benefits.

The achievement of naturalness is at least in part accomplished by making what are really only arbitrary or ideologically informed relations appear as if they are innocent and necessary. The success of the rhetoric of this definitional imperialism depends on its ability to make those arbitrary relations appear as natural to the shopfloor, such that they can do nothing but nod in agreement to the sense, the appalling obvious sense, of what is being said. Thus, when the presented definitions of management forge the relationship between, say, 'participation' and 'consultation' arbitrarily from amongst all the myriad possible associations that could have been made, it is the task of rhetoric to make that relationship appear to the audience as wholly natural and right.

The assumed source of the text itself contributes to the achievement of naturalness. But more important would be a matching of the adopted rhetoric with the background expectancies of the intended audience and a locating of the relationships within an ideological discourse that is shared by the audience. Again 'participation' is singular in this regard. Once the association is formed between 'participation' and '(industrial) democracy', the way is opened up for a tapping of the ideological discourse that is indexed by that latter notion, one that is assuredly shared and familiar to all members at Tridy. This displays the interrelated feature of discourses.

Embodied in such an ideological discourse are arrangements for shared values. On this view, ideology is not something other than the discourse, not some rarified confection of beliefs and opinions, but a more or less established and commonly shared set of interrelationships that provides a distinctive texture of meaning around value and belief items. An ideological discourse might be said to be just that established and shared chain of signifiers where the relations and interrelations between items appear as (morally?) natural and right. The provision of one or more items from that chain in a particular piece of talk gives an index and an entree to the rest of the texture or discourse. Such discourses are naturally highly bounded, that boundedness being added to by breaches being in various ways sanctionable by those who position themselves as guardians and interpreters of the discourse. Ideology is thus seen as part of the mechanism by which meaning is controlled, and closed.

An ideological discourse not only provides this sense of naturalness and order, but also provides the grounds and the categories of inclusion. The established boundaries of the discourse mean that certain items and certain relations are ruled out in various ways and on various grounds. It is easy to see on this basis where the struggle for power enters in at the level of discourse. It is clear already that those in control of the policing of the boundaries are in a position of power. The edges of the discourse are in need of protection to retain control of the closure on potential meanings emerging. The development of unwanted and uncontrolled relations in the border regions can significantly alter the whole of the discourse. This is potentially subversive, especially if such relationships threaten to challenge the required naturalness of the established relations and to reveal them as merely conventional, arbitrary or ideological.

Participation as a newness, as otherness, has this potential quality. It is in danger of realigning the relationships within the established company discourse. It could subvert the supposed naturalness of the relations between such items as, say, 'control' and 'hierarchy' or 'management prerogative' and 'decision-making', and so on; the reader can doubtless explore some of those likely relationships for him or herself. The company is already taking a risk by the introduction of the item at all. The need exists then for the introduction of the term to be controlled and guided. Its relation with items already in the discourse and with fresh ones drawn from outside needs to be monitored very carefully so that there are no drastic unintended consequences.

The talk of management assumes for itself a privileged position that gives it the sole right to delineate the meaning of the term and its relationships. It claims the right to speak adequately and sensibly about participation whilst at the same time denying the veracity of any other talk which might so presume. It does not do so in absolute terms, but claims the right specifically in relation to the context of Tridy. This is a sensible move since management talk already assumes a privileged position in relation to company affairs; a privilege that is, incidentally, largely acquiesced to and colluded with by most company members. Indeed, the fresh presentation of participation trades on and exploits this agreed authority of management talk to apply itself to, and define, all major matters relating to the company.

There are many points in the text where participation is returned to domains of discursive familiarity by rhetorical means. It is only possible here to illustrate that process with one or two examples. It may help, then, to analyse in some detail certain of the more salient textures,[33] instances where the language is more obviously ideological, rhetorical and reflexively supportive of the dominant social formation — either in terms of the wider society or localized in relation to the company.

Some of the most strongly articulated and sophisticated textures occur in the talk of senior management in those contexts where it seeks to define and present participation to the workforce. The illustrations will be drawn from that body of talk.

PARTICIPATION AND HISTORICAL INEVITABILITY: TEXTURE

In the early stages of the scheme various internal documents were produced by the personnel department that spoke about participation. In these documents 'participation' is again engendered in the signifying process. One of the relationships entails 'participation' and 'change'. At some points change has a further specificity, being cast in terms of change in (managerial) style and skill — an interesting arrangement on its own that develops into an elaborate texture. However, participation is also related to 'change' in terms of a set of other, more general relations.

The 'participation–change' relationship operates a double movement. First, participation is held to entail internal change in management style and skill — part of a change exercise initiated by the company. Secondly, it is conceived as part of a more general, society-wide change. As stated in the document 'Discussion Document on Worker Participation':

> ... changing times will inevitably mean greater participation of staff at all levels. A state of planned change is preferable to precipitated action forced by pressure of events.

> ... accelerated change involving greater participation reflects trends both political and educational.

At other points there are express attempts to link participation with an overall background of 'forces' in society that are said to have a direct bearing on the industrial scene. In one document these various 'external forces' are identified in the 'overall background': they are (a) educational, (b) social, (c) political, (d) legal. Each item reflects an intertext surrounding public discourse on the issue of industrial democracy. 'Political' refers to the renewed interest of political parties in the issue at that time and the publication by all political parties and affiliated bodies of documents setting down more or less specific views on the issue. 'Legal' partly indexes a fear that government action was imminent and the company might find themselves saddled with legislation for which they were ill-prepared and have some participation scheme foisted upon them (possibly with statutory trade union involvement). With regard to 'education' and 'broader social forces', in the wider discourse about participation reference is often made to an increasing democratization in society's other institutions and in social life generally and that this should/will be reflected more in our industrial and commercial institutions.

In one company document that seeks to provide an 'up-to-date assessment of the small experimental "worker involvement project" in the Chemical Plant at Tridy' (note the choice of words and relationships here), there is inserted a host of textual gleanings related to this socio-politico-legal movement. By this juxtaposition the former is incorporated into the latter. Management talk indexes these other, already elaborated, portions of discourse on participation.

In all this there is a rhetorical attempt to relate participation to an inevitable social and historical process. The words reflect a strong social determinism. The fact of participation cannot be ignored. There are forces in the wider society, beyond the control of the company, that mean that participation, in some form, has attained an importance and an inevitability and that it must be responded to at some point.

What these associations also achieve rhetorically is a distancing of the need for, and the generation of, participation from the company. At other points in the text the language around participation employed by senior management created a texture of 'ownership' — '*our* scheme', 'how can *we* involve *our* employees', '*managerial* style', etc. Here, however, the genesis of and obligation for participation are located outside the company in social forces and the march of time. Now the talk presents the company as only responding to the power of events beyond their direct control. Participation is not really their idea, it does not belong to them, they are not responsible for its emergence or its need at Tridy. This goes some way towards deflecting any criticisms of their motives for introducing the scheme (which certainly emerged). It directs potential criticism away from the company to factors outside — the imponderables of societal and political process. If participation goes wrong it is not the company who are to blame but politicians, the educators and the nature of historical change.[34]

The rhetoric also possesses a more positive force as well. It ties the talk of senior management (and thereby 'the company') to wider creditable sources. It demonstrates to those who might question the need for and the importance of participation that it already has a place in the lofty world of national politics (of all persuasions, most usefully). It seeks to show that 'the company' are in touch with the tide of history and the complicated processes of society. These portions of company documentation that reference these wider forces succeed in tying participation to those other worthy political and academic discourses that also tackle these issues and that talk about 'progress' in society. But more importantly, they locate their own moves to initiate participation within a wider scheme of historical and social processes. The introduction of participation at Tridy is made to appear as part of an historically inevitable process. Any move to challenge the need for or the sense of introducing participation at Tridy is forced, then, to go against not only the wisdom of political and academic opinion but also the very march of historical progress. To challenge participation at this point is to appear reactionary, as someone out of touch with the natural processes in society, and to misconceive history. This is quite a lot to oppose.

The relations present in these documents are clearly very limited and partial. There are diverse shades of opinion in those areas of wider discourse, some of which run counter to that presented. The company documents are constructed to access that portion of the intertext that supports the relation of participation to historical and social inevitability. They work an exclusive movement that elides other areas, and, knowledgeable of the gaps in the discourse of their audience, marks off the available alternatives.

But there is yet another turn in the rhetoric. The company at the same time are able to assert their independence, to claim the right to control the introduction and development of participation at Tridy. The very inevitability of industrial participation and the assumed impending legislation is also used as a rationale for the company introducing a scheme off their own back and in their own way. This is coupled to expressions of fear about legislation forcing upon them a particular and potentially inappropriate format of participation. The talk here maintains that it is in the interests of nobody at Tridy to have this happen.

Working together, these rhetorical movements serve to present the company as competently and knowledgeably aware of wider events and involved in the inevitable tide of history, but also assure their members that they can control that movement for their benefit and not subject them to unwarranted and inappropriate interference. The company had the foresight to anticipate events and act accordingly. If participation is inevitable, as is part of the suggestion, then it is surely better that a sensible management preempt events and create a scheme that is more directly suited to the wishes and needs of its members.

Still yet the texture moves and works. It relates participation, in this arrangement, back to the general company discourse (company culture perhaps). It relates to aspects of the company discourse that traditionally present the company as progressive, modern, caring and paternalistic.[35] This discursive arrangement is already familiar to the shopfloor and other organization members.

There is a kind of 'grammar of motives' here. The 'cause' of participation is said to reside in a range of interrelated 'external forces'. These motives are constructed in context and made to serve particular rhetorical purposes. The relation of participation with these forces ultimately connotes a sense of social and historical determinism. The theoretical sense of this remains unexplicated and is merely indexed. The notion of historical and social determinism is taken as an adequate (at least in part) explanation of the presence of participation. The ideological force of this is the extent of the acceptance, and perceived naturalness, of historical and social 'forces' as being responsible for, or as determining of, features in the social realm, such as greater or lesser participation. The fact that the nature of those 'forces' remains largely unexplored is not the point. It is of interest to note only that the invocation of such 'forces' — that set of relations — is taken as an adequate explanation of the development of participation — or even that it is simply assumed to be adequate. Whether it appears adequate to the audience depends upon the extent to which they share in that ideology.

Participation is made to exist within a broader sense of societal progress — society is seen as in a state of change. There are movements in the political, social, legal and educational realms. Furthermore, they are all moving in the same direction — towards greater participation. Suggesting this, and that the industrial sector *must* follow that motion, confirms a conception of a unitary society with all elements formed together into a cohesive whole. That series of relations, 'society – cohesion – unity – stability', is of course itself an ideological construction. Participation is part of this unitary picture and is a movement within the general and natural movement of the cohesive body of society. The 'forces' that create that movement are unchallengeable and unstoppable, ergo so is participation. This is the way things are, it is the way things are going.

STRUCTURING PARTICIPATION: THE PYRAMID

At another point in the development of the scheme, the managing director undertakes a formal presentation of what he sees as the future development of the scheme and its ultimate structural form. The presentation took the form of a slick, well-rehearsed speech accompanied by overhead slide and chart illustrations.

The most significant portion of the presentation concerned the use of two slides and accompanying talk that purported to display how the existing and proposed structure of participation matched and fitted into the general structure of the organization (see Figures 1 and 2). The slides employed the metaphor of the pyramid to represent both the traditional structure of the company and the development of participation.

In broad terms the presentation accomplished two rhetorical movements. It represented the first coherent and structured view of participation to emerge at Tridy. It posited a total picture, placing participation directly in the context of Tridy and relating it to future plans and developments. It also related participation to familiar ways of representing and talking about things within the company.

The presentation offered an overall picture and a contextualizing of participation at Tridy. For many other organization members it provided a possible framework to which they could now attach a series of amorphous and vague relationships dispersed across a number of seemingly unrelated and unrelatable discourses. Such structuration and totalizing certainly operated to control meaning and to close off meaning as far as other organization members

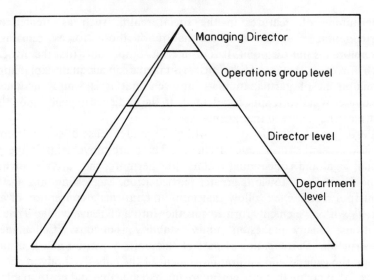

Figure 1 Traditional structure

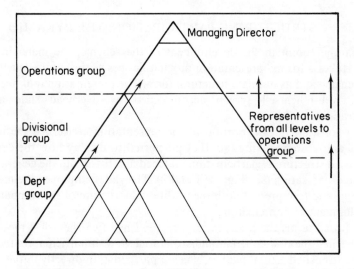

Figure 2 Development of participation

were concerned. For some, participation had become an enigma, a problem in need of resolution. Here a partial resolution or a route to resolution is offered. The messiness and nebulous nature of participation is, at least temporarily, smoothed out and clarified. There is a new unity and cohesion. The circling, unconnected meanings; the uncertainty; the dispersal and the plurality are catered for. Order is restored; clarity is restored; unity is restored. Everything that an organizational heart could desire. The fuss of many and meandering meanings is curtailed and foreshortened. The unfettered are given credible connections and boundaries are established. Most significantly, the meanings dispersed across other regions of discourse and the associations with strange discourses are cured. Participation is related strongly to a familiar area of discourse. And it is fixed, made steady. There is indeed a structuring of process. The convolutions of meanings emerging in process are ironed out and placed neatly in a frame; one of geometric precision. This is particularly so when one considers that the managing director is also presenting a history. He is not only giving details of future plans but also a *post hoc* account of the creation and building of the scheme. The formalist structure that he provides glosses the contingent and emergent quality of that process. It belies the uncertainty, the feeling-of-the-way, the unanticipated and the unstructured reality of the method of proceeding. In its stead is placed a careful, thoughtful, ordered and rational account.

Other textures have related participation to familiar fields of discourse external, as it were, to the company and its affairs. *This* texture provides the necessary connection between participation and the common discourse of the company. The supposed existing structure of the company is overtly displayed in the graphic metaphor of the pyramid. The pyramid speaks of levels: levels within the company. The company structure is said to be represented by this pyramidal shape, with its apex, its various levels and its base. The structure is, obviously, a metaphor for the existing power arrangements of the company. The levels refer to the formal rights and positions of people in the decision-making processes of the company. Increasing levels indicate increased rights and invested authority to take decisions, to be in control, to punish and reward, to direct and lead. The pyramid is the whole of the factory. At the top is the managing director; at the bottom are the shopfloor personnel. Each department is further represented by the mini-pyramids embedded in the larger. The relations of geometry are duplicated in each department; each department is assumed to have broadly the same structure as the company as a whole.

This structure is a familiar and widely experienced one, the metaphor common, even if not conceived of exactly in the graphic form presented. The discourse surrounding that structure would be widely shared and employed to articulate the experience of many in their working lives. The images of top and bottom and of levels, for instance, would seem to be rooted in much habitual talk about organizations and issues of industrial relations. Such a structure is wholly traditional and one that is expected and accepted by most industrial participants in England. It is seen as a natural arrangement and thereby serves ideological purposes. That the shopfloor concur largely with that image is at least partially confirmed by some of the traditional and collusive comments made by them in the early conversations I had with them, and by the fact that they did not react to this presentation negatively. Indeed quite the opposite, they readily accepted the presentation and were relieved to have that sort of clarifying structure provided for them. There was never, at any point, a suggestion that the structure was in any way inappropriate or inaccurate.

There is a double rhetorical play at work here. In the first place there is the move to present the existing company structure in terms of the graphic metaphor of the pyramid, with all the implied connotations and the organizational discourse thus indexed. Then there is a second move to relate participation directly to this structure. The second is an explicit act of inclusion. Participation too is made into a framework, into a structure that is then inserted into the existing organizational structure, filling it completely. The two structures are made to appear in isomorphic relationship to each other. The now presented structure of participation is made to completely overlie the existing and traditional structures of the company's formal power relations. The movement is subtle, since in the same motion participation is transposed into a structure and brought into direct confluence with the presented structures of the company's normal arrangement. It is both ordered and related to the discursively familiar at the same point.

Let us be clear. The graphic metaphor of the pyramid is firstly made to present the organizational structure of the company's power relations. That is the first rhetorical move. It exploits a known and presumed shared conception of traditional organization. It exploits the background expectancies of the company members. There is familiarity here: a well-known ground and a dimension of discourse that is understood and accepted. At the same time participation is also made a structure. It ceases, for the moment, to be an emergent process and is fixed as a structural form. And that form is of the same substance as the structure of the existing company organization. Participation becomes a static series of formal relationships in the company. Participation is made to depend on the relations and levels already said to be present in the company. It is made to rely upon the extant power relationships, the established authority positions and the accompanying rights of decision-making, control and responsibility. Finally, the structure of participation thus established is put into correspondence with the traditional structure and the two become one: interdependent and inseparable.

The ambiguity and dispersal of participation, its otherness and newness, are retrieved at several points. The naturalness of the link between the supposed organizational arrangements of the company and the formal structure in the form of the pyramid is ideologically rooted. These are exposed, common and accepted arrangements. They are wholly familiar, legitimate and right. They are, of course, essentially ideological relations that have come to assume the position of natural ones in most domains of discourse in the western industrial world. They are like incorrigible presuppositions; and they are reflexively self-supporting. All organizational talk tends to be cast in that form (even participation, so it would seem); it provides the answers to its own questions; its effectiveness is judged in relation to its own discourse — thus, in one sense, all talk about organizations tends to reconfirm the rightful dominancy of those relations. Participation, then, is made to become a part of those relations and thereby to share in their naturalness. Where before participation had been locatable in unfamiliar discourses, if at all, here it can be grounded in something that is not only familiar but natural to the point of immutable. Participation is no longer so strange, so external. It inhabits the lasting and abiding structures of western industrial life,

More pertinently, it is enclosed in that linguistic and graphic arrangement that is said to adequately represent affairs at *Tridy*. It is part of the company. It is shown to be accommodated by the normal and traditional structures of Tridy, something people are familiar with, can operate in with ease, and can talk around. Participation is no longer positioned outside the company as some alien and potentially disturbing element; it is made to cohabit the same space as the existing structures of the company. It is a sweeping act of inclusion that takes participation in, rehabilitating it from its mystery and its floating, non-aligned power. It is placed in the company of the familiar, it becomes the familiar, it need no longer be feared or misunderstood.

The rhetorical strategy here operates as a short cut. It is a significant move that so readily relates participation to the structures of the company, exploiting the naturalness of those arrangements and making participation a part of them. There was a need to begin to relate participation to the familiar discourse of the company, both to control it and to make it comprehendable and no longer a source of anxiety. Without this rhetorical ploy there would doubtless have been the need for a good deal of protracted interactional work whereby the various signifiers connected to participation were gradually connected to those others that were already common coinage in the company discourse. By this direct association of participation with the formal structures of the company it is immediately, if indirectly, associated with all of the familiar discourse of the company; it is incorporated into that established network in which matters of industrial relations and other company affairs are normally spoken about.

There is a strength that turns back on itself here too. If one considers some of the other areas of the texture built up around participation, particularly those where it is shown up as valuable, right and good,[36] then there is a way in which the linking of existing company language, structure and philosophy with participation turns around to reinforce and reaffirm that prior language. For example, if participation is associated with 'progressiveness', then the linking of participation with existing company arrangements suggests the latter are at least conducive to progressiveness. In other words, the language built up around participation that prizes it,really becomes transferred, osmosis-like, on the basis of the close-forged link, from participation to the *status quo*.

The rhetoric here also participates in that movement which one of the textures, that around the language of science,[37] has begun. Participation is now shrouded in a language of order, rationality and logic. The figural language of structure, of plans and programmes, polices the meanings of participation into a coherence and order that belies its naturally uncharted and wild development. The disparate and unconnected meanings and associations are marshalled into an intelligible whole. The process, so contingent, unplanned and off-the-cuff, is transposed and corsetted into a structure. It is made to conform to standards of rational development. The organizational values of order, clarity, coherence and planning are demonstrated to apply in the case of participation. It is more acceptable, palatable and recognizable that way.

A DIAGRAM OF POWER

These illustrative textures are just two drawn from a range of others. Amongst those that again are more obviously ideologically informed are those developed around the relations 'participation–representational democracy', 'participation–science', 'participation–rationality' and 'participation–change'. Some of these have already been alluded to in what has gone before and it should be clear that they have no real independence or mutual exlusivity — they are all embodied in the same text. It should also be made clear that even the full set originally desedimented cannot be taken as complete, final and absolute. Even, within these presented textures, the evacuation is partial; there are further possible appliqués and threads that have not received treatment here. The availability of more space and time would still render the task of unpicking the whole text impossible.

What I hope has been demonstrated thus far is the relationship between those textures and ideology and rhetoric and how this operates a closure on the meanings in the context of Tridy. It is also hoped that the potential of the outlined social critical practice can now begin to be appreciated.

Each texture operates a movement towards closure. It does so in part by indexing a particular wider discourse that offers reflexive support for the coherence and sense of the texture, by making available particular positions of intelligibility and by operating an inclusive–exclusive practice. At the same time, textures have, both within themselves and in the relations between them, points of contradiction, omissions and aporia. Points where the rhetoric that offers a finite and closed texture and an ordered set of meanings is inadequate to mask the arbitrariness or ideological nature of the constructions. These are further points of potentiality. They offer a possible ground for contestation in relation to the espoused project. They can be exposed and space made for critique and counterposition. Thus in the effort of closure, in the continued movement and productivity of text and the spaces within and between textures and discourse, resides the site of political activity and the exercise of power.

Textures index and become embedded in discourse. Each discourse offers itself as truth; proposes to talk knowledgeably about the real. As is perhaps already clear, discourse is the site of a particular episteme. It has its own incorrigible propositions, its own canons of truth. It is a way of ordering, a way of saying how things are. Discourse is a vehicle or instrument of espoused knowledge. As such, each arena of discourse, even each relation or texture indexing an area, aspires to '... designate such matters as relevance, propriety, regularity, conviction and so forth' (Said, 1978, p. 706). Knowledge is assertive and it excludes alternatives.

Bersani (1977) talks about the exercise of power as 'diagramming' — that is, as an ordering of knowledge within a particular discursive frame. But, of course, it is a particular ordering; it excludes and offers a closure on other modes of attaining meaning. Michel Foucault also maintains that discursive practices are characterized by:

... a delimination of a field of objects, the definition of a legitimate perspective for the agent of knowledge, and the fixing of norms for the elaboration of concepts and theories. (1977, p. 199)

They attempt to articulate an enclosed space, a specified ground that is adequate, final for the purposes for which it is made to apply. At their most elaborated and most inclusive they seek to totally claim an area of knowledge such that it is virtually impossible to think or speak outside of them — for to do so is to speak the untruth, the meaningless or the mad. Clearly the totalizing aspect of discourses is variable. Some achieve this archexclusivity, others are less secure, more fluid and permeable. But each discourse aspires to such totality.

For Foucault forms of knowledge, or claimed knowledge, are domains of discourse and are strategies of power. Discourse is central to the notion of power; it is, for Foucault, at once the *object* of the struggle for domination and the *means* by which that struggle is engaged. Talking about reality, ordering experience, forming textures and relations in ways that include and exclude is an exercise of power in a most fundamental way. Discourse and power occupy the same ground; to lay claim to a discourse is to seize a form of power, and any seizure of power is an appropriation of discourse.

Foucault, however, goes to great lengths to show how the will to power is habitually hidden in discourse that presents itself as innocent. This presence in discourse effaces itself — it becomes invisible, Foucault suggests, for political reasons. The will to power inherent in discourse is disguised; it is thus more covert and invidious. A naked will to power is unpalatable, and furthermore is more readily countered. Discourses present themselves as innocent; as sensible, objective and exclusive orderings and selections of experience. While it is true that some discourse domains are clearly and obviously political and are areas of debate and controversy, others do not have the appearance of being exercises of power. But these differences only reflect different moments in a process, not absolute differences. Discourses of knowledge present themselves as rational

—say a logical rationality, or a moral, or a socio political, or an economic rationality — but, it is suggested, each of these is only a rationalization of power: the will to power disguised by a supposed rationality.

Foucault is attempting to move beyond the sort of 'textual isolationism' (Said, 1978) that he sees Derrida ensnared in and to show how texts are an integral part of, and not merely an accessory to, the social processes of differentiation, exclusion, incorporation and rule. The full force of rhetoric must be appreciated. The construction of discourse as an exercise of, and/or will to, power is hidden by the rhetoric that enables discourses to present themselves as innocent, as speaking clearly, objectively, naturally and truthfully, to the extent that many appear as neutral.

The construction and presence of any discourse immediately, at the same time, drives something else out: discourses occupy a space that excludes. They dislodge or displace other, and other possible, discourses. At a lower level, the interpolation of certain textual relations lessens the possibility of others being able to occupy that space, particularly so if those relations index and connect with a dominant extant discourse. Such textual relations serve to provide positions of intelligibility. Such talk achieves a situating of potential meaning relations within a discourse that is familiar, accepted, even taken-for-granted. The series of relations around 'participation–representational democracy' seemed to achieve this admirably in the context of Tridy. That texture served to link participation into a major hegemonic discourse in society, one that has most vitally carved out an exclusive place. The invocation of that discourse was sufficient to place participation in a significant relationship that served some important purposes. It gave the audience the chance to locate participation in a discourse that secured and bounded much of its meaning. Other textures provided a similar service, as we have seen.

Part of the movement to closure is this incorporative practice, but at the same time it also operates an exclusive practice. The obscuring of alternatives was particularly telling for the shopfloor membership at Tridy as it became apparent they were unable to locate participation in any vital discourse of their own that offered an interrogative position *vis-à-vis* those positions provided by the proffered discourse. The notion of location and place here is significant.

If we return to the level of the signifier, what we encounter with Foucault is an added sophistication. That is, it is important not only to consider the signifier, but also to explore its place — a place not in abstraction, not innocent, but a place within a discourse with all the power it possesses, its place in a discursive matrix that includes and excludes and that has its own place amongst others. That placing, then, has a force. Signifying in place *is* — rather than merely represents — an act of will with ascertainable political and intellectual consequences (Said, 1978, p. 709). It is an act that is an attempt to locate and occupy a position, to give a position of intelligibility that offers knowledge: a willful ordering of things in particular ways. It is, then, an act of power. Power is not possessed, not necessarily privileged, acquired or preserved by formal positions, but that which is exercised in these placings themselves. The exercise of power becomes recognizable in the overall effect of these strategic positionings.

Serial acts of signifying in place are themselves an exercise of power, relating specific utterances to discourse and ideological practice. Creating the relation 'participation–science' is an example here. The placing of the signifier in that relation also places it in the discourse of science and as such is a political and ideological move. Its place in that discourse, with the authority that discourse possesses *vis-à-vis* other discourses present or possible in our society and in that context, serves to exclude others and to include participation in that dominant will to knowledge — a way of speaking about and ordering reality in truthful, objective and neutral ways. Its ability to be so placed also, of course, serves to reflexively reinforce the power of that discourse.

It is in this sense that power is said to be everywhere, omnipresent. It does not proceed from a seat or origin of power, its exercise is found always, and everywhere, in these surface practices; *in every act of signification.*

We might go further and suggest that social relations of difference are themselves the embodiment of discursive practice. There are arenas of discourse that form and perpetuate the difference between manager and subordinate for instance. Verbal enactments made possible by those discourses that engender differences of relation also reflexively reconfirm those differences.

Each time a signifying practice is engaged in, then, there is an exercise of power. It is an attempt to control meaning, an attempt to propose one series of relations rather than another, an attempt to valorize one discourse rather than another. It is an attempt thereby to provide closure, to exclude and to incorporate. This is facilitated by a discursive practice that already creates subjects and positions them. Those positionings are also points of differentiation. They engender at the same moment a subject's ability to engage in certain types of discourse and an exclusion from others. This provides a position of intelligibility from which that, and other, discourses can be apprehended.

I hope the earlier illustrations have gone some way to show how the talk around participation at Tridy enacted these practices, how particular relations emerged and how those relations either directly indexed certain discourses or else, by forming a complex texture, locked relations into discourses. I hope something of the positioning practices involved has also been revealed or can be readily conceived of. The emergent talk at Tridy can usefully be conceived of in terms of an exercise of power; of attempted closure on meaning and of discursive practices that retrieved participation to places in an existing ideological arrangement. However, as already suggested, the closure of meaning and the totalizing of discourse struggle against the continued productivity of text and the movement of meaning.

Bersani (1977), whilst articulating the 'diagramming' of power, also asserts that it 'leaks'. Power too is a ceaseless activity, never final and absolute. Power is an activity always present in all these small relations and it is released in every signifying practice. Bersani talks of the state and its ordering attempt to immobilize the release of power in all these microconfrontations. But every act of signification is a site of productivity, as we have seen. However rigidly positioned, however pervasive the discourse mode, the possibility at least always exists of a countermanding relation of signifiers being constructed. In this sense every exercise of power inscribes the potential for resistance. The exercise of power is always directed, so in a simple sense relations of power by definition include the adversary role. If there were not relations of difference (even among subjects) there would be no signifying practice of any meaning, and no sense in an exercise of power.

Part of the 'leaking' of power is, Bersani maintains, the fact that the exercise of power is invariably in excess, an excess that releases counterpositions. The aspired-to closure and totalizing of an exercise of power, the will to power, almost inevitably defeats its own object Foucault also maintains. As Bersani (1977, p. 5) puts it, it does so '. . . by always producing in excess of the calculable requirements of a strategy of domination'. That excess is partly the result of the productivity of language but partly the result of the practical need to say more. The latter may take the form of a metacommentary on one's own prior constructions, or a simple repetitiveness that is never exact replication but always a difference, or 'a supplementary bavardage which may lend itself to a regrouping of several elements in the networks of power' (Bersani, 1977, p. 5). All this overflowing disrupts the attempted coherence. It is a release, a release of signifiers and textures that can be assimilated and reconstituted by others — and, what is more significant, reconstituted into an oppositional frame.

For example, managers in their presentation of participation were obliged, simply by the reoccurrence of situations and by the obligations perceived in different contexts, to represent it variously. In doing so it is put inevitably into new and different relations. The plurality of meaning becomes more apparent at each turn. The aspired-to coherence becomes increasingly more impossible. It is here particularly that the lesions, the tears in the fabric of the text, appear and the possibilities of a rereading and a counterpractice become apparent.

Similarly, no texture is able to claim for itself a clear-cut linguistic domain whose borders effectively enclose meaning. Particularly at their interstices, there is often a collision, an unhappy adjacency where one texture undercuts the aspired-to logic, coherence and closure of the other. An example here would be the tension between the emergent texture of historical inevitability and that texture that talks of participation being provided by a caring company for the good of the workforce — an internal generation. Also, relations and the textures merely index discourse arenas; the articulation of those discourses is necessarily very partial and consequently leaves much open space to be exploited and occupied. It is in these areas that the very possibility of a counterlanguage develops.

The exercise of power, then, is a diagramming, an ordering of knowledge within a particular discursive frame. But it is also a productivity, a release and an overflowing that provides the possibility of an interrogative practice and a rediagramming, or at least a chance 'to provoke a mutation in the diagram' (Foucault, 1975, cited in Bersani, 1977). A chance to expose lesions in the text and to exploit them.

Every resistance to the exercise of power is, of course, a counterexercise of power. The power of a signifying practice can only be countered by another signifying practice. The exercise of power, then, is also an attempt to contain the signifying responses of others — by positionality, by indexing dominant discourse arenas; by the rhetoric and a reliance on ideology. Thus, the attempt in the talk of management to provide a rightful, coherent and enclosing sense around 'participation' — to make its textual relations appear right, obvious and natural — is also an attempt to foreclose upon any alternative signifiying response; to make alternatives unspeakable, if not unthinkable.

One could return here to the 'sociological story' that had continued to work very hard in this research practice. That is, one might begin to conceive of power in terms of the ability to define situations, power as the engagement of a signifying practice that constructs a texture of relations that occupy a space in interaction and a social realm, that is accepted as an adequate or right textual covering of the experience or phenomena faced by the participants. At a different level, it is the hegemony of certain discursive frames and practices that attain a dominance by succeeding in a claim to speak knowledgeably and morally. It is the ability to offer an account that is accepted (if only temporarily) as *the* account.

Despite the concentration on textual matters thus far it is important to make clear, first that non-linguistic forms of signification can be involved in the exercise of power, and secondly that there exist certain institutional arrangements, themselves fortified and recreated in discursive practice, that have a tendency to provide certain parties to a situation with a right and an ability to control to an extent the means of the production of signification and its release and flow. Examples that come most obviously to mind include management's ability to control the construction of the minutes of meetings, and their capacity to control the construction of agendas. But in other, more complex situations, management has an authority and capacity to access various information sources on site, and to control the production, release and flow of significations. All of this and more facilitates, *inequitably*, the ability to engage in a signifying practice that constructs an account and that offers up an authoritative set of meaning relations. It permits management again to create a discourse that presents itself as a knowledgeable discourse. This additional mundane facility is enabling of their appropriating the discourse of knowledge already invested in that discursive arrangement that positions them as 'managers' and by extension as 'experts' (knowers) in particular appropriate arenas. It is they that are held to have 'knowledge' about 'company' matters —that is their privileged discourse.

Significations, then, enter the conflictual arena of competing interest groups — indeed constitute that difference — as real and positive forces. As Hall (1982, p. 70) puts it:

> The signification of events is part of what has to be struggled over, for it is the means by which collective social understandings are created — and thus the means by which consent for particular outcomes can be effectively mobilised. Ideology on this perspective, has not only become a 'material force'... (but is) real because it is 'real' in its effects. It has also become the site of struggle (between competing definitions) and a stake — a prize to be won — in the conduct of particular struggles.

The power struggle at Tridy is manifested to a large extent in the attempt by management's signifying practice to construct a text around participation that aspires to the status of a preferred and limited range of meanings. It is embodied in the movement to maintain coherence and legitimacy in the account offered. There is an internal power struggle, as it were, for that text to police its own boundaries, to halt the potential proliferations of meaning. There is a power struggle also to maintain that version and to prevent alternatives arising and the possibility of the development of a signifying practice from other participants that might come to take the form of a counterlanguage. It is an attempt at closure, it is an attempt to stem the surplus, the overflowing of meaning, it is an attempt to locate and employ ideological discourses and to paper over and disguise the lesions. But the movement of text continues. It is ineluctably the site of productivity, and thus the potential for rereading, adjusting, mutating and countering is also always present. The control of the means of production of texture and discourse and the entrenchment of certain types of discourse arena often ensure that such an interrogative option is not realized and the counterlanguage remains only in potentiality.

NOTES

1. The research is reported more fully elsewhere: see Westwood (1983).
2. The nomenclature of the 'exercise' was problematical to the company then, and remains so here now.
3. I take this to be a sufficiently well-known and extensive research and theoretical corpus as to not warrant referencing here.
4. Notably Berger and Luckman (1967), but also see Holzner (1968) and Jehenson (1974).
5. Scott and Lyman (1970) being the chief exponents.
6. Informed by K. Burke oeuvre — see Overington (1977). But see also

Messinger *et al.* (1962), Dewey (1969), Burns (1972), Boland and Young (1972), Brissett and Edgley (1975) and Edgley and Turner (1975) for more recent and applied elaborations.

7. Ethogenics is a term coined by Rom Harré to describe a research practice developed by himself. Not all his work falls under this label but see Harré (1977; 1979).

8. The notion of 'sociological story' is taken from Davis (1974).

9. The 'story' of the definition of the situation has a legitimate starting point in the work of W.I. Thomas (Thomas and Znaniecki, 1927; Thomas, 1937; 1951) but more recent theoretical contributions come from Stebbins (1967; 1969; 1970), Vernon (1965), Newcomb and Turner (1965), McHugh (1968), Ball (1972) and Perinbanayagam (1974). It is a notion that also appears frequently in the work of Erving Goffman (especially Goffman, 1959). There is in addition a diverse body of empirical work employing the concept.

10. I am now unable to trace the point at which the shift became a possibility. The reality, of course, is that the research trajectory is, as I suspect is common, somewhat disjunctive. However, I believe this perspectival move may have been initiated by the following comment from Robert Moore: 'Hearing what people *mean* rather than what they say, involves the use of sociological imagination that lies closer to skills in literary criticism' Moore (1972).

11. New Criticism represents a loose school in, largely American, literary criticism. Major apostles include J.R. Ransom, Cleanth Brooks and W.K. Wimsatt, whose work in turn owes much to T.S. Eliot and I.A. Richards. Some useful brief summaries can be located in Hawkes (1977), Norris (1982) and Culler (1981).

12. One of the strongest attacks on 'the Intentional Fallacy' is provided by Wimsatt (1970).

13. Saussure's work has been revitalized in more recent times partly by its reinterpretation by the post-structuralists. The seminal work remains his *Course in General Linguistics* (trans. 1974). Valuable commentaries are provided by Culler (1975; 1976) and Jameson (1972).

14. Something of a summary of this movement is provided by Hawkes (1977). Post-structuralism is a rather amorphous critical school and cannot be said to constitute a cohesive body of theorizing. It is commonly held to include the work of Derrida, Foucault, Barthes (latterly), Kristeva, DeMan, Girard, Said and Marin, although certainly the first two would probably wish to disown the attribution of the label. Some recent commentaries include Harari (1979), Young (1981) and Said (1978). The rubric 'Deconstruction' is employed by some authors to index portions of the same kind of critical practice (see Norris, 1982; 1983; Culler, 1983; Hartman, 1979.

15. In the past Foucault, Barthes and Derrida were considered part of the same

movement that was said by some to also include Levi-Strauss (see e.g. Lane, 1970). But it is clear that post-structuralism would find much to distance itself from in the version of structuralism pursued by Levi-Strauss.

16. Barthes' more recent work (e.g. Barthes, 1977; 1974) provides an auto-criticism of his earlier attempts at a scientific semiology (Barthes, 1963) and even the metalanguage contained in *Mythologies* (1973, originally published in 1957).

17. 'Sign' is, of course, the crucial concept of semiology. It is not a new concept — the first theory of signs was developed by the Stoics — however in modern times the deliberations of Saussure have led to its reemergence. See Saussure, 1972, pp. 60 ff.

18. A text that makes much of this materiality and is one of few attempts to explicate the relationship between signification and ideology and move semiotics towards Marxism is that by Coward and Ellis (1977). See also some sections of Silverman and Torode (1980).

19. For an explication of this notion and of this general sense of the productivity of language see Barthes (1981) and Derrida (1970).

20. Silverman and Torode (1980) see Garfkinel's ethnomethodological practices as still within the interpretist framework, although working at the limits.

21. The notion of text is more forcefully articulated by Barthes (1977; 1981).

22. It is around this point that Foucault takes issue with Derrida. Foucault accuses him of pedagogy. He criticizes him for an intellectual elitism and feyness in engaging in interminable linguistic games that always fail to grapple with anything that affects people's life concerns (see Said, 1978, pp. 702ff). As Said (1978, p. 703) puts it, the two hold different notions of *praxis* of text. Foucault relates text to power — he sees texts as discursive events related to the place of discourse in the struggle for power. This is something returned to later in the chapter.

23. A point made much of by Wootton (1975). For a very lucid discussion from within the ethnomethodological paradigm see Coulter (1971).

24. It has not been possible here to reveal much of the complexities of that position. Useful commentaries/readers are available in those texts cited under note 15, plus Lane (1970) and Macksey and Donato (1970).

25. A point made, incidentally, by Giddens (1976).

26. For a fascinating exploration of the photographic form of signification see Barthes (1982).

27. It is not being proposed that this is the only appropriate level of analysis, but that it is the most powerful if we are interested in meanings and their production encountered in social interaction.

28. How could such judgements be made in any case without the assumption of a metaposition within a presumed superior discourse?

29. What is being referred to here has an affinity to the notion of *aporia* and

aporetic logic for which see Derrida (1976; 1978; 1973) and DeMan (1979).

30. Perhaps the ethnomethodological programme begins to fall down where it fails to make the link between 'interpretive practices' and ideology.

31. A notion of some complexity dealt with at perhaps the greatest depth in the work of Kristeva.

32. As already indicated, early management talk elided the use of the item 'participation'; it spoke instead of 'worker involvement exercise'; 'consultation'; 'working groups', and so on.

33. Note the possibile substitution here of 'connotational clusters' or 'vocabularies/rhetoric of motive'. The notion of 'connotational clusters' is elaborated in the work of Kenneth Burke (see Burke 1950; 1969). 'Vocabularies/rhetoric of motives' is derived, of course, from C. Wright-Mills and Burke again, but an interesting account is provided in Taylor (1979).

34. The indexed 'evolutionary' explanation of the development of participation in the talk of management here is analysed and most cogently critiqued by Ramsey (1977).

35. These are some aspects of the company's existing discourse or culture revealed in an analysis of other signifying material not reported here (see Westwood, 1983).

36. Other portions of the text had established participation in relation to such things as 'progress', 'rightness', 'socially just', 'modern', '(more) rational', and so on.

37. This was an extended and complex texture possessing much force. Space precludes its elaboration here.

Organization Analysis and Development
Edited by I. L. Mangham
© John Wiley & Sons Ltd.

The Pathos of Bureaucracy

CHAPTER **9**   *Peter Cumberlidge*

Amongst the mêlée of diverse activity that marks the familiar, grinding process of our economy, tucked well back behind the rhetoric of politicians, trade unionists and captains of industry, and, ironically, under the good cover provided by the bulk of current affairs comment and academic investigation alike, a daily personal struggle continues to be waged by members of the workforce. This is a struggle enacted at a microcosmic level and generally in rather mundane terms. It is rarely self-conscious and, where perceived as such by those concerned, it is usually poorly articulated. To me, it seems to resemble a kind of lay appreciation of two old and conflicting schools of thought — the materialists and the idealists if you like, or perhaps more recently the behaviourists and the social interactionists.

For academics, these broadly opposed views of socioeconomic activity tend to live on as partisan positions within the social sciences and to provide convenient paradigms for research and discussion by their respective protagonists. For many others, in the relatively silent majority who hold no specific brief to analyse, a more catholic model of their place within the scheme of things appears to be commonly held — an intuitive model probably, yet often incorporating a dialectic recognition of what both these schools represent. In crude outline, this dialectic might be said to reflect the tension between an individual's perception of his freedom to act and, on the other hand, his invariably coexistent perception of the determining constraints imposed by the institutions to which he belongs.

This tension, as Weber and others have pointed out, is the almost inevitable fate of those who work within bureaucracies. Weber, however, chose not to address fully the more fundamental questions of how this more or less intense state of partial subjugation has become so pervasive within the western world and, more interestingly, what kinds of effect this has had, and continues to have, upon either willing or unwilling participants. Weber's seminal analysis of bureaucracy was far-reaching, but his standpoint was essentially neo-rational and did not extend to considering employees' experience of and reactions to the formalized milieu in which they worked.

207

It is possible to argue that Weber was a materialist in at least this limited sense. One of his central observations was that '... the purely bureaucratic type of administration is, from the purely technical point of view, capable of attaining the highest degree of efficiency and is in this sense formally the most rational known means of exercising authority over human beings'.

If, however, you investigate bureaucratic organizations from an interactionist point of view, you soon encounter a curious amalgam of, so to speak, materialist and idealist material. This mix will include individuals' own highly varied interpretations of bureaucracy, a likely common thread being a strong tendency to accept that the organizational structure has a natural and self-evident authority.

The extent to which this authority is resented seems to vary widely. The disparity between an individual's personal aspirations and what he is able to draw from his position within a bureaucracy may be highly significant or of no apparent consequence. Imagine, on the one hand, a high level of tension — a pathological state to the neo-rationalist — with close parallels to Marx's notion of alienation. Of this, Marcuse has written:

> For the vast majority of the population, the scope and mode of satisfaction are determined by their own labour; but their labour is work for an apparatus which they do not control, which operates as an independent power to which individuals must submit if they want to live. And it becomes the more alien the more specialized the division of labour becomes. Men do not live their own lives but perform pre-established functions. While they work, they do not fulfill their own needs and faculties but work in alienation.

Whether or not you see this as an extreme argument is largely a matter of politics, but the Marxian view of alienation must define, at least, one end of a continuum of tension. The opposite pole might represent a state of apparent harmony, in which the employee fundamentally internalizes the bureaucratic ideal and then expresses his own needs in these same terms. He does this not just because he wishes to be a good employee, but because he believes sincerely in the code of ethics and practice that the organization subsumes.

This idea of a continuum of tension between an individual and his work began to emerge empirically in the course of a recent research study within the highly bureaucratic world of local government. In this we were concerned principally with examining the notion of group decision-making, with specific reference to one particular interdepartmental team. As part of the investigation we attempted an analysis of personal interest for each of the team members and this was one of the first stages in the formulation of a model to represent group objectives. In fact the concept of group objective became increasingly blurred as the research proceeded, but it was nonetheless valuable in the effort to understand some of the determinants of group decision-making.

It is clearly important to distinguish between what an individual may state as a personal objective and motives that might be inferred from his behaviour and from his interactions with other people in the organization. One member of the team we were working with was often to be heard espousing an ambition to 'get to the top', earn a high salary and to lead a dynamic working life 'up where the action was'. He would frequently make this point with apparent seriousness, yet his performance within his own department and at team meetings did not usually match those of a man determined to succeed in the terms he was proclaiming.

Significant also, perhaps especially within local government, is the question of the moral judgements that other employees may hold, and wield, concerning the cultivation of individual interests within their organization. A curious ambivalence about the 'proper' pursuit of ambition is often to be found amongst the staff of bureaucracies. It is generally agreed that it is a 'good thing' for officers to be hardworking and competitive, with an eye to the furtherance of their careers. Yet there are usually rather definite social pressures applied to overambition. Beyond a certain acceptable degree of zealousness, colleagues may start to communicate perjorative evaluations about someone who is seen to be principally concerned with his own advancement and not enough about 'the job', his department, the public or the working group of which he may be a part.

Foreknowledge of these subtle but real sanctions can tend to limit the extent to which an officer will even articulate, let alone pursue, ambitions which could be interpreted as 'using' the organization for his own ends. But what range of such ambitions are we talking about? Our analyses of the personal interests of the members of our chosen interdepartmental team drew upon numerous interviews, recordings of meetings, notes taken during and after informal discussions and even social gatherings. From this considerable weight of material we were able to define a number of important categories, some of which applied to most of the team members and others which were rather more idiosyncratic.

In deriving these categories, we endeavoured to construe the concept of personal interest widely enough to take account of more than merely selfish behaviour on the part of the actors concerned, but not so widely as to dissolve the notion in a definitional short circuit. Parsons (1960) has referred to this problem:

I do not think it is useful to postulate a deep dichotomy between theories which give importance to beliefs and values on the one hand, and allegedly 'realistic' interests, e.g. economic, on the other. Beliefs and values are actualised, partially and imperfectly, in realistic situations of social interaction and the outcomes are always codetermined by the values and the realistic exigencies; conversely, what on concrete levels are called 'interests' are by no means independent of the values which have been institutionalised ...

It is also useful to differentiate between means and ends, so that we can make some judgement about when to stop probing behind what people tell us. Maslow (1954) has observed that:

If we examine carefully the average desires that we have in daily life, we find that they have at least one important characteristic, i.e. that they are usually means to an end rather than end in themselves ... Usually when a conscious desire is analysed we find that we can go behind it, so to speak, to other, more fundamental aims of the individual.

One of the most frequently subscribed to categories of personal interest had to do with team members' perceived chances of internal promotion. The following quotations are indicative of this preoccupation:

The point is, you've got to be careful not to hide your light under a bushel. I know people say that anyone can get promoted in local government if they hang on long enough, but I reckon that's all changing these days. Anyway, the quicker you get promotion the quicker your salary goes up and that's what it all boils down to in the end doesn't it?

By and large, if you keep doing a good job you get noticed, although there are some who always seem to float up through the pile quicker than others, regardless of their performance.

I mean it's obvious that salary is important, but there's more to it than that. There's the status that goes with promotion, I'm sorry to say, the recognition that you are a cut above the rest. It's sad in a way, but everyone is looking for it — the wife, the kids, the bank manager. So promotion is always there at the back of your mind whenever you are working, particularly at meetings.

These were all comments made in response to questions, put to each member individually and over a period of time, about how they imagined that their performance at team meetings was influenced by factors relating to themselves personally rather than to the organization that employed them.

Some of the members expressed, if you like, an apparently negative interest in promotion, although in at least the first of the following quotations the professed unconcern was probably symptomatic of a lingering resentment at being passed over:

I don't give a damn about promotion quite frankly. I've been here a lot longer than most of them and I always say what I think even if I do sometimes tread on a few toes. Nothing anyone can do can affect me one way or the other, but I've seen a few pull themselves up by saying the right thing at the right time to the right ear.

I don't really worry about promotion very much. I just get on with my job and let other people play politics. Life's too short for getting involved with all these devious strategies.

I reached my sticking point a long time ago. All I want is a quiet life with just enough challenge to keep me interested. The others can get worked up if they want to, but I'm not one for chasing premature heart attacks.

There is a general recognition in these last three responses that promotion is something that most officers chase as a matter of course. These negative assertions are as important as the positive ones for illuminating this particular category, but they also uncover a second category of personal interest — the desire for a quiet life, without undue pressures and, in the last two cases, free from conflict.

Most of the team members identified with a third category, closely related to the last but rather more positively articulated. We called this the pursuit of job congeniality and it appeared to be a highly prevalent dimension of personal interest, not only within the team but in local government in general:

One of the key things for me is that I enjoy coming to work each day. I think a lot of us in local government feel that, so there's a tendency for us to try and arrange our work programme so that it contains a minimum of unpleasantness. That's why you'll find that most of us on the team will avoid direct conflict. We usually manage to work things out without getting heated and involved in interdepartmental bickering. Even the most ambitious officers prefer a pleasant working day, given the choice.

I suppose it's a very clubby sort of atmosphere and we like to keep it that way. There's nothing worse than getting up in the morning knowing that there's a load of hassle waiting for you at the office.

Politics do go on, but it tends to be higher up amongst the directors. They are always trying to outmanoeuvre each other, to increase their budgets and extend their influence. Down at our level it's imitation politics really, with one or two notable exceptions. We like to get things done, don't get me wrong, but preferably in an amicable sort of way without any aggro.

This selection of categories has been introduced simply to illustrate some of the ways in which personal interest has been expressed by, if you like, some real members of an existing bureaucracy. As part of the process of building up a picture of group decision-making, we were also interested in our team members' definitions of their collective purpose.

In this it is clearly necessary to consider the distinction between corporate or bureaucratic purpose in Weber's organizational sense (Weber, 1947) and the kind of formulation of group objectives that may occur either completely outside the context of formal administrations or within a local subgroup convened under the auspices of an existing bureaucracy. March and Simon (1958) have noted that:

The bureaucracy is a set of relationships between offices, or roles. The official reacts to other members of the organization not as more or less unique individuals but as representatives of positions that have specified rights and duties. Competition within the organization occurs within closely defined limits; evaluation and promotion are relatively independent of individual achievement.

This rather pure concept of bureaucracy must be regarded as an ideal type and appears in practice in various stages of dilution. But its most fundamental characteristic is the backing and demands of a 'legal' authority.

Of this legality, Weber himself has observed (Weber, 1947):

> ... Obedience is owed to the legally established impersonal order. It extends to the persons exercising the authority of office under it only by virtue of the formal legality of their commands and only within the scope of authority of the office.

Corporate objectives that have no foundation in a formal organization, but which are understood and recognized in terms of collective interests or group membership, have a rather more elusive nature. The allegiance accorded them by participating individuals, and the various ways in which they are referenced, may be more difficult to uncover than either explicit or implied rules of bureaucracy. Such objectives are often believed by group members to exist, somewhere and somehow, yet they may not appear in any tangible form and may be rarely addressed or articulated.

Our own team seemed to fall some way between these two extremes. It had its roots in a parent bureaucracy, yet it had no formally laid down terms of reference. The team was set up to deal with a specific housing problem but then evolved to meet a continuing demand. At the beginning the members had only a hazy idea of what they were being asked to do, yet the team soon became established as a more or less permanent institution. When we asked members individually about the objectives of this institution, we obtained a diverse set of responses. For example:

> I don't think we've ever set down our objectives properly. R might have proposed something at the first meeting and then we just took it from there. It was in 1975, when we had a large quantity of marginal housing in the city. That was just after reorganization and you probably remember that interdisciplinary working was a big buzz-word. The then chief executive reckoned that these problem areas involved conflicting but not very powerful interests and so he conceived this idea of an interdepartmental team to iron out the conflict. Feather in his cap at the time I suppose. It was all decided above us though. We just got the memos saying that we'd been selected as members and R's memo appointed him as coordinator. He got things going really.

> I've never been too sure what we've been supposed to be doing. We've got no real power. We make informed recommendations which draw upon our different areas of expertise. We're almost a kind of planning committee I suppose, in the very wide sense, but we actually take the initiative and then follow the project through to completion. The areas we try and sort out are the neglected parts of the city — maybe neglected by the council, neglected by private owners, neglected by companies. You know that small estate just behind the industrial block — it's rather smart now but it wasn't then. That was our first project and our objective was really a kind of tidying up operation. We've been tidying up ever since, but a lot of what we do never gets noticed, never gets any publicity.

R, the coordinator of the team, attempted a characteristically more structured explanation of their objectives:

> Well I'll tell you what I've tried to keep us heading towards. There are really three stages to the job, as I see it. First, we're always trying to make sure that we're as up-to-date as possible with the state of all the housing in the city. We maintain a register of all properties that are known to have fallen below, or are about to fall below, a habitable condition — whoever they belong to and whatever the cause.
>
> Now from this register, and our own local knowledge, we also keep an action list of properties that we think can be brought back to scratch. That's the list we use at meetings.
>
> Finally, for each case on the action list, everyone looks at all the pros and cons and we try to come up with a workable improvement plan. But we've got no executive power, we can only recommend — we make recommendations to the Housing Committee, to developers, to architects, to private individuals. We work a bit behind the scenes as you know.
>
> But there's a lot of different criteria to be weighed and balanced. That's where our skill and experience come in — we've got representatives from all the necessary disciplines. In practice, of course, strategies often suggest themselves. There are usually so many constraints of one sort or another that we're pleased to get anything done that puts housing units back into useful stock.

Now whatever you might argue about the practical or theoretical validity, or indeed utility, of using group objective as an explanator of collective decision-making, it is clear that these three team members, at least, have such a concept in mind themselves, or at any rate they can recognize it when they are asked questions about it. R has put his own ideas of their group objectives in comparative detail. The first respondent explained how things got started and he seemed to infer that some kind of group objective took shape under R's guidance. More importantly, it seems to me, he has an implicit belief that such a collective purpose really ought to be there somewhere, even if he can't quite put his finger on it at the moment.

The second respondent admits at the beginning that he's never been to sure what the team's brief has been, yet at the end of his reply he comes up with the notion of 'tidying up', which for him seems to sum up what the team has actually been working towards.

What people tell you, of course, when you ask them questions, may or may not reflect how they behave. And even if you think you've got hold of an accurately expressed motive, the relations between motive and action may be rather complex. But because employees of a bureaucracy are invariably prone to talking about goals in one form or another, they can't help but become important facets of even an interactionist analysis of corporate behaviour.

Cyert and March's (1963) treatment of organizational goals has provided some insight into this tricky concept. In developing their theory of corporate purpose, they begin by viewing the organization as a coalition, noting that:

> ... over a specified (relatively brief) period of time we can identify the major coalition members; or, for a particular decision we can identify the major coalition members. More generally, for a certain class of decisions over a relatively long period of time we can specify the major classes of coalition members. As a result, we will be able to develop models of organizational decision making (for the short run) that pay only limited attention to the process by which the coalition is changed ...

In the ensuing analysis, Cyert and March uncover some of the complications in thinking about corporate purpose, they point to philosophical difficulties surrounding the definition of such a concept, and then they go some way towards formulating ideas which take these problems into account. Yet in so doing they seem to be employing, almost unconsciously, an epistemology which somehow cannot preclude the phenomenon of organizational goal in very much a systems sense. It is also significant that Cyert and March refer to 'the problem of collective goals', a problem, that is, from the theorist's point of view.

The problem is summarized by Cyert and March as follows:

1. People (i.e. individuals) have goals; collectives of people do not.
2. To define a theory of organizational decision-making, we seem to need something analogous — at the organization level — to individual goals at the individual level.

Cyert and March, it seems to me, have the same kind of ambivalence about corporate purpose as do many employees of corporations. They can't quite pin it down because it seems rather diffuse, but they think it ought to be there somewhere, albeit in a highly theoretical form. They recognize the existence of goal conflict within organizations and, in so doing, put together one of the earlier models of company politics in that genre that has been developing since the late 1950s.

The company politics paradigm, if I might so describe this seam of research and literature, takes as its starting point an accentuated version of goal conflict. Most organizations, it argues, are rife with intrigue and political manoeuvring. There is conflict at all levels — conflict between individuals, conflict between departments, conflict between individual goals and company goals. Cyert and March begin in a rather mild way:

> In keeping with virtually all theories of organizations, we assume that the coalition represented in an organization is a coalition of members having different goals ...

But their position appears to escalate towards a more anarchic view of organizations:

... most organizations exist and thrive with considerable latent conflict of goals. Except at the level of non-operational objectives, there is no internal consensus. The procedures for 'resolving' such conflict do not reduce all goals to a common dimension or even make them obviously internally consistent.

Once again, though, their concept of resolution seems to presuppose an authoritative, if elusive, sense of direction along which that resolution might be made. That is to say, this early formulation within the company politics paradigm still recognizes and depends upon the existence of an organizational *status quo*, without which conflict cannot be recognizably defined and political manoeuvring has no meaning.

Later protagonists of this school adopted essentially what might be called a 'real-life' perspective of organizations, which accepted conflicts of interests as a starting point and organizational politics as a natural state of affairs. These analysts were trying to get at the goings-on behind the scenes. They were trying to look behind the respectable bureaucratic front to see how organizational life was really lived, for example Argyris and Schon (1974), Axelrod (1977), Brewer (1973), Eden (1978), Lerner (1976), Mangham (1978), Mumford and Pettigrew (1975), Perrow (1972), Pettigrew (1973), Radford (1977).

They found, amongst other things, numerous pockets of unofficial activity, much of it initiated by self-interested employees who would not always sit down quietly to pursue, single mindedly and according to the book, what they understood by their organizational goals. They found power struggles, intrigues, departmental coups, bluffs and double bluffs. They also found a worldly sophistication and a rather tarnished veneer of cynicism. Yet the inference tended to be that by their cunning, these ambitious and successful officials had somehow been able to liberate themselves from their employing organization and, as men of the world, had been able to further their own positions as well as getting the job done. Within the literature of the organizational politics paradigm, successful politics usually represented a partial escape from the enslaving chains of bureaucracy.

More recently, writers such as Robert Presthus (Presthus, 1978) have preferred to concentrate on updating the traditional bureaucratic model of organizations, rather than fashioning specific 'real-life' aspects of the working world into some kind of pseudo-modern school of its own. The contemporary bureaucracy, Presthus argues, still exhibits the full range of characteristics that Weber was at pains to set out. What is important to recognize now is how today's officials react to those characteristics, what expectations they have of their own place within their chosen bureaucracy, and how, realistically, they interpret their own lives in its service. For we are all well socialized into both the official and the unofficial world. We know, long before joining the race, what kinds of niche modern organizations are able to provide for us. We know what is expected from us in return. From an increasingly early age, we are only too familiar with the deal.

Even though it has vaguely immoral associations, status is widely recognized to be a key driving force within the modern bureaucracy, more particularly as opportunities for prospering outside the big organizations become yet more severely constrained. Presthus notes that:

> The difficulty of achieving independence through owning one's business, a difficulty which reflects the trend towards bigness and concentration; the employment of the 'independent' professions on a bureaucratic, salaried basis; the devaluation of the term 'professional' — all seem conducive to increased status anxiety and striving ... size and anonymity result in sustained attempts to preserve status in compensation for the loss of autonomy. C. Wright Mills speaks of the status panic that characterizes life in the white collar world.

The contemporary view of bureaucracy does not preclude individual conflicts of interest, or the political manoeuvring that follows from it. Indeed, it is an irony that these have become subsumed into the ethos of modern organizations, have become accepted as part of the script.

Yet, at the same time, it is important not to place too much emphasis on the machismo of politics and double-dealing, and not to overrate the power that would be mobilized by the promise of the trappings of status. Bureaucracies have their more mundane aspects as well, with which most of us are only too familiar. Large chunks of organizational life are characterized by a comradely acceptance of routineness and boredom. We frequently encountered this phlegmatic ennui in our dealings with our 'subject' team and elsewhere in local government — encountered more of it, indeed, than we came across the cloak and dagger.

The members of our team knew each other well and some had even been to school together. They were all of a similar seniority and each was located somewhere near the middle of his available career progression. None of the members was particularly ambitious or unambitious. Few could recall what had led them into local government and why they had stayed. It was just one of those things, R said one afternoon. You just followed the path ahead and suddenly, here you were, approaching middle age with all the responsibilities of family life and a sense of time having passed you by.

Thankful enough, they seemed to be, for an occupation with relative security and respectability. Unfulfilled, on the whole, by the contract they seemed to have with their organization but, on the other hand, never expecting too much.

Opportunities for political manoeuvring were limited. The members were occasionally frustrated by this or that technical restriction, sometimes caught up in interdepartmental bickering, and they were often irritated by what they saw as the vacillations of their immediate superiors. For the most part, however, they worked steadily and peaceably within well-defined limits of discretion.

These three quotations from team members serve to illustrate their general acceptance of unexciting routine:

Sometimes, with these meetings, the biggest problem is just surviving the boredom. These cases can go on for months and months and the same old arguments and details keep turning up. I often wonder how many people there are across the country sitting in dreary conference rooms wishing they were somewhere else. Millions of pounds ticking away in dead words ...

I must admit that a lot of the work is just routine and not what you'd call exciting. Occasionally we get the odd spark of interest — there was that court case last month where the owner of one of the properties on the list was up for running a house of ill-repute. Not that we ever got any perks in that direction ...

I sometimes think that local government runs on boredom. It's the fuel that keeps us all going. We seem to thrive on hefty great chunks of it. This team is no exception I can assure you, for all that it's supposed to be at the forefront of the city's housing problems ...

This, in a sense, is the very antithesis of organizational politics. Here are the grey regions where neither corporate goals nor personal goals, whatever we conceive them to be, can raise their heads high enough to stem the enveloping tedium. Along with the tedium can come un-intention and a marked indifference to outcomes, which can often provide the most complicated circumstances for an analyst trying to unravel how a particular decision came to be made. R, the coordinator of our team, once made the following observation:

Very occasionally I just lose interest altogether — not often but it does happen. It's usually with cases where none of the people involved are especially interested either and then you seem to be banging your head against a brick wall. After a while you think 'What the hell?' Then the meeting loses direction and any old thing can happen — it depends what kinds of silly suggestions come up.

This is hardly a state of alienation in the Marxian sense, since the official, R, still maintains a kind of theoretical allegiance to his work and his office. He knows well what he 'ought' to be doing, but he has switched off temporarily and is freewheeling for a while. He is neither enthusiastic about his bureaucratic commitments nor actively antagonistic. This state of indifference is common within organizations, but it is not well covered by the literature.

Yet another seam of research into bureaucracies has its roots in the methods and concepts of systems analysis that gained such momentum in the 1960s. The modern systems analysts remain, essentially, structuralists although their arguments have been increasingly modified to take due account of the people who work within the structures. Ranson, Hinings and Greenwood, (1980) attach to this school and they have developed an evolutionary model of organization which says that, over long periods of time, institutions adapt to and are contingent upon the circumstances that they have encountered in history.

Ranson *et al.* (1980) point out that:

> The concept of structure is usually understood to imply a configuration of activities that is characteristically enduring and persistent; the dominant feature of organizational structure is its patterned regularity. Yet descriptions of structure have typically focused on very different aspects of such patterned regularity. Some have sought to describe a structure as a formal configuration of roles and procedures, the prescribed framework of the organization. Others have described structure as the patterned regularities and processes of interaction ... The continual counterposing of framework and interaction is unhelpful because of its implicit and inaccurate opposition of 'constraint' to agency.

This is an allusion to a phenomenon similar to the tension with which we introduced this essay — the tension between forces imposed by an existing structure upon participants and, on the other hand, the participants' perception of the flexibility of that structure and of their freedom to act within it — or to change it. Ranson *et al.* (1980) go on to say that:

> The recent works of Bourdieu (1971; 1977; 1979) suggest a more fruitful perspective, focusing upon the interpenetration of framework and interaction as expressing a relationship that is often mutually constituting and constitutive ...

The implication here is that institutional structures are at least in part maintained by the participants' continuing definition of the *status quo*, and participants must also include the clients of the organization. The bureaucracy, in the end, is held together and perpetuated because all concerned behave as though it is a bureaucracy.

Yet it is likely that few of the modern systems analysts would subscribe to that view. They are rather inclined, it seems to me, to hold that it is somehow it is the structures themselves in some reified sense that wield the power that shapes employees' behaviour. This power is often seen to be independent of social construction and acts, as it were, like a magnet.

Ranson *et al.* refer to this 'magnet' model when they say:

> Much comparative research in organizational analysis has in fact examined the contextual determinants of structural variability in organizations. This has become known as the 'argument from contingencies' (Lawrence and Lorsch, 1967) which suggests that the relationship of structural characteristics to be found in any organization — the particular constellation of rules, differentiated labour and hierarchy, for example — arises because of the pressure of contingent or situational circumstances.

But how does this evolution take place? Not, presumably, by some mysterious, impersonal process of osmosis. Contingency forces can only be executed by individuals within the organization who have been able to gauge some kind of mismatch between their organization's external environment and the output with which it is responding. They have not only got to perceive this mismatch — they have also got to believe, for one reason or another, that it is their business to do something about it.

Of course certain elements of context may be strongly established either by statute or by tradition. It is also a familiar feeling to many participants in bureaucratic decision-making that events have determined themselves almost independently of attempts to contribute to a debate or to otherwise intervene.

In this last respect, Friend and Jessop (1969) have observed that:

> Any form of planning activity by a local authority must take place within a procedural setting which is laid down in the standing orders of Council, and in the more specific instructions to individual committees. Although each local authority has a measure of autonomy in developing these procedures within the legal constitution of the local government system, no local rules of procedure can in themselves do more than provide a basic framework within which groups and individuals can act. Inevitably, certain patterns of behaviour and expectation evolve which tend to become an integral part of the local government system even though they have no procedural basis.

This is another structuralist argument, despite its recognition of locally developing customs. These customs become part of the structure, ready to act upon all those who come along behind. The vital processes by which participants derive meaning from the procedures that they encounter are not addressed. Saunders (1979) is more aware of these processes:

> It has become a sociological cliché that the formal structure of an organization does not necessarily indicate what actually goes on within it . . .

Saunders goes on to say that:

> Both functionalist (e.g. Blau, 1963) and interactionist (e.g. Silverman, 1970) approaches to the sociology of formal organizations have stressed the need to examine how members routinely accomplish their 'roles', and it follows that the analysis of the formal organizational framework of local authority decision-making can only be a first step in understanding how policies come to be made . . .

It is an arresting characteristic of bureaucracy that, whichever school of analysis happens to be paying it attention — be they endeavouring to assert its functional and rational aspects; or if they eschew these and are more attracted by the manoeuvrings behind the scenes; whether they are principally concerned to clarify bureaucratic objectives or to uncover personal goals being pursued 'under cover' — indeed, almost regardless of a theorist's point of view, it seems that Weber's original conception of a formal bureaucracy is invariably accepted as a fixed and given background to whatever else is thought to be going on. Organizational theorists appear, on the whole, to be as well imbued as the rest of the working population with stable traditional images of how bureaucracies go about their business and how officials ought to be behaving within the confines of a bureaucratic contract.

The functional sociologist may concentrate on roles, considering role definitions that are prescribed, apparently, by the organization and examining role expectations and interpretations held by employees and clients. For the theorists of the organizational politics school, the structure of bureaucracy often appears as a familiar backdrop against which and under whose auspices officials are able to pursue their own secular interests, however they care to define them. You can argue that this perspective carries with it the illusion of an employee's freedom to act, although Presthus (1978) has referred to the fate of typical upward mobiles '... as likely to remain happy prisoners in the iron cage'. The modern structuralists, on the other hand, hold a more obviously bleak view of organizations. The future is written, they conclude, in the cumulated events of history. Our institutions respond ponderously to the environment they encounter, rather in the manner of a large, unwieldy organism. The working population locked up inside might as well be riding within the Trojan horse for all the control they are able to exert upon their destiny.

The interactionists impute degrees of freedom to participants in bureaucracy, but it is freedom of a subtle kind. Officials are at liberty to construe and, in this way, to configure their own working lives and define their own relationships with bureaucracy. But employees are stuck, unfortunately, with the language of the day. This allotted currency embodies well-worn clichés about occupation, the obligations that go with it and the benefits it imparts in return.

There are theorists who acknowledge this and recognize the pervasive processes by which values can be inherited along with language. Bachrach and Baratz (1963) have been concerned to highlight the means by which important policy issues may be decided by default, as it were, through either the management or the unintentional reinforcement of publicly accessible meaning (Pettigrew, 1977). In such cases, the end consumers of policy outcomes may not be aware that a decision, as such, had effectively been taken, and perhaps had not considered that things could have turned out differently.

Bachrach and Baratz observed that:

> Many investigators have also mistakenly assumed that power and its correlatives are activated and can be observed only in decision-making situations. They have overlooked the equally if not more important area of what might be called 'nondecision-making', i.e. the practice of limiting the scope of actual decision-making to 'safe' issues by manipulating the dominant community values, myths, and political institutions and procedures. To pass over this is to neglect one whole face of power.

Bachrach and Baratz refer to a state of 'false consensus' in which members of a given population appear to stand in agreement about a current state of affairs without being aware that an opportunity existed for a different state to pertain.

This is a similar notion to Lukes' three-dimensional view of power (Lukes, 1975), which focuses upon the way in which political agendas may be controlled. Both ideas owe a debt to Marx's concept of false consciousness and they are, in a sense, just as elusive. Merelman (1968) has criticized what he refers to as the neo-elitist critique of power, and argues that:

> The argument on the problem of 'false consensus', as it is presently stated, is not an empirical argument, though it makes certain dubious empirical assumptions. Rather, it is a purely deductive, tautological theory which, if one accepts its empirical assumptions, does not admit of empirical proof or disproof ... the argument does not allow us to distinguish between 'real' and 'false' consensus.

However, it is not our intention here to become embroiled in a debate about political manipulation. Our concern here has been more straightforward: simply to underline a recurring phenomenon that was thrown up, albeit as an aside, by our recent research into aspects of group decision-making. This phenomenon is the apparent pervasiveness, among its participants, of reinforcing definitions of bureaucracy and of the bureaucratic ethos of working life.

More surprisingly perhaps, such reinforcing definitions appear to be held, sometimes implicitly, by theorists from a wide range of schools of thought. The Weberian model of bureaucratic structure seems to be woven strongly into our working culture.

You may, if you react to it at all, find this phenomenon reassuring and take from it a sense of security and stability. You may, conversely, feel just a tinge of regret that the invisible 'iron cages' have come to dominate so much of our working lives. More pragmatically, if you are a professional observer, you may be largely unaffected by pathos in bureaucracy and just take heart that it provides so much good material with which you can ply your trade. Robert Presthus, at any rate, remains essentially fatalistic:

> Set against the material hegemony and financial resources of modern industrial structures and the functional need for national economic growth to provide employment, all buttressed by the dominant values of materialism and success, which remain salient because they have no saturation value for those who accept them, the rationale of contemporary advocates of 'open organizations' seems rather utopian ...

A final quotation from our team interviews is equally resigned:

> It's a job anyway. You've got to do something to pay the mortgage, run the car and keep the kids in new shoes. But I sometimes wonder who I'm working for and where the treadmill ends. I suppose, come to think of it, you're in the same sort of boat. I mean you've got the same kind of deal haven't you? You've got to churn out your analyses of us in order to keep your sponsors happy.

I seem to remember making an elaborate reply that was distinctly lacking in content, and then I changed the subject rather quickly.

Organization Analysis and Development
Edited by I. L. Mangham
© John Wiley & Sons Ltd.

Social Beings as Hostages:

Organizational and Societal Conduct Answering to a Siege Paradigm of Interaction

CHAPTER 10   *Andrew Travers*

SUMMARY

In this mainly theoretical chapter the development of Erving Goffman's concept of 'frame' into the new concept of 'ritual realm' (described as that frame in which a person may achieve his or her maximum social importance) is facilitated and extended by the incorporation of Freud's siege schema and Ivan Morris's tragic hero schema.

Freud's model of the melancholic's psyche, when used to open up the 'person' into various realm roles, shows how ritual realms are often under siege. Thus there emerges the proposition that social beings are the self- or other-taken hostages of ritual realms. The state of framelessness (Goffman's 'negative experience') is considered for the light it throws on realm generation, and as a result self-belief is discovered to be a socially perverse and supremely individualistic self-framing that may hold its own against antagonistic, besieging frames. The special cases of particularly powerful self-framings are examined with the help of an ideal type derived from Ivan Morris's Japanese tragic heroes, after which it is suggested that what could be called 'the ritual order' might structure some apparently non-utilitarian conduct. Lastly, the advantages for organizational and societal analyses of seeing social beings as hostages are discussed.

INTRODUCTION

Since this chapter is primarily intended to add a ritual dimension to Erving Goffman's frame, it is necessary for me to begin with a short recapitulation of the main ritual terms I developed in my PhD thesis (Travers, 1981). After doing this I isolate what I think has been a neglected feature of Erving Goffman's major work *Frame Analysis*, which is its spirit, one of levity I conclude. The levity that is the spirit of frame analysis is of course a powerful argument for 'keying' frames ritually and thereby attempting to make them as serious as the human beings who use them. This is what I do in the section entitled 'What is a Ritual Realm?' but before answering that question I provide the reader with a

223

very brief epistemological account of frames and ritual realms which has the general purpose of emphasizing the importance of human perception in the matters of framing experience and experiencing ritual power.

After establishing the ritual dimension of frames I use one of Freud's most schematic psychic models in order to give 'ritual realm' a quasi-spatial description that compels the idea that ritual realms are sieges with perpetrators and hostages. Then I present two long examples of ritual realms which I hope will impart something of the experience they offer participants.

Finally the dramatic parabola of an extreme type of realm hostage is drawn, after a discussion of framelessness has shown how self-belief ('faith') of the sort held by Japanese tragic heroes is the only route from framelessness to a totally social life.

RHETORIC OF RITUAL SOCIOLOGY

The sociological explication of ritual phenomena has a strong rhetorical component (in the Burkean sense) since ritual phenomena, more than most social phenomena, are dependent in their analyses on the language of their presentation. A brief resume of my PhD thesis (Travers, 1981) will make sense of this assertion, and it will also introduce the concept of 'ritual realm' from the other side of frames, as it were, before I go on to firmly embed it in Goffman's frame analysis.

In Travers (1981) I make the case that persons can and ought to be seen as ritual beings who gain or lose 'ritual power' through their performances in interactions. Agents like role and self disappear in my ritual rhetoric to be replaced by the idea of 'possession', and a possession is a person inasmuch as she[1] seems like an envoy from a ritual realm. Except as it is implied (to the exclusion of all other frames or realms) by competent dramatic enactments, a ritual realm has no reality. It can be compared to the dimension of perspective in a two-dimensional painting of three-dimensional space: the ritual dimension (like space) makes various kinds of significant sense for the conduct (the paint) that actually indicates it. (In the same way, physically absent connotation and denotation give a word, *qua* lexical item, the meaning that supplies the correct denotation and connotation.) Thus ritual realms in general are not quite the same as David Cole's (1975) *illud tempus*, though the *illud tempus*, the spirit zone to which actors in peak performances have easy access, is certainly a ritual realm. Possession, then, emerges as a ritually-boosted version of Goffman's 'demeanour' (1972), but just as Goffman's demeanour requires the apposition of 'deference' so possession is not completely comprehensible without an answering state in its audience. This state, the interaction reciprocal of possession, I call 'rapture' (to distinguish it from Goffman's 'engrossment' and 'involvement'), but rapture, I point out, is the limit of possibility and only elicited by profound, original possession, when it resembles Aristotle's (1975) catharsis (which occurs for audiences of staged tragedies).

My rhetoric deliberately eschews Goffman's terminology of involvement and engrossment because it is at pains to suggest that in the case of rapture there is a total identification of audience and performer (implying the absolute collapse of social distance). Thus an enraptured person, being a person who is 'moved' or 'transported' (and transported to no other rhetorical location than a ritual realm), is not best described as someone who, though engrossed or involved in a focus of interest, stands apart from it. Sociologically an enraptured person cannot stand apart from an enrapturing possession, for she and the performer are as one, in some other reality than their bounding time and space (this formulation, I believe, is more accurate than Goffman's, and lends itself with less difficulty to the viewing of interaction not as the separate behaviour of separate persons but as collaborative frame production that utterly discounts the separateness of interactants). Goffman's involvement and engrossment, though on their way to rapture, unfortunately allow a fallback to Meadian or Blumer-like calculation that in analytically sheering off the human potential for rapture in every interaction cannot motivate the need for ritual realms, which of course even low involvement and engrossment bring into being. That is why I prefer the term rapture, despite the fact that it is, as I said, a limit of possibility.

The ritual rhetoric of possession and rapture derives from ritual power which itself originates in Goffman's ritual frame (Travers, 1982), and the three terms, possession, rapture and ritual power, generate the fourth term, ritual realm, which elucidates the other three.

This chapter, like Travers (1981), starts out from a firmly established feature of Goffman's sociology, but my use here of Goffman's *Frame Analysis* to strengthen the concept of ritual realm means that I shall only incidentally consolidate the other ritual terms. By approaching ritual realms this time from the new direction of Goffman's frames, I am able to say more about the ritual nature of persons and, in particular, the new idea of persons as hostages (to ritual realms) becomes inevitable.

This text, then, is heavily invested with a consciousness of persons as possessions whose variable ritual power variably enraptures others, and so it is only fitting to refer to it as ritual sociology (the kind of sociology whose guiding assumptions differentiate it from non-ritual sociologies in which the conception of a person as having the ability to perform compelling original conduct is not analytically functional). The rhetoric of ritual sociology, moreover, just because it constantly refers to ritual phenomena, also differs from other sociological rhetorics (especially those with 'non-style' styles, as Gusfield (1976) puts it) in being reflexively aware that its effectiveness may come in part from the self-development of a ritual realm whose ritual power, insofar as it has this, must depend upon the form of its words.

It is not to be supposed, however, that phenomena like ritual power, rapture and possession can only acquire their full meaning in a specifically ritual sociology. Other types of discourse, when highly sensitized to such ritual qualities as honour and inspiration, often effectively express ritual realities. Thus the following quotations from Tom Wolfe's (1979) *The Right Stuff* suggest the very nature of strong ritual power:

> ... in this fraternity, even though it was military, men were not rated by their outward ranks as ensigns, lieutenants, commanders, or whatever. No, herein the world was divided into those that had it and those who did not. This quality, this *it*, was never named, however, nor was it talked about in any way.
>
> As to just what this ineffable quality was ... well, it obviously involved bravery ... the idea here ... seemed to be that a man should have the ability to go up in a hurtling piece of machinery and put his hide on the line and then have the moxie, the reflexes, the experience, the coolness, to pull it back in the last yawning moment —and then go up again *the next day*, and next day, and every next day, even if the series should prove infinite — and, ultimately, in its best expression, do so in a cause that means something to thousands, to a people, a nation, to humanity, to God.
>
> That unmentionable *stuff*, after all, involved a man hanging his hide out over the edge in a hurtling piece of machinery. And such unmentionable payoffs it brought you! One, which he had started receiving even *before* this morning, was a look. It was a look of fraternal awe, of awe in the presence of manly honor ... It was the look that came over another man when one's own righteous stuff triggered *his* adrenalin.

And exactly what I mean by possession and rapture is caught in the following quotation from Nathaniel Hawthorne's (1965) *The Scarlet Letter*:

> The eloquent voice, on which the souls of the listening audience had been borne aloft as on the swelling waves of the sea, at length came to a pause. There was a momentary silence, profound as what should follow the utterance of oracles. Then ensued a murmur of half-hushed tumult, as if the auditors, released from the high spell that had transported them into the region of another's mind, were returning to themselves, with all their awe and wonder still heavy on them. In a moment more, the crowd began to gush forth from the doors of the church. Now that there was an end, they needed other breath, more fit to support the gross and earthly life into which they relapsed than that atmosphere which the preacher had converted into words of flame and had burdened with the rich fragrance of his thought.
>
> In the open air their rapture broke into speech. The street and the market place absolutely babbled, from side to side, with applauses of the minister. His hearers could not rest until they had told one another of what each knew better than he could tell or hear. According to their united testimony, never had man spoken in so wise, so high, and so holy a spirit, as he that spake this day; nor had inspiration ever breathed through mortal lips more evidently than it did through his. Its influence could be seen, as it were, descending upon him, and possessing him, and continually lifting him out of the written discourse that lay before him, and filling him with ideas that must have been as marvellous to himself as to his audience.

THE SPIRIT OF FRAME ANALYSIS

Since the concept of ritual realm is so intricately bound up with Goffman's frame and since the spirit of Goffman's (1975) *Frame Analysis* is so extraordinary, I think it is necessary for me at this juncture to describe what I feel is the spirit of frame analysis and to indicate how this will affect my argument.

Most commentators[2] have overlooked or played down (perhaps out of a kind of scientific embarrassment) what I take to be the genial nihilism of Goffman's introduction to *Frame Analysis*. This nihilism, I believe, blends Goffman's impatience towards rival sociologies with a resigned detachment from social life and compounds the two with a methodology that is openly unrepentant of its arbitrary procedure.

Goffman begins by flatly stating that people do not define situations. If they did, he says, social life would be 'wished' further than it is into 'unreality', and there is no point in doing this because 'social life is dubious and ludicrous enough already'. Thus Goffman dismisses a considerable body of symbolic interactionist work that is founded on the assumption that people do ongoingly define their social situations.[3]

Having begun in this cavalier fashion, Goffman goes on to assert that the span and level of the events he will focus on are arbitrarily chosen. Not only that, but a strip of activity (which is later defined as a 'primary framework') is neither a natural nor an analytic division: it is an arbitrary slice. Participants in a strip of activity, furthermore, may well have several different motivational relevancies, but none of those, though they may be as valid as Goffman's, need coincide with his. No justification is offered for this orientation to the phenomena.

Next we are reminded that our experience of the world may be generated by a number of rules. Goffman, like other analysts (he names Garfinkel), will only find between five or ten, but 'thousands more' could be listed. No argument is proffered in favour of Goffman's rules over Garfinkel's or over anybody else's.

Finally, Goffman says that when he analyses a strip of social activity he selects just one out of the many things going on, and selects this, the reader is left to assume, just because it suits his analysis. Disarmingly, Goffman does declare that this method of selection is a 'bias', but the bias should be welcomed because it is in favour of 'unitary exposition and simplicity'. It follows from this (in Chapter 1), and quite unblushingly, that a primary framework is an 'operating fiction'.

Frame Analysis, Goffman says, is written in ordinary language because this language is flexible enough for his purposes, but he doesn't say why, though he does say that the work will not adopt full methodological self-consciousness lest it displace its substance with nothing but that self-consciousness.

As if all this is not enough, Goffman leaves the reader in doubt *vis-à-vis* the work's status. He cheerfully announces that he has perpetrated a 'mentalistic adumbration'.

I can think of several possible responses to Goffman's levity towards what is his longest and conceivably his most forbidding work. One can simply ignore the levity, as it has so far been ignored. Or one can attribute the levity to Goffman's sardonic taste for puncturing pompous illusions. Or one can regard it as a sign of his exasperation with methodological and phenomenological debate. Or one can read the levity as a deliberate methodological nihilism of the same order as that of *Gender Advertisements* (1979), where Goffman matter-of-factly owns that the data (pictorial advertisements in newspapers and magazines) prove nothing, being merely the 'effective depiction of a theme' (the text of *Gender Advertisements* quite openly admits to being 'generalization-by-pronounce-ment', a procedure halfheartedly defended as — in the absence of proof — the discovery and presentation of a theme).

I myself feel that all these responses are appropriate. So where does that leave me, who would use Goffman's frame as a means of legitimizing an essayistic analysis? Perhaps I should not venture my own answer to that question but just remind readers of the widely-held view that science comprises the works of politically rather than epistemologically acceptable practitioners.

So the spirit of frame analysis is sociologically cynical (to say the least) as well as being playful (in the game-playing sense — Goffman refers to himself and to the ethnomethodologists, separately at their work of reality generation, as 'players'). I have drawn attention to it in order to prepare the reader for a ritual argument that is not meant to be either cynical or playful. The ritual sociology that follows is an adjunct to existing analyses and its principal purpose is to add another dimension (the ritual dimension) to social life, doing so in a way that prejudices the reader in favour of including ritual considerations in her own view of social life. Of course I implicitly argue that omission of the ritual dimension must condemn a social analysis to a process of becoming decoupled from what the persons analysed find most important, and thus, I hope, it becomes evident that there is a warrant for regarding my analysis as something more fateful than sociological game-playing. So ritual realms, in giving some frames a ritual dimension, may have a seriousness, then, the lack of which in *Frame Analysis* much more effectively supports than would a frame analysis conducted in a spirit of sociological uplift.

THE ONTOLOGICAL STATUS OF RITUAL REALMS

It may not seem obvious that ritual realms are only real as interpretative dimensions of the conduct whose ritual power depends on seeming to originate in them. The following brief philosophical excursus, however, should recommend such a view of ritual realms, and it will have the additional function of providing a suitable frame for the ritual realm. So this section can be read as an introduction to the ritual realm of ritual realms.

Philosophers have always had difficulty saying why a particular reality is real in itself, but this difficulty is sidestepped if realities are differentiated according to how they are made real by human attention and interest. It will follow that the real becomes that which at the current moment is treated as having paramount interest. William James almost took up that position, but like Brentano and the phenomenologists he could not quite bring himself to deny that the world of the senses would always be the most real world. Like James, Alfred Schutz differentiated interest-generated worlds, but he too fell in with commonsense and gave 'the working world' preferential status. Goffman in *Frame Analysis* seems to have successfully avoided James' and Schutz's temptation to prefer a certain type of reality, and in the discussion of frames there is no latent assumption that it could be useful to say that a commonly experienced reality should be regarded as having reality apart from the experience of it. (Crook and Taylor (1980) accuse Goffman of near relativism here, but they ignore both that Goffman is only addressing interaction reality and that Goffman's epistemological argument, such as it is, is only intended, as I see it, to dispose of the possibility of frames being non-perceptually 'actual'.) In fact Goffman pronounces that 'a reader's involvement in an episode in a novel is in a relevant sense the same as his involvement in a strip of "actual" experience. When James and Schutz spoke of something being "real after its fashion" and of "multiple realities", it was potential for inducing engrossment that they really had in mind' (Goffman, 1975, p. 347).[4]

So Goffman uses the word frame to mean what is real for interactants, and nothing more. However, in his analysis he often has recourse to the terms 'world' and 'realm', distinguishing world from realm by saying that a realm is only a world if it is 'actual', which is to say, in a rather Schutzian fashion, if it is experienced as comprising real things. I have adopted this usage of realm because the defining quality of a ritual realm is that it isn't actually there (so to speak). Thus I don't have ritual worlds and do have ritual realms.

Ritual realms, whether in each particular case or as a class, are unlike worlds and frames in that their explanation works best in textual performances that seem to have a modicum of ritual power. This means that the ritual realm is given some sociological viability if the reader of ritual rhetoric is brought to a state in which it would be perverse of her to detach herself from the ongoing narrative for the reason that it might not be sociology that she is reading. However, because ritual conduct is said by ritual rhetoric to be always aspiring to originality, there can never be an exhaustive account of ritual realms, for there will always be new ones that won't quite resemble old ones. Talking about ritual realms, then, is like telling a code, and telling a code, as Donald Wieder (1969) has shown in the case of the 'convict code', is an integral part of the conduct it interprets, rendering any sociological description as one further instance of 'the product which results from the uses of practices whereby "telling the code" is achieved' (Wieder, 1969). A code, therefore, can never be completely told, since each telling (in the case of the ritual code a telling is the creation of a ritual realm) is a further interpretative act informing all future tellings.

I might add here that it is just because ritual realms are cogent that there is a temptation to explore them as if they exist (apart from conduct) in various psychological constructions such as Jung's archetypes and Freud's ego–id–superego. Psychological constructions, of course, when they have the enormous power of Jung's and Freud's, are invaluable testaments to the ubiquitous presence of ritual realms, without which, I contend, there would be much less inclination to look beyond (as it were) a person's visible conduct for its full meaning.

WHAT IS A RITUAL REALM?

Although most frames are not ritual realms, all ritual realms are frames. So a delineation of Goffman's frame will define the non-ritual form of a ritual realm, and lead to a frame-based account of ritual realms.

A frame is both the organization governing an event and the organization of persons' subjective involvements in that event. A primary framework changes something meaningless into something meaningful by the imputation of human motive and human intent, and events are perceived in terms of primary frameworks. The framework, an 'operating fiction', provides a description of 'what is going on' (Goffman, 1975). In short, a frame is organized so as to be perceived: the organization of what is perceived is the perception of what is perceived.

The primary frameworks of a group are central to its culture, and a group's framework of frameworks is its belief system or 'cosmology' (Goffman says no more than that).

Primary frameworks can be 'keyed' (transformed) and when keyed they will be described not in terms of the transformed activity but in terms of the key (e.g. people playing at fighting are not fighting but playing). Keyed frames can be rekeyed (adding a 'lamination') and the outermost layer of a frame is its 'rim' (frames are labelled by the label of the rim). If the key of a frame is hidden from those who are framed, the frame may be said to be 'fabricated', either in a benign or an exploitative manner. But, whether keyed or fabricated (a key can be fabricated and a fabrication keyed), a frame, of however many laminations, is both the understanding of what it is and the action that fills it.

In practice, then, we have numerous frame descriptions of strips of social life and these descriptions are prompted and then confirmed or altered by the conduct of the persons in the strips. There is only one case of there being no frame available for description and this Goffman calls 'negative experience', when 'reality anomically flutters' (1975, p. 379). Usually negative experience is manufactured by persons with the most framing power (those who are socially sanctioned to create untenable positions for others) but social sabotage (such as heckling) can effectively anomize the higher status interactants. Negative experience is analytically similar to Goffman's embarrassment (1972) and, until it becomes positive, it draws attention away from the official frame. (Negative experience is not to be confused with 'out-of-frame activity', which is systematically disattended activity that includes several subordinate channels used by interactants to edit frames as they succeed one another.)

Goffman says that an essential characteristic of a frame is that it is what people 'get caught up in, engrossed in, carried away by' (1975, p. 6) and that it is what a person is 'alive to at a particular moment' (1975, p. 8). Without 'subjective involvement' in a frame there cannot properly be said to be a frame for the person in question. So involvement is the *sine qua non* of being in a frame: no involvement, no frame. Above all else, says Goffman, keyed primary frames (especially dramas and contests) 'provide engrossables — engrossing materials in which observers can get carried away, materials which generate a realm of being' (1975, Chapter 3). And engrossment is 'a psychobiological process in which the subject becomes at least partly unaware of his feelings and his cognitive attention' (1975, p. 346). This kind of engrossment is the same as involvement, which (in *Behavior in Public Places*) is said to mobilize a person's 'psychobiological resources' so as to 'sustain cognitive and affective engrossment in occasioned activity' (1963, Chapter 3). Thus a frame is social activity whose meaning exacts partly involuntary attention from its participants.

A frame will only be a ritual realm, however, when ritual factors are in play, that is, when it has the capacity to raise or lower the interaction status (Goffman's concept) or ritual power (Travers, 1982) of one or more participants. But, since almost any frame contains the theoretical possibility of one or more interactants gaining or losing ritual power, a ritual realm must be a type of frame created in part at least for the purpose of manipulating the ritual power of one or more interactants. Therefore ritual realms are those frames employed by the interactant who has the 'gain strategy' of Goffman's doctoral thesis. Such an interactant 'is interested in raising the definition that others present have of him and/or lowering the definition they have of someone else who is present', for 'in Dixon, as apparently in other subcultures of our society, few persons can consistently forego the opportunity that small interplay presents to engineer a favorable image of themselves' (Goffman, 1953, p. 249). So, directly devolving from ritual realm, we get 'ritual strategy', the interaction conduct by which a person creates a flattering ritual realm in which she appears to belong (belonging to a realm is the same as being natural within it, and being natural, Goffman says, is not just acting as if at ease but behaving as if the apparent frame is unproblematically the real frame). Ritual power thus accrues to she who can summon morally attractive realms as the seemingly correct locations of what in Anglo-American usage is often termed her 'real self'. As Goffman says: 'To be able to alter this balance [of motivational forces] at will is to exert power' (1975, Chapter 12). Power is exerted according to the effectiveness of ritual strategies in building ritual realms that displace competing realms and frames.

One of the main disadvantages of Goffman's frame is that it forces an analytic picture of interaction as a series of realities, each one discrete from its neighbours, and this picture runs contrary to the commonsense feeling that persons in interaction are sufficiently mutually monitored to maintain perduring individual frames for the interactants whatever the current frame may be.[5] A ritual realm, on the other hand, in having more ritual power than an ordinary frame, is bound to be engrossing until some frame or realm of greater ritual power occurs. Certainly other frames will be operational but, it is suggested here, they will be subordinate to various ritual realms and will far from exhaust interactants' ongoing involvements. What I mean by this is that a person can be in two or more frames at once when one of those frames is a ritual realm. I don't know why Goffman never considered the possibility that persons can be involved in several frames at once. Perhaps he anticipated problems of establishing a frame priority that can only be measured in terms of inaccessible subjective involvement. These problems, however, do not arise with the distinction of ritual realm from frame, because a ritual realm, in being defined as having ritual power, must always be more involving than a non-ritual frame.

Another analytic advantage of ritual realms emerges here: they are not as choppy and discontinuous as frames. This is because they remain real until, so far as the participants are concerned, all their ritual power has gone. Thus exposure to a powerful realm followed by a withdrawal from that realm does not entail that the realm withdrawn from ceases to exert power. The withdrawing person will remain under the influence of the realm until some other realm takes its place, and, until this happens, the original realm will continue to be more influential than succeeding frames.

Persons may define themselves, therefore, through their abilities to create realms. Thus a skilled ritual strategist can gain ritual power by seeming to belong to a favourable ritual realm. This is in line with Goffman's (1975) idea that every situation gives a 'human effect' which seems to point to a self. But it only points: 'What they [other people] discover from their gleanings [of a self generated in the contrasting streams of a person's behaviour] will apparently point to what this fellow is like beyond the current situation. But every situation he is in will provide his others with such an image. That is what situations can do for us. That is a reason why we find them (as we find novels) engrossing' (Goffman, 1975, p. 299).

So, to recapitulate, it can be said that the main difference between a Goffman frame and a ritual realm stems from ritual rhetoric's concept of ritual power (which is a corollary, never developed by Goffman, to his variable 'engrossment' or 'involvement'). An understanding of ritual power allows us to see, distinct from other behaviour, conduct that is performed to exact more or less involvement than the performer would be due in her status according to any other social order than the interaction order. It follows from this that some interactants may have the dramatic ability to use ritual strategies as self-framing devices that bring into an interaction ritual realms which alter the current balance of ritual powers either by a radical reframing or by realm superposition over frames.

In this chapter, for reasons of space, I ignore the topic of ritual strategies and concentrate on ritual realms, but before saying more about ritual realms I should note that they will be best approached empirically by a study of ritual strategies in interaction, for just as much as when the strategies fail (children's naive boasting, for example) as when they succeed, a realm is promoted, the one uninhabitable and the other inescapable.

In the next section I shall emphasize the pervasive social power of ritual realms by invoking the concept of siege as Freud implicitly uses this in his paper 'Mourning and Melancholia' (1915).

FRAMES AS SIEGES

In this exposition of Freud's siege model (and at times elswhere) there are some apparent contradictions in the usage of terms like ego and self and person. These result from the narrative not fully articulating a siege model of persons in interaction. The narrative can't do this because the siege model itself is being argued from a non-ritual starting point.

Freud's (1915) melancholic experiences the loss of a beloved object (not necessarily a person) and is thereby expelled from the ritual realm wherein she enjoyed an involvement describable as love for the realm's perpetrator. But, since the willingness to be absorbed in this other ritual realm is in no wise diminished by her expulsion, the melancholic suffers a severe ritual setback. She must now either consider herself worthless (for being so considered by the worthiest love object she knows) or else somehow acquire a self-saving rituality. Thus she chooses to save herself (in defiance of the physical bereavement) by replacing the love object with a split-off portion of her own ritual realm (Freud calls this 'ego-identification', and says that the process is unconscious). The lost realm is reinstated — magically — as a realm under the direct jurisdiction of the melancholic (who denies the manoeuvre by performing it unconsciously), so that there seems to be no bereavement. But of course there is (and it is her unconscious knowledge that this is so which induces the melancholic to revile herself, just as if the value of the internalized other is only guaranteed by her own devaluation). In this way a person becomes her own hostage to a perpetrator's realm: she makes herself captive psychobiologically. And it is precisely in order to justify her captivity that she gives over her psychobiological resources to a perpetuation of the other's realm. There are now three possible outcomes (besides melancholia). Either suicide (which confirms that expulsion meant the end of a liveable social life) or release into a new realm (the realm, for instance, of psychoanalysis) or reinstatement in the original perpetrator's realm.

The Freudian ritual model, it can be seen, discloses a possible structure of the relation between ritual realms and psychobiology. And that the model is derived from the case of pathological mourning argues its ritual applicability, since in ritual terms it would be expected that explusion into realmlessness would be the equivalent of 'ritual death' (Travers, 1981, pp. 356–360). The model also underlines the life-and-death nature of realm involvement, as well as indicating how a realm operates to ensure its social impregnability. But are these sufficient reasons for its use here? I think so, because it is a model, unlike any other that I know of, specifically devised to account for the consequences of an ego being overwhelmed by another object (which is practically to say, in my rhetoric, 'enraptured' by another object).

According to the Freudian model, then, a person in interaction may allow herself to be absorbed into another's realm so that afterwards she may remain its hostage, actively abetting the perpetrator. I call this a siege situation because it has a perpetrator, hostage(s) and a context of besieging realms that would break it down. Perpetrator, hostage(s) and besiegers should be regarded as having only contingent correspondence with discrete physical persons. They may be, as in Freud, entirely intrapsychic constructs or they may be differentially embodied in ongoing interactions.[6] I can say this because the siege model (being a ritual model), in not replicating the configurations of bodies in space, harks back to the analysis in Travers (1981) where the extreme possibility of an audience being totally enraptured by a perfectly controlled performance gives the analytic status of unity to audience and performer (they are 'as one').

Freud's melancholic is besieged when she holds out against deritualizing reality by using an intrapsychic manoeuvre that feeds a ritual realm. My contention here is that this melancholic is the type of any interactant whose sense of what she really is threatened by currently contradictory evidence. I further contend that this type of interactant (except in the rare cases of those who command in every social situation genuinely involved deference) must be the type of every interactant for substantial passages of her social life.

The word siege (when it describes frame as ritual realm) has a meaning, I think, that is closer to the phenomena than alternative weaker terms like sacred territory (which, while capturing the idea of liminal sacrosanct reality, conveys nothing of that reality's social trials). More importantly, 'siege', in opening up the person into a triumvirate[7] (perpetrator, hostage, besieger), has much greater ritual flexibility than Goffman's (1975) quartet of 'figure', 'principal', 'strategist' and 'animator'. And, to repeat, an advantage for interaction analysis of splitting a person (or persons) in these three ways is that it disembarrasses the analysis of any notion that the little social system of an interaction is not firstly a system and only secondly the contributory conduct of beings considered as separate.[8] (There is no conflict here with Goffman's assertion that it is 'a lamentable bias' to think of a person as 'somehow more than social, more real, more biological, deeper, more genuine' (1975, p. 270).)

Arising out of the siege model is a projection of social life as successive ritual framings brought about by successive perpetrators. Obviously a perpetrator holds hostage both her own and others' psychobiological reality, for the bodies and consciousness of an interaction are dedicated to its ritual form. Furthermore, since a person in ritual sociology is not a person unless ritually framed (framelessness, as will be seen, is social extinction), a person is perpetually besieged, as hostage or perpetrator, and the realm besieged itself lays siege to other realms.

Now I can add to what I said in the previous section about the perduring nature of 'personal' ritual realms. Goffman's notion of 'rendition', which he defines as a 'mini-keying' of frames (such that their style of 'playing' can come to be seen as pointing to a person 'behind' the frame-maker), is a guide. But mini-keying does not quite square with Goffman's regretful concession that a person is socially constructed to appear isomorphic with her psychobiology, for Goffman himself wants to say that a person in talk 'frames himself from view' (1975, p. 547), which I take to mean something like 'creates the frames that are experienced as their creator'. This is better expressed by Goffman in 'Footing' (1981), where he says: 'It is as if they [the listeners] were to look into the speaker's words, which, after all, cannot be seen. It is as if they must look at the speaker, but not see him.' What the listeners (and the speaker too) must experience, I suggest, is the one ritual person to which the current frame allows greatest intelligibility, and this person is not so much a member of the interaction in the other interactants' eyes as an envoy from a seemingly constant ritual realm. So I am saying here that persons ritually frame themselves with sufficient consistency to acquire unitary ritual appearance. And my analysis suggests a reason for this: that, if ritual power is to be obtained, it needs to be obtained by an identifiable agent (Goffman's 'figure') or the agent, in not being seen to obtain the power, will remain ritually powerless (less than a person).

The outcomes of sieges (ritual death, ritual rebirth, ritual reinstatement) can be seen now as the possible outcomes for any interactant who has experienced a powerful ritual realm, for such a realm will continue to dominate her until she ceases to be a ritual being or until the realm is replaced by a new one or until the old one is rebuilt. I suggest, therefore, that profound and momentous experiences of social life do not readily release interactants into other experiences unless these seem to be similarly profound. This is a way of saying that the psychobiological remainder of a person in interaction, though it will always be claimed in some part by the current frame, need not be treated as an analytically awkward lump of matter but is best thought of as being the hostage of previous realms. Moreover, it is just this held-back (by other realms) aspect of persons in interaction that commonsense urges is the only real person (that is, the potential for a maximum ritual life).

Thus the nature of those ritual realms that have most power over a person can give a full ritual account of that person. An aggregation of such realms will provide a cultural profile of a social being, and this profile will have little to do with the actual moral conduct of the person. But, unlike her moral conduct, a person's ritual profile will be a true guide to the attempted self-presentations of the person in future interactions. This is because the moral meanings that have most power over a person shape her conduct (Travers, 1981, pp. 295–303) so as to display these to others, and these meanings do not need to provide a logic of her past and future conduct except insofar as it is purely expressive (though it may be instrumental as a consequence of being expressive).

The siege paradigm, particularly as it is facilitated by Freud's model of the melancholic psyche, thus accounts for the disposition of people to feel that they are being perfectly candid with one another even while they are trying to show themselves in the best possible light. They may be behaving like Goffman's (1959) 'merchants of morality' but, I suggest, they are performers held hostage by past performances that have overwhelmed them, and as such they are not the cynical calculators for whose depiction Goffman has so often been criticized.[9] Their greatest moral delict, from a siege point of view, is simply their capacity for getting caught up in performances that encourage emulation.

(The foregoing may be seen as a piece of text that was once held hostage by Goffman but is now trying to perpetrate a more powerful ritual realm.)

TWO EXAMPLES OF RITUAL REALM

A full sociological account of the nature and extent of ritual realms must await at least a provisional survey of ritual strategies, for only the presence of ritual strategies shows that a frame is also intended to be a ritual realm. Meanwhile it can be said that ritual realms may be of almost any size, from the microscopic gesture to full-blown cosmologies (such as the major religions). The realms presented here have spatial–temporal boundaries explicable in non-realm terms, but they may be distinguished from non-ritual frames by their capacity to invest participants with membership that goes far beyond affiliation to or co-presence in a fleeting, contingent frame. Strong emotions, self-definition and highly motivated conduct (to use non-ritual terms) are at work in these realms. Participants are not merely framing themselves but are as it were thoroughly steeping themselves in a reality that is theirs alone.

While they are in these realms the participants can be seen only with an effort as belonging to other frames, and the participants in each case have an apparent willingness to jointly create a realm that seems to them not to have been so created (but to be there apart from its constitutive conduct). These realms are powerfully characterizing for the participants, who seem to experience them as of much more social consequence than frames that would reveal themselves as simple conveniences of social organization.

Another observer of the following realms might have written very different notes of the same phenomena and called them valid data just as I do. Obviously the writing is influenced by predispositions not only to see selectively but to see in some lights and not in others. The data are therefore already a jumbled kind of theory: the phenomena they purport to record are simply not tractable to brief verbal notations that will not show great variability dependent on the writer's current assumptions. The best that can be said about this scientifically hopeless state of affairs is that there may be more to be gained than lost by the collection of these sorts of data.

Example One: The Rehearsal Realm

The first example of a ritual realm might be given the general title of 'Rehearsal'.[10] This Rehearsal realm lies somewhere between an unpractised, groping familiarization with the playworld that is being rehearsed and an actual performance of that playworld. It can be seen that in the absence of the director the rehearsing proceeds by fits and starts. None of the interactants, however, is willing to attack the realm until it has been collectively subverted from within, when, very interestingly, it appears to have collapsed of its own accord. From the Rehearsal realm the actors draw their ritual power of 'professional actors'. That is why they cannot attack the realm directly, despite their evident weariness, for if they put an early stop to the Rehearsal realm they jeopardize their standing as actors. The playworld helps here. The actors are able to interact at delicate moments as the characters whom they are bringing into being by rehearsal. Thus, when their interactions are destructive of the playworld, the fact that they partly originate in a fictional frame enclosed within the Rehearsal realm validates the rehearsal (and so endorses the Rehearsal realm) in that it is empowering play characters to have effect beyond their playworld. The whole process as I have recorded it shows the subtlety of a coordinated realm collapse that yet invests the realm with ritual power even as it collapses:

The cast begin a scene that almost at once threatens to founder because Bromden is not there to say his lines (he is away recording voiceovers with B, the director). But Warren keeps the action flowing by addressing himself to an imaginary Bromden, and Nurse Flynn helps out by reading Bromden's lines. Nevertheless, after only two runthroughs, the cast fall into discussion.

Martini repeats other people's points before saying, several times: 'Let's try it.'

They do try a few ideas. However, discussions between each runthrough of smaller and smaller pieces get longer and longer. Interest is shifting from action to motivation, which is to say from practicality to potentiality, from the text to infinity.

Big Nurse describes how she now sees herself in her opening scene, and this is an interpretation that, if adopted, would totally alter the conception of the play that the company has taken the last two weeks to work towards collectively. But, when nobody takes Big Nurse up on this, she starts demanding ideas to 'help' her where she feels 'a bit odd'. Nurse Flynn, finally, is the one who responds, and soon the rehearsal becomes a dialogue between Big Nurse and Nurse Flynn, in which they try to define what McMurphy is really up to in the ward. None of the actors during this dialogue relinquishes his or her stage position. Thus the playworld imposes its structure on the rehearsal world: in both worlds the nurses try to control social reality, and in both worlds Big Nurse has greater power than Nurse Flynn. Harding yawns without covering his mouth. Surely he is in character here, because I cannot think that he would do that normally. Billy says nothing. That too would be the character, not the actor. Only Martini has the temerity to inject remarks such as: 'We'll see when we do it.'

At 7.15 pm Warren breaks his silence and asks the company: 'Shall we try it?'

This almost starts everyone off, but just before they 'try it' Nurse Flynn puts a spanner in the works by asking Big Nurse a direct question, which Big Nurse answers in detail. Martini is moved to remark that if Big Nurse were to do what she is now suggesting 'it would make a baddie out of her too early'. She counters this criticism and then, without Martini being able to head her off, broadens the discussion to her role in the play as a whole. Finally, realizing that Martini is impatient, she does return to the point he made, and says, of her revisions: 'This is the way B [the director] wanted it.' Nobody seems to believe her, but nobody objects, though Martini mildly challenges the absent director by saying: 'I don't necessarily agree with it.' Now a long silence endorses the challenge, until Martini defuses the situation by saying: 'Shall we whack into this anyway?'

Lethargically the cast take up positions for the scene in which Big Nurse publicly embarasses Billy about his girlfriend.

Hardly have they started when Billy stops it.

He does not 'feel happy'.

Again the playworld imposes its structure on the rehearsal world: the scene whose rehearsal Billy has interrupted is the one in which he vainly begs Big Nurse not to disclose his shameful secrets. And, just as in the playworld, the scene is now restarted in the face of Billy's stuttered protestations.

Big Nurse interpolates a directorial comment, but nobody hears, because all are listening to Warren, who has taken over from Nurse Flynn the job of reading Bromden's lines. A few more lines and Nurse Flynn makes a directorial comment. Again no reaction. Nurse Flynn senses her slight gaffe of trying to apply the brakes when momentum is gathering, and asks: 'Is it all right to stop now?' Everybody laughs, after which there is quite a lot of chit-chat before they restart.

It is going quickly now, with one jarring (and new) wrong note, that Big Nurse is still smoking the cigarette she absentmindedly lit during the last break. And then right in the middle of one of her own longer speeches Big Nurse requests ideas about her motivation. As she addresses the cast she further breaks character by making a gesture Big Nurse would never use. She pulls her scarf up over her mouth.

While Big Nurse is talking through her scarf, something interesting occurs between Martini and Cheswick. Cheswick was going to butt into Big Nurse's peroration when Martini distracted him by prodding with an index finger at his (Cheswick's) left temple. (One should remember here the bit of sideplay that Martini and Cheswick worked out a few days ago: Martini jabs both his index fingers into Cheswick's temples, causing Cheswick to react with a convulsive shudder as if he has been given ECT.) Cheswick leans away from Martini's finger, quivering ever so slightly, and in so doing forgets what he was about to say to Big Nurse.

Before they can start, Cheswick raises the subject of smoking on stage (presumably this was what he had been intending to confront Big Nurse with just before Martini jabbed his temple). Cheswick says that if all six patients smoke they will 'cloud the air'. As everybody falls to musing about the clouding of the air, the deputy stage manager breathlessly enters, apologizing for her absence.

The DSM sinks into the settee.

And then Harding instigates further discussion of motivation, which Nurse Flynn cuts short with the general remark: 'Work time?'

Nurse Flynn is actually referring to the unit of one scene which they have labelled for convenience 'Work Time'. But everybody looks upset as if she had drawn attention to the possibility that the work of rehearsing is being shirked. Aware of this misunderstanding and in an attempt to minimize the disturbance it has caused, Nurse Flynn wades into the talking she has just abridged, and gives it new life. Soon they are all wondering aloud how things will work out once the DSM has borrowed the necessary brushes and mops for Work Time. During this, Nurse Flynn leaves the stage area and goes to the settee where she sits next to the DSM, at the centre of volubility. Cheswick observes: 'He [the director] said there's going to be aluminium ring round the wall.' (Martini at this point returns from the lavatory.) Nurse Flynn steers the conversation to the topic of the water bottle prop in the previous production. It was always being spilled. Cheswick comments: 'I didn't care.' Martini replies: 'That was the trouble.' Then Martini adds: 'Not very professional.'

Meanwhile Big Nurse is developing an amusing fantasy on the theme of cleaning the ward. She cleverly exaggerates just a bit at a time and all of a sudden, it seems, arrives quite logically at a prospect of the actors and the entire company being washed off the stage into the auditorium on a rip-tide of froth and suds.

Huge laughter, followed by a guilty silence.

Martini takes it upon himself to end the evening's efforts with the question: 'Has this rehearsal fallen apart, or what?'

To which, as if astonished by a shambles she had no part in creating, Big Nurse brightly replies: 'It's splitting at the seams.'

Without saying anything, Billy and Cheswick start clearing the stage area, and the rest follow suit.

Example Two: The Good Time Realm

The second example of a ritual realm is one that I have observed many times in very similar forms.[11] It is a realm in which a large number of young men and women (during the months of observation) found it important to participate on a regular basis, and for these people the realm represents a 'Good Time'. Many participants (in other contexts) expressed attitudes to the effect that it was immoral not to have a good time when it was available, and non-participants were regarded by the participants as not fully comprehensible. In fact, the ability to voluntarily abstain from the realm was seen as betraying a sort of bloodless, neutered personality that was less than human. So this communal Good Time ritual realm functioned to separate those who did and did not frequent it, and the demarcation between the two resultant groups ran along a line that was more sharply drawn than (and not coincident with) boundaries of class, age group, fashion group, subculture or any other sociological category. The participants in the realm thought of themselves as being human in a different way from other people, and they recognized their communality, elsewhere, just as easily as they recognized non-members as being ritually strange.

Outsiders who did not visit the realm tended to have fantastic ideas about the pub which was its physical site, stigmatizing it as a den of iniquity, a thieves' kitchen, a drug dealers' emporium and a near brothel. These exaggerations expressed the feeling that the Good Time realm must be deeply polluting. So the realm was ritually powerful, but negatively so, even to those who shunned it:

The cool air blowing gently in through the open doors may be a slightly unwelcome reminder of the day they have left behind to the young men who have come here straight from work, but it does not give them gooseflesh. In the gloom, their tattooed arms are moving glasses of beer about, from counter to lips, from lips to counter, as if patiently at the work of rearranging the fine detail of a scene that will never ever be a tableau. But, though there is a feeling of slow motion, pints are being downed swiftly enough, so swiftly indeed that the drinkers give the impression of firmly disbelieving that their getting drunk could follow upon the drinking. This early in the evening the landlord without any apology in his bearing is carrying crates (empty and full) back and forth between his customers, who readily stand out of his way and who, none of them, show any inclination to disturb the quietness by feeding a coin into the jukebox. The barmen, still sleepy from afternoon beds, are not yet chatting with one another, let alone with the customers whose eyes they avoid while covertly drawing on last forbidden cigarettes before the evening gets going.

Daylight gradually dies and the rows of bottles behind the bar shine more and more brightly under the neon tubes set above them. A young man, coming in, looks but can't see into the pub's darkest corners as, pausing on the threshold, he automatically shuts the doors behind him.

Two solitary men, holidaymakers or travellers, take up positions three yards apart at the long bar.

Most of the early drinkers go home about now to their dinners.

An off-duty barmaid, excited by the prospect of an evening on the town, makes an entrance with her boyfriend (just behind her), and one of the barmen bestirs himself to show an interest in her, congratulating her on her white low-cut dress (a dress too easily stained to be worn when working behind the bar). The barmaid introduces the barman to her boyfriend, after which an air of false joviality hangs over the trio's interaction, with both men colluding to keep the girl in high spirits. She is one of those girls who occasionally looks very pretty but tonight she is more odd than pretty, made odd possibly by her mistaken feeling that this is one of her pretty nights. Pretty or odd, whichever she is, she never stops sucking hard on a king-size cigarette, as if the smoke feeds a love-starved self-image. The boyfriend tells the barman that after a couple of drinks in another pub he and the barmaid will eat an Indian meal and then go on to a nightclub, and while he is saying this the barmaid drops her cigarette end to the floor (that the cleaners not the barstaff clean), grinding it out with the toe of a very high-heeled white shoe.

'Have a good time,' says the barman.

From the door the barmaid looks back and gaily waves goodbye.

A group of under-age girls come in. They buy their drinks separately (fruit juices and, in two cases, halves of sweet cider) and then sit around a circular table which is too small for all their glasses, handbags, cigarettes, lighters. The jukebox comes on, and plays: 'When two tribes go to war ...' One of the girls, to entertain her friends, sings along louder than the jukebox. Much giggling and squeaking.

Two youths who have been at the pool table since opening time give way to another pair who are on their first pints of the evening.

The two solitary drinkers at the long bar are lost in a whole row of men, some with women in tow, and, behind this wall of backs, other men press forwards, holding out five- and ten-pound notes to signal that they want service. The barmen, flashing smiles, are wide awake now, and their banter comes to them effortlessly and, although they would never admit it, they are enjoying their work. A few older couples during the last half hour have claimed the quieter tables away from the jukebox (playing non-stop, and much louder than before). These couples, on finishing their drinks, leave the pub in search of a quieter environment.

The cannabis smokers have occupied their usual seats near the door into the Gents (they do their dealing in the lock-up cubicles) and a joint, passing from hand to hand, adds its smoke to the pub's cigarette smoke. Some drinkers, sniffing the aroma of cannabis, seem to feel a satisfaction that this pub is where the action is.

It is no longer possible to go from one part of the pub to another without constantly having to say 'Excuse me', and at the bar, because of the number of customers, service has slowed down, though the barmen are working faster than ever. Change is being given at such a rate that the landlord several times has to empty plastic bags of coins into compartments of the three electric tills, and at any given moment eight or nine hands are waving paper money at barmen rushing by. The two solitaries, having been pushed into contact, are conversing so deeply that they don't feel the need to move aside for the men behind them shoving forwards. The landlord tours the pub picking up much-needed glasses. He lifts them, a dozen in each hand, over the human barrier at the bar while, behind his back, a girl from time to time slips a sherry glass into her handbag.

The regular customers who see one another every day in the town, when they barely exchange nods, smile widely as, bearing drinks, they brush shoulders, and now and then they even stop to share a joke against outsiders. The circular group of girls near the jukebox (which has been playing at maximum volume for the past hour) is twice its original size from an influx of young men. Egged on by her friends, one girl is hungrily kissing one of the young men. Two of the labourers who came to the pub straight from their buidling site at half-past five lurch from side to side as they go to the Gents for the fourth or fifth time this evening. Pool playing has been abandoned because there is not enough space around the table to make a shot without having the cue jogged. Laughter erupts everywhere. Eyes glisten. Groups of people sing along with the songs on the jukebox. Even the bearded and bejeaned veteran hippy, who is assumed to be a Drug Squad detective (there to spot the main dealer among the cannabis smokers), is the worse for drink, and perilously close, I feel, to blowing his cover in the interests of greater conviviality. Complete strangers are striking up friendly conversations whose topic with surprising frequency is the surrounding drunken throng.

It is as if the pub is approaching a critical mass and that, after reaching it, nothing less than an orgy will result, but at this precise moment, as it does every evening, the crowd begins to thin out.

Those of the couples bound for late-night discos and nightclubs are sneaking away as if leaving a party whose host (even though there isn't one) must be dodged lest he forcibly detain them. The remaining majority do not notice the departures or notice the tempo slowing. Time for them has so completely disappeared that a bell ringing out and a voice calling after it 'Last orders please!' comes as a shock.

But time, after having been stopped, suddenly accelerates as final drinks are bought.

'Hurry up please! Ladies and gentlemen!'

Men stare at pints they can hardly bring to their lips without spillage.

'Drink up please! Time gentlemen please!'

Beering is being poured slowly into nearly overflowing throats.

'Let's have your glasses! Ladies and gentlemen! Please!'

Men set down empty glasses. Their eyes are glazed like those of boxers not knowing if they've won or lost. 'Drink up now please!' Barmen whisk away the glasses, empty the ashtrays, wipe the tables.

'Come on! Let's be having you! Haven't you got any homes to go to?'

The landlord draws the curtains, opens wide the windows and the doors, and switches on the overhead fluorescence. So the pub is no more homely than a railway platform as the stragglers going out say their inordinate goodbyes. Some regulars will not leave until they have shaken hands with the barmen, who, knowing that release is nigh, generously humour their customers. The landlord stations himself by the door and receives, poker-faced, a number of manly leavetakings such as would befit the conclusion of important business.

THE DRAMATIC PARABOLA: PUTTING SOCIETY IN THE WRONG

Since I have strongly implied that being a person means belonging to a ritual realm, it would follow that consideration of the state of not belonging to any ritual realm will add to an appreciation of ritual realms by drawing attention to their human necessity.

Obviously, to go realmless is to go frameless, and framelessness, according to Goffman, is 'negative experience' (negative because it takes its character from what it is not and 'what it is not is an organized and organizationally affirmed response' (1975, p. 379)). Negative experience, however, is not a kind of unemotional alienation, for the unframed interactant finds her predicament and its causes urgent matters with which she is 'unreservedly engrossed' (Goffman, 1975). But how can Goffman say that framelessness is engrossing when he has defined a frame as social reality made real precisely by its capacity to engross? Isn't framelessness a frame, albeit of a disorganizing kind, by Goffman's own definition (Scheflen's (1973) microanalysis of schizophrenic frame-breaking in fact shows that the conduct involved may be highly organized, and so too does McDermott's (1977) microanalysis of 'unruly' classroom behaviour)? The only way framelessness isn't a frame, I think, is through a construal of the social being experiencing it as non-social, and this is more or less how Goffman portrays the unframed person, as 'flooding out', 'opting out' and 'giving up control' (Scheflen and McDermott suggest that seemingly uncontrolled conduct is actually conduct organized in a different way to its contextual conduct, but I would say that it is organized so as to be unframeable). I shall take Goffman's lead and describe as realmless any person who, whatever her apparent social life, cannot become more involved in any available realms than she is in her state of being uninvolved in them. So realmlessness is an active involvement in the inability to feel that realms are involving in any other aspect except that of their being uninvolving. Clearly such a state is destructive of the self if the self is understood as a social phenomenon, for the self presented by a realmless person must be ritually dead (and thus fairly soon responded to as such). The realmless person, then, is caught in a vicious circle, finding realms less and less engrossing the more she feels a realmlessness that in making realms even less engrossing makes her more realmless yet, and so on. She is like a depressive who is increasingly unable to entertain alternative responses to the world other than depression as the depression becomes increasingly more profound than any other possible response.

Perhaps it is a measure of the self-destructive power of realmlessness that persons for whom only shameful realms are possible will choose shame rather than realmlessness. And it must be easier to be socially disgraced (centred in a disgraceful realm) than to feel that the disgrace is meaningless, or the social forces of condemnation would not have the general effect of keeping people from warranting it. Realmlessness might function socially, therefore, as a potential state, the depersonalizing nature of which ensures that sooner than enter it persons will occupy almost any conceivable realm. This being so, one must assume that persons will be moved to try to adopt realms more powerful than their own by performing acts expressive of the self-belief that they should be rightfully framed in a better realm (where realmlessness means self-destruction, it is in order to ritually speak of upward realm passage as requiring self-belief). There will have to be a socially unrealistic bootstrapping principle at work in this process: past evidence weighs against a person who would be better framed than she currently is, and her self-framing as a better person is carried out in the face of social scepticism (I don't refer here to status passages ordained by societal arrangements but to moral ascendance). If the framing works (if, that is, it begins to look cogent), it will eventually confirm itself as having been appropriate all along (the Prince Hal syndrome). 'Faith' operates here, for realm promotion must be achieved by the generation of conduct geared initially to a completely unsupported expressive self. Conversion experiences will be of this type: without reference to evidence or rationality, persons, as they say, are 'born again' (that is what I mean by reframing as a result of belief).

The more sustained and elevated the act of faith, I suggest, the more ritual power it will exert. The Japanese tragic hero, as he is rendered by Ivan Morris (1980) in his book *The Nobility of Failure*, illustrates this contention very clearly and also shows how ritual power may be boosted by self-belief committing the believer to physical destruction. The following extraction of an ideal type from the nine tragic heroes analysed by Morris charts a moral career (Morris calls it a 'dramatic parabola') of the self-believer which I think is often, in less sharp form, emulated by many ritually vital persons. In addition, the ideal type reveals a so far underemphasized possibility for the hostage, that she might experience her role as personally fulfilling. (At first glance the ideal type of the tragic hero might seem very different from Freud's melancholic, but I think the two have much in common. The Japanese tragic hero is a hero and is tragic because the realm that gives him social eminence is doomed. Unless he gives up his beloved lost cause, he too is doomed. But just like the Freudian melancholic, he will not give up the realm that made him what he is. And of course he goes to death by suicide, as does the melancholic in the extreme of melancholia. Perhaps there is a difference in the manner of his going to his death, but even here Freud would account for the elevated mood during the downward path of his parabola as the mania that can alternate with depression without curing it.)

The Ideal Type of the Japanese Tragic Hero

The Japanese tragic hero, who always emerges in a period of unrest or war, has a number of invariable attributes. Most importantly, he (I use 'he' and 'himself' because all Morris's heroes are male) is uncompromising and singlemindedly sincere, showing no sign of caring for fame, rank, money or his own physical welfare. His knowledge of his society is intuitive rather than empirically based, and under no circumstances will he manoeuvre or negotiate or make trade-offs in order to achieve mundane success. His character is passionate, spontaneous and trusting. He is pure of heart, imaginative, courageous and, in battle, daring. He will defy convention and commonsense alike while comporting himself with extreme control, and yet he sooner finds fault with himself than with others. Living frugally but at a higher emotional level than most men, he wages war against whatever strikes him as evil and unjust.

This hero type usually enjoys brilliant success in his early years, achieving a rapid upward propulsion accelerated by his unswerving moral rectitude. Then, at his peak (the crest of the parabola), there is a moment of confrontation with the inevitability of ultimate failure. This is when self-belief is thoroughly tested, and found proof against everyday reality. No compromise is accepted. There will be no reframing. In every case the hero now commits himself to the end, and the very attributes that carried him so high — his sincerity, courage and refusal to be dishonest — plummet him to disaster and defeat. He is betrayed and outwitted by more worldly men, but he goes down bravely, poignantly and tragically towards a glorious failure, 'flinging himself after his painful destiny' in a 'death frenzy' (Morris, 1980).

Death is always by suicide, and carried out so as to testify to the hero's sincerity and to vindicate his honour (honour would have been lost in the indignity of capture). The outcome of the hero's career is not simply a temporary setback but usually the 'irrevocable collapse of the cause he has championed' (Morris, 1980). History shows the hero's struggle (politically, not ritually) to have been not only useless but also counterproductive. Yet the hero becomes a legend who is remembered long after his adversaries are forgotten, and each tragic hero becomes the subject of survival and reincarnation myths. He enters a sacred realm of his culture and does so not because of his early achievement but because of his later self-sacrifice to a realm that had become politically untenable.

The brilliantly successful novelist Yukio Mishima (who himself committed hara kiri when Japanese servicemen refused to rise up and follow him in a doomed attempt to reinstate their emperor as a god) sums up the moral philosophy of a tragic hero when he says that 'the way of the sage is in the public realm alone ... Even the superior man, if he knows the good but fails to act upon it, is transformed into a pygmy' (quoted in Morris, 1980 pp. 97–8), and (in a quoted letter to Morris) 'I have believed that knowing without acting is not sufficiently knowing and that the action itself does not require any effectiveness'.

Intimations of a Ritual Order

Thus the dramatic parabola is a classic career of a person first perpetrating a ritual realm of extraordinary social power and then, finding himself the revered hostage of this realm, choosing to go on believing in himself and validating the realm despite and even because of its terrible political unreality, up to the point where by his self-destruction he assures the realm an existence independent of him in perpetuity.

Such a moral, self-believing line (the antithesis of going realmless), I suggest, is followed by any person when she commits herself to realities over and above her psychobiological convenience (convenience is the lowest form of ritual life), whether these realities be nation or religious belief or vocation or principle or conviction or family, to mention just a few possibilities. And yet the line is scarcely acknowledged in sociological accounts of, for example, upward and downward social mobility, though it must be plain that even the choice not to follow it will have considerable social meaning for those who make it.

An important consequence for organizational and societal analysis of taking persons' dramatic parabolae into account (whether followed or not followed) is the necessity to gauge the power of various realms in terms of actual conduct that would seem otherwise gratuitously principled. And the awareness of realm-generated conduct of the dramatic parabola type will throw into relief those conditions whereby political reality, as if irrationally, is sacrificed to moral integrity. Thus many unfathomable disputes and conflicts can be redeemed to the realm of sociology when their ritual order is discovered.

So it may be that conflict resolution in some circumstances may be dependent on the creation of new realms that will exert more ritual power than the previous conflicting realms: people will have to believe in the peaceful future for it to come to pass (just as, for example, the IRA and UDR don't). Belief is all, perhaps, and the belief will have to morally elevate the believers, or it won't stand any chance of becoming a belief. That may be why lost causes can be so attractive (and destructive of less attractive social aims), since the more lost they are the more they ritually justify themselves to otherwise unclaimed ritual beings. In a fully ritual world there is no standpoint between right and wrong, and a fully ritual person to himself or herself is always right, and the more right the more lost, as, for example, Jack Abbott (1982):

You think I just see one side of them [the guards]? They have a good side — but, as I said, only when there is a knife at their throats: they obey violence. They obey it in their hearts, as do all animals.

A prisoner does not.

A prisoner rebels even with the knife at his throat. That is why at this time he is a prisoner. It is the essence of being a prisoner today. He cannot be subdued. Only murdered.

This is true in spite of himself.

Those who are neither guards nor prisoners are nevertheless either oppressed or oppressors. There is not a true 'mixture' of these two terms. There is always a principled contradiction.

There is a 'gray area' inhabited by most people in European industrial societies. It is like the dry foliage that surrounds a fire that will spread and consume it. Everything in the world is committed to the flames, no matter our wishes.

When they came in their jackboots and kick in your door, that 'gray area' of your existence will be no more. You will join in our struggles in spite of yourself.

The 'gray area' deludes itself. Tells itself the conflict can resolve itself peacefully, or that it is not *real*.

CONCLUSIONS

1. Organization Research

In this chapter I have advanced a view of social life as being composed of ritual realms and their perpetrators and hostages. How can this view be employed in the analysis of an organization, for example? Clearly, a first step would be the isolation of dominant ritual realms (which may not include a realm collectively identified as the organization in question). Then it would be necessary to group the organization members (across hierarchical, professional, trade union and technical lines) by reference to their dominant realms. Next, a survey of the ritual strategies enacted within the organization would show not only who are the most and least effective perpetrators but also the 'shadow organization' of failed realms (and the potential for instatement of the shadow organization). Thus several involvement maps of the organization could be drawn so as to yield up the ritual order of the organization. The stability or instability of the organization's ritual order will give a strong clue to the ease or difficulty of organizational development, as well as identifying the best areas in which to initiate change. And how the ritual order fits with other organizational orders such as the legal, economic, status and technical orders will show why some or all of these are functional or not according to official or unofficial criteria.

These brief indications may bear some general expansion, in particular around the point that the ritual order may not be isomorphic with other organizational orders. One problem here is that there has yet to be an organizational study exclusively and consciously focusing on the ritual order. This is understandable in view of the very nature of ritual phenomena, which will always emerge most strongly when non-ritual structures seem to be breaking down or to be losing their power. At their most salient, ritual phenomena tend to occur just when the concept of organization itself begins to look unstable and inapplicable. Weber's notion of 'charisma' will explain how this happens (I refer to Weber so as to anchor the discussion to a sociology whose implications for organizational theory are well known). Weber (1974) says that 'charisma knows only inner determination' and that 'its attitude is revolutionary and transvalues everything'. When there is a grouping around a charismatic leader, 'the master as well as his disciples and followers, must stand outside the ties of this world, outside of routine occupations, as well as outside the routine obligations of family life'. Thus the organization coming into being around a charismatic leader will be what Weber calls a 'charismatic structure', and this structure 'in contrast to any kind of bureaucratic organization of office ... knows nothing of a form of an ordered procedure of appointment or dismissal'. One might say then that charismatic structures are barely organizational and yet clearly, if they are to prevail through time and in the absence of the originally ritually powerful leaders, these structures will determine the organizations that finally reify the founding faith. (An example would be how the church of Rome grew out of the charismatic structure of disciples to the Messiah in Israel.) Of course such charismatic structures are extreme cases of ritual orders, when other orders are overshadowed by the ritual component. But it may be hypothesized from what has been argued thus far that in origin most organizations will have been touched by charismatic leadership. And it is easy to see that the development of an organization will proceed most rapidly from just those places within it where charismatic figures are prominent enough to initiate non-destructive change (of course change may be promoted by any number of non-ritual reasons, but I am suggesting here that a relatively stable organization will be most fluid where there is charisma).

The implications for organizational research are fairly plain. Where such research finds that strictly laid down organizational procedures are not being adhered to or are even being flouted, then it will be probable that a major organizational source of ritual power will have been located. This is the moment when most organizational research becomes confounded by the data, wanting to say that the data are not really organizational data, belonging to a part of the organization that according to non-ritual lights is disorganized. But a ritual view of organizations will find this kind of destructuring or (in Victor Turner's phrase) 'liminal' data the key to organizational change as it is occurring. So a general research rule may be adduced from the foregoing. That in organizations where procedures are no longer working properly, new organizational structures may be emerging which will be best understood as having ritual moment. In these organizations the isolation of a ritual order will indicate what kind of accommodations will cause least organizational dysfunction. Clearly, direct opposition and conflict with a faction that is already impatient with the old orders will only serve to further empower this faction's impatience.

Not all organizations, however, will seem to be ritual battlefields, but it may be said that wherever organizational members have more than a merely rational–pragmatic interest in their work the ritual element will be present, demanding a specifically ritual analysis to rescue it from classification as organizational 'noise'. Naturally the importance of ritual analyses of organizations will not be seen until we are in a position to compare such analyses with other kinds of analysis. This chapter has argued, among other things, that the starting point for a ritual analysis of an organization will be the definition of dominant ritual realms, a research task probably best undertaken through deep interviewing of members in order to discover how they are hostages to what realms. Participant observation will then be profitable since the researcher's perception will be guided by a latent structure whose delineation in practice will safely proceed independently of other distracting orders.

2. Goffman's Emptiness

Crook and Taylor (1980) criticize Goffman's frame analysis for not developing analytic tools which 'would allow him to consider the possibility that engrossment might be a function of the significance which a person attaches to the contents rather than the form of experience'. This chapter, has I think, supplied just such an analytic tool, the ritual experience, whose exploration will have as much to do with content as form. Also Crook and Taylor say that Goffman is not 'able to suggest that the "motivational relevancies" which generate such significance might be related to a person's history as part of a social rather than an experiential structure'. But the ritual realm concept allows just this, because ritual realms are perduring agent-identifiable frames. So I feel that what Crook and Taylor refer to as 'the emptiness at the centre' of *Frame Analysis* is potentially filled by ritual conduct.

3. Future Realm Research

Finally I would like to indicate a research initiative that I think would complement my proposed collection of ritual strategies. This would be to look at actual sieges so as to isolate recurrent structures that might apply to everyday interactions. The very propensity of almost any kind of siege anywhere in the world to immediately take first place in news items, I think, suggests that sieges have considerable resonance in mass societies. Just what this resonance is and how far it reaches into everyday life would be questions to be answered by siege research, which would come at ritual realms structurally (while ritual strategies establish them inferentially).

NOTES

1. Throughout this chapter I use 'she' in place of 'he' and 'her' in place of 'his'. This may be regarded as positive discrimination or linguistic folly.

2. In no particular order: Crook and Taylor (1980); Gonos (1977); Ditton (1976); Jary and Smith (1976); Craib (1978); and Manning (1980). These are the principal commentators, but there are many others.
3. And also some work that is not specifically symbolic interactionist such as Becker *et al.* (1961).
4. Crook and Taylor (1980) are anxious to have Goffman meaning that his primary frameworks are primary in an ontological sense, but when Goffman says that novels and actual experience are equivalent in terms of their comparable capacities to engross I think he is carefully opting out of the very ontological debate that Crook and Taylor assume he is engaging in.
5. Sharron (1985) is particularly critical of the way frame talk subverts a sense of ongoing reality, and he altogether abandons frame analysis in favour of William James's 'stream of life'.
6. I don't find it strange to use Freud's intrapsychic constructs socially, any more, I imagine, than Freud found it strange to use the Greek drama of *Oedipus* (an exceptionally social phenomenon) to explain psychological events.
7. Triumvirate is a man-centred term, but I can't think of a similar woman-centred term.
8. Pittenger *et al.* (1960) have expressed this point with exceptional vigour, and Bateson (1971) iterates the same point. Many microanalysts, including, notably, Albert Scheflen, Carl Couch and Ray Birdwhistell, have made it a central operating assumption.
9. Gouldner (1970) seems to be the instigator of this type of criticism.
10. Taken from participant observation of a theatre group in 1980. I call the actors by the names of the characters they play.
11. Taken from participant observation in a small town between 1981 and 1983 for a project called 'Ritual Strategies of the Unemployed'.

References

Aarne, A. A. (1964). *The Types of the Folktale*, translated by S. Thompson. Helsinki.

Abbott, J. H. (1982). *In the Belly of the Beast*. London: Hutchinson.

Abercrombie, N. (1974). Sociological indexicality, *Journal for the Theory of Social Behaviour* **4**, 89–95.

Abrahams, R. D. (1968). Introductory remarks to rhetorical theory of folklore, *Journal of American Folklore* **81**, 146.

Ackoff, R. L. (1979). The future of Operational Research is past, *Journal of the Operational Research Society* **30** (2), 93–104.

Ackoff, R. L. and Emery, F. (1972). *On Purposeful Systems*. London: Tavistock.

Allen, T. J. (1966). Performance of information channels in the transfer of technology, *Industrial Management Review* **18** (1), 87–98.

Allen, T. J. (1971). The international technological gatekeeper, *Technology Review* **73**.

Allen, V. L. and Scheibe, K. E. (eds) (1982). *The Social Context of Conduct*. New York: Praeger.

Althusser, L. (1971). *Lenin, Philosophy and Other Essays*. London: Monthly Review Press.

Anderson, P. A. (1983). Decision-making by objection and the Cuban missile crisis, *Administrative Science Quarterly* **28**, 201–222.

Ansoff, H. I. (1979). *Strategic Management*. London: Macmillan.

Argyris, C. (1971). Management Information Systems: the challenge to rationality and emotionality, *Management Science*, 275–292.

Argyris, C. and Schon, D. A. (1974). *Theory in Practice: Increasing Professional Effectiveness*. San Francisco: Jossey-Bass.

Aristotle (1975). *Poetics*. London: Everyman.

Asch, S. E. (1955). Opinion and social pressure, *Scientific American*, November, 31–35.

Atkinson, J., Cuff, E. and Lee, G. R. E. (1978). The recommencement of a meeting as a member's accomplishment. In J. Schenkein (ed.) *Studies in the Organization of Conversational Interaction*, Vol. 1. New York: Academic Press.

Atkinson, J. M. and Drew, P. (1979). *Order in Court*. London: Macmillan/SSRC.

Attewell, P. (1974). Ethnomethodology since Garfinkel, *Theory and Society*, 179–210.

Averill, J. R. (1980). A constructivist view of emotion. In R. Plutchik and H. Kellerman (eds) *Emotion: Theory, Research and Experience*. New York: Academic Press.

Axelrod, R. (1976). *Structure and Decision*. Princeton: Princeton University Press.

Axelrod, R. (1977). Coping with deception. Working Paper, Department of Political Science and Institute of Policy Studies, University of Michigan.

251

Axelrod, R. (1979). Argumentation in foreign policy settings, *Journal of Conflict Resolution* **21** (4), 727–745.

Ayer, A. J. (1936). *Language, Truth and Logic*. London: Gollancz.

Bachrach, P. and Baratz, M. S. (1963). Decisions and non-decisions: an analytical framework, *American Political Science Review* **57**, 632–642.

Bailey, F. G. (1969). *Stratagems and Spoils*. Oxford: Blackwell.

Baldwin, J. and McConville, M. (1979). *Jury Trials*. Oxford: Oxford University Press.

Ball, D. (1972). The 'definition of the situation': some theoretical and methodological consequences of taking W. I. Thomas seriously, *Journal for the Theory of Social Behaviour* **2** (1), 61–81.

Bannister, D. and Fransella, F. (1971). *Inquiring Man: The Theory of Personal Constructs*. London: Penguin.

Barish, J. (1981). *The Anti-Theatrical Prejudice*. Berkeley: University of California Press.

Barnes, B. and Law, J. (1976). Whatever should be done with indexical expressions, *Theory and Society* **3**, 223–237.

Barthes, R. (1963). *Elements of Sociology*, translated by Annette Lavers, London: Cape.

Barthes, R. (1973). *Mythologies*, translated by Annette Lavers. London: Paladin Granada.

Barthes, R. (1974). *S/Z*. New York: Hill and Wang.

Barthes, R. (1976). *The Pleasure of the Text*. New York: Hill and Wang.

Barthes, R. (1977). *Image–Music–Text*, translated by S. Heath. London: Fontana.

Barthes, R. (1979). From work to text. In J. Harari (ed.) *Textual Strategies*. Ithaca: Cornell University Press.

Barthes, R. (1981). Theory of the text. In R. Young (ed.) *Untying the Text*. London: Routledge and Kegan Paul.

Barthes, R. (1982). *Camera Lucinda: Reflections on Photography*, translated by P. Howard. London: Cape.

Bate, P. (1984). The impact of organizational culture on approaches to organizational problem-solving, *Organization Studies* **5** (1), 43–66.

Bateson, G. (1971). In N.A. McQuawn (ed.) *The Natural History of an Interview*. Chicago University of Chicago Library Microfilm Collection of Manuscripts on Cultural Anthropology, No. 95, Series XV.

Bateson, G. (1972). *Steps to an Ecology of Mind: Collected Essays in Anthropology, Psychiatry, Evolution and Epistemology*. New York: Ballantine Books.

Becker, H.S., Geer, B., Hughes, E.C. and Strauss, A.L. (1961). *Boys in White*. Chicago: University of Chicago Press.

Bell, P.B. and Staines, P.J. (1979) *Reasoning and Argument in Psychology*. London: Routledge and Kegan Paul.

Bennis, W.G. (1965). Theory and method in applying behavioural science to planned organizational change, *Journal of Applied Behavioural Science*, October–December.

Benso, J.K. (1977). *Organizational Analysis: Critique and Innovation*. Beverly Hills: Sage.

Berger, P.L. and Luckmann, T. (1966). *The Social Construction of Reality*. Doubleday: New York.

Berger, P.L. and Luckmann, T. (1967). *The Social Construction of Reality*. Harmondsworth: Penguin.

Berne, E. (1964). *Games People Play*. London: Deutsch.

Bersani, L. (1977). The subject of power, *Diacritics* **7** (3), 2–21.

Blau, P.M. (1963). *Exchange and Power in Social Life*. New York: Wiley.

Blau, P.M. (1974) *On the Nature of Organizations*. New York: Wiley Interscience.

Blumer, H. (1969). *Symbolic Interactionism: Perspective and Method*. Englewood Cliffs, New Jersey: Prentice-Hall.

Bogdan, R. and Taylor, S.J. (1975). *Introduction to Qualitative Research Methods*. Chichester: Wiley.

Boland, J. and Young, T.R. (1972). The Dramaturgical Society, Paper presented at the Annual Meeting of the American Sociological Association, New Orleans, August.

Booz, Allen and Hamilton (1968). *Management of New Products*. Chicago: Booz, Allen and Hamilton.

Booz, Allen and Hamilton (1981). *New Product Management for the 1980's: Phase I*. Chicago: Booz, Allen and Hamilton.

Bourdieu, P. (1971). The thinkable and the unthinkable, *Times Literary Supplement*, October 15, 1255-1256.

Bourdieu, P. (1977). *Outline of a Theory of Practice*. London: Cambridge University Press.

Bourdieu, P. (1979). *Algeria, 1960*. Cambridge: Cambridge University Press.

Bowen, K.C. (1979). Personal and organizational value systems: how should we treat these in OR studies?, *Omega* **7** (6), 503-512.

Brewer, G.D. (1973). *Politicians, Bureaucrats and the Consultant*. New York: Basic Books.

Briskman, L. (1981). Creative product and creative process. In D. Dutton and M. Krausz (eds) *The Concept of Creativity in Science and Art*. The Hague: Nijhoff.

Brissett, D. and Edgley, C. (eds) (1975). *Life as Theater: A Dramaturgical Sourcebook*. Chicago: Aldine Press.

Brooks, R.C. (1957). 'Word-of-mouth' advertising in selling new products, *The Journal of Marketing*, October, 154-161.

Brown, D. and Kaplan, R.E. (1981). Participative research in a factory. In P. Reason and J. Rowan (eds) *Human Inquiry: A Sourcebook of New Paradigm Research*. Chichester: Wiley.

Bruno, A.V. (1973). New product decision making in high technology firms, *Research Management*, September, 28-31.

Bujake, J.E. Jr (1972). Ten myths about new product development, *Research Management*, January, 33-42.

Burgon, B. (1982). *The Gramophone* **60**, October.

Burke, K. (1936). *Permanence and Change*. New York: New Republic Inc.

Burke, K. (1950). *A Grammar of Motives*. Los Angeles: University of California Press.

Burke, K. (1969). *A Rhetoric of Motives*, California edition. Berkeley: University of California Press.

Burns, E. (1972). *Theatricality: A Study of Convention in the Theatre and in Social Life*. London: Longman.

Burns, T. and Stalker, G. (1961). *The Management of Innovation*. London: Tavistock.

Burrell, G. and Morgan, G. (1979). *Sociological Paradigms and Organisational Analysis*. London: Heinemann.

Burton, F. and Carlen, P. (1977). Official discourse, *Economy and Society* **6** (4), 377-407.

Cameron, W.B. (1954) Sociological notes on a jam session, *Social Forces*, 177-183.

Carter, C. and Williams, B. (1957). *Industry and Technical Progress: Factors Governing the Speed of Application of Science*. London: Oxford University Press.

Centre for the Study of Industrial Innovation (1971). *On the Shelf: A Survey of Industrial R and D Products Abandoned for Non-Technical Reasons*. London: Centre for the Study of Industrial Innovation.

Cicourel, A. (1967). *Method and Measurement in Sociology*. New York: Free Press

Clark, D.L. (1985). Emerging paradigms in organizational theory and research. In Y. Lincoln, *Organizational Theory and Inquiry: The Paradigm Revolution*. Beverly Hills: Sage.

Clegg, S. and Dunkereley, D. (1980). *Organization, Class and Control*. London:

Routledge and Kegan Paul.

Clements, P. (1983). *The Improvised Play: The Work of Mike Leigh*. London: Methuen.

Cohen, M., March, J. and Olsen, J. (1972). A garbage can model of organizational choice, *Administrative Science Quarterly* **17** (1), 1–25.

Coker, J. (1964) *Improvising Jazz*. Englewood Cliffs, New Jersey: Prentice-Hall.

Cole, D. (1975). *The Theatrical Event: A Mythos, a Vocabulary, a Perspective*. Middletown, Connecticut: Wesleyan University Press.

Coleman, D.W. (1970). An innovation system for the larger company, *Research Management*, September, 341–349.

Coleman, D.W. (1974). Research-based venture companies — the link between market and technolgy, *Research Management*, May, 16–20.

Coleman, J., Katz, E. and Menzel, H. (1957). The diffusion of an innovation among physicians, *Sociometry* **20**, 253–270.

Collier, D.W. (1970). An innovation system for the larger company, *Research Management*, September, 341–349.

Collier, D.W. (1974). Research based venture companies: the link between market and technology, *Research Management*, May, 16–20.

Collins, R. and Makowsky, M. (1972). *The Discovery of Society*. New York: Random House.

Comanor, W.S. (1967). Research and technical change in the pharmaceutical industry, *The Review of Economics and Statistics*, 182–190.

Cook, M. (1979). *Perceiving Others: The Psychology of Interpersonal Perception*. London: Methuen.

Cooley, C.H. (1902). *Human Nature and the Social Order*. New York: Scribners.

Coulter, J. (1971). Decontextualised meanings: current approaches to Verstehende investigations, *Sociological Review* **19**, 301–23.

Coulter, J. (1979). *The Social Construction of the Mind*. London: Routledge and Kegan Paul.

Coward, R. and Ellis, J. (1977). *Language and Materialism: Developments in Semiology and the Theory of the Subject*. London: Routledge and Kegan Paul.

Craib, I. (1978). Erving Goffman: Frame Analysis, *Philosophy of the Social Sciences* **8**, 77–86.

Crawford, C.M. (1983). *New Products Management*. Homewood, Illinois: Richard D. Irwin.

Crenson, N.A. (1971). *The Un-politics of Air Pollution: a Study of Non-decisionmaking in the Cities*. Baltimore: John Hopkins.

Crook, S. and Taylor, L. (1980). Goffman's version of reality. In J. Ditton (ed.) *The View from Goffman*. London: Macmillan.

Crossman, R. (1975). *The Diaries of a Cabinet Minister, Volume 1, Minister of Housing 1964–66*. London: Hamilton and Cape.

Culler, J. (1975). *Structural Poetics: Structuralism, Linguistics, and the Study of Literature*. London: Routledge and Kegan Paul.

Culler, J. (1976). *Saussure*. London: Fontana.

Culler, J. (1981). *The Pursuit of Signs: Semiotics, Literature, Deconstruction*. London: Routledge and Kegan Paul.

Culler, J. (1983). *On Deconstruction*. London: Routledge and Kegan Paul.

Cyert, R.M. and March, J.G. (1963). *A Behavioral Theory of the Firm*. Englewood Cliffs, New Jersey: Prentice-Hall.

Davis, F. (1974). Stories and sociology, *Urban Life and Culture* **3**, October.

Davis, P.J. and Hersh, R. (1981). *The Mathematical Experience*. Harmondsworth: Penguin.

DeMan, P. (1979). *Allegories of Reading*. New Haven, Connecticut: Yale University Press.

Derrida, J. (1970). Structure, sign and play in the discourse of the human sciences. In E. Donato and R. Macksey (eds) *The Languages of Criticism and the Sciences of Man.* Baltimore: John Hopkins.

Derrida, J. (1983). *Speech and Phenomena, and Other Essays on Husserl's Theory of Signs,* translated by D. B. Allison. Evanston, Illinois: Northwestern University Press.

Derrida, J. (1976). *Of Grammatology,* translated by G. C. Spivak. Baltimore: John Hopkins.

Derrida, J. (1978). *Writing and Difference,* translated by A. Bass. London: Routledge and Kegan Paul.

Derrida, J. (1981). *Positions,* translated by A. Bass. London: Athlone Press

Dewey, R. (1969). The theatrical analogy reconsidered, *American Sociologist* 4, 307–11.

Dickson, G. C. (1981). An empirical examination of the willingness of managers to use utility theory, *Journal of Management Studies* 18 (4), 423–434.

Diesing, P. (1972). *Patterns of Discovery in the Social Sciences.* London: Routledge and Kegan Paul.

Ditton, J. (1976). Review of 'Frame Analysis', *Sociology* 10 (2).

Donato, E. (1970). The two languages of criticism. In E. Donato and R. Macksey *The Languages of Criticism and the Sciences of Man.* Baltimore: John Hopkins.

Douglas, J. D. (1977). Existential Sociology. In J. D. Douglas and J. M. Johnson (eds) *Existential Sociology.* London: Cambridge University Press.

Duda, R. O. and Gaschnig, J. G. (1981). Knowledge based expert systems come of age, *Byte,* September, 238–281.

Eden, C. (1978). Operational research and organization development, *Human Relations* 3 (8), 657–674.

Eden, C., Jones, S. and Sims, D. (1979). *Thinking in Organizations.* London: Macmillan.

Eden, C., Jones, S., Sims, D. and Smithin, T. (1981). The intersubjectivity of issues and issues of intersubjectivity, *Journal of Management Studies* 18, 37–47.

Eden, C., Smithin, T. and Wiltshire, J. (1980). Cognition simulation and learning, *Journal of Experiential Learning and Simulation* 2 (2), 131–143.

Eden, C., Smithin, T. and Wiltshire, J. (1985). *COPE User Guide and Reference Manual.* Bristol: Bath Software Research.

Edgley, E. and Turner, R. E. (1975). Masks and social relations: an essay on the sources and assumptions of Dramaturgical Social Psychology, *Humboldt, Journal of Social Relations* V3 (1).

Eisner, R. and Strotz, R. H. (1963). Determinants of business investment. In *Commission on Money and Credit – Impacts of Monetary Policy.* Englewood Cliffs, New Jersey: Prentice-Hall.

Enos, J. (1962). Invention and innovation in the refining industry, National Bureau of Economic Research, *The Rate and Direction of Inventive Activity.* Princeton: Princeton University Press.

Evan, W. M. and Black, G. (1967). Innovation in business organizations: some factors associated with success or failure of staff proposals, *Journal of Business* XL (4), October, 519–530.

Filstead, W. J. (1970). *Qualitative Methodology: Firsthand Involvement with the Social World.* Chicago: Markham.

Fisher, W. R. (1978). Towards a logic of good reason, *Quarterly Journal of Speech* 64, 376–384.

Fisher, W. R. and Sayles, E. M. (1966). The nature and functions of argument. In G. R. Miller and T. R. Nilsen (eds) *Perspectives on Argumentation.* Chicago: Scott Foresman.

Foucault, M. (1975). Ecrivain non: un nouveau cartographe, *Critique* 3, 1226.

Foucault, M. (1977). *Language, Counter-Memory, Practice,* edited and translated by D. F. Bouchard and S. Simon. Ithaca: Cornell University Press.

Freeman, C. (1971). The role of small firms in innovation in the United Kingdom since 1945, Report to the Bolton Committee of Inquiry on Small Firms, Research Report No. 6. London: HMSO.

Freeman, C. (1974). *The Economics of Industrial Innovation*. Harmondsworth: Penguin.

Freud, S. (1915). Mourning and melancholia. In *The Standard Edition of the Complete Psychological Works of Sigmund Freud*, Vol, XIV. London: Hogarth Press and Institute of Psycho-Analysis.

Friend, J. K. and Jessop, W. N. (1969). *Local Government and Strategic Choice*. London: Tavistock.

Galbraith, J. K. (1967). *The New Industrial State*. Harmondsworth: Penguin.

Garfinkel, H. (1967). *Studies in Ethnomethodology*. Englewood Cliffs, New Jersey: Prentice-Hall.

Geach, P. T. (1976). *Reason and Argument*. Oxford: Basil Blackwell.

Geertz, C. (1975). *The Interpretation of Cultures*. London: Hutchinson.

Gibson, R. E. (1964). A systems approach to research management. In J. R. Bright *Research, Development and Technological Innovation*. Homewood, Illinois: Richard D. Irwin.

Giddens, A. (1976). *New Rules of Sociological Method*. London: Hutchinson.

Gilbert, G. N. and Mulkay, M. (1982). Warranting scientific belief, *Social Studies of Science* 12, 383–408.

Gilot, F. and Lake, C. (1964). *Life with Picasso*. New York: McGraw-Hill.

Glaser, B. G. and Strauss, A. L. (1967). *The Discovery of Grounded Theory*. Chicago: Aldine.

Globe, S., Levy, G. W. and Schwartz, C. M. (1973). Key factors and events in the innovation process, *Research Management*, July, 8–15.

Goffman, E. (1953). Communication conduct in an island community, PhD thesis, University of Chicago.

Goffman, E. (1959). *The Presentation of Self in Everyday Life*. New York: Doubleday.

Goffman, E. (1963). *Behavior in Public Places: Notes on the Social Organization of Gatherings*. New York: The Free Press.

Goffman, E. (1972). *Interaction Ritual: Essays on Face-to-Face Behaviour*. Harmondsworth: Penguin.

Goffman, E. (1975). *Frame Analysis: An Essay on the Organization of Experience*. Harmondsworth: Penguin.

Goffman, E. (1979). *Gender Advertisements*. London: Macmillan.

Goffman, E. (1981). *Forms of Talk*. Oxford: Blackwell.

Goldthorpe, J. H. (1973). A revolution in sociology?, *Sociology* 7, 449–62.

Gonos, G. (1977). 'Situation' versus 'Frame': the 'Interactionist' and the 'Structuralist' analyses of everyday life, *American Sociological Review* 42, 854–867.

Goodwin, P. D. and Wenzel, J. W. (1979). Proverbs and practical reasoning: a study in socio-logic, *Quarterly Journal of Speech* 65, 289–302.

Gouldner, A. (1970). *The Coming Crisis of Western Sociology*. London: Heinemann.

Gozzi, C. (1890). *The Memoirs of Count Carlo Gozzi*, two volumes London.

Grabowski, G. H. (1968). The determinants of industrial research and development: a study of the chemical, drug and petroleum industries, *Journal of Political Economy* 76, 292.

Green, E. I. (1965). Organizing for research. In E. Dale (ed.) *Readings in Management*. New York: McGraw-Hill.

Griliches, Z. (1957). Hybrid corn: an exploration in the economics of technological change, *Econometrica* 25, October, 501.

Gruber, W. H. and Marquis, D. G. (eds) (1969). *Factors in the Transfer of Technology*. Cambridge, Massachusetts: MIT Press.

Gruber, W. H., Poensgen, O. H. and Prakke, F. (1973). The isolation of R and D from corporate management, *Research Management*, November, 27–32.

Gusfield, J. (1976). The literary rhetoric of science: comedy and pathos in drinking driver research, *American Sociological Review* **41**, 16–34.

Hall, S. (1982). The rediscovery of ideology: return of the repressed in media studies. In M. Gurevitch, T. Bennett, J. Curran and J. Woollacott (eds) *Culture, Society and Media*. London: Methuen.

Hamberg, D. (1964). Size of firm, oligopoly and research: the evidence, *Canadian Journal of Economics and Political Science* **30** (1), 62–75.

Hansard, Weekly (1983). 13th July, c. 892.

Harari, J. V. (ed.) (1979). *Textual Strategies: Perspectives in Post-Structuralist Criticism*. Ithaca: Cornell University Press.

Hare, A.P. (1985). *Social Interaction as Drama*. Beverly Hills: Sage.

Harré R. (1974). Some remarks on rule as a scientific concept. In T. Mischel (ed.) *Understanding Other Persons*. Oxford: Blackwell.

Harré, R. (1977). The ethogenic approach: theory and practice. Reprint from *Advances in Experimental Social Psychology* V, 10, Academic Press.

Harré R. (1979). *Social Being*. Oxford: Blackwell.

Harré R. and Secord, P. F. (1976). *The Explanation of Social Behaviour*. Oxford: Blackwell.

Hartman, G. (ed.) (1979). *Deconstruction and Criticism*. London: Routledge and Kegan Paul.

Hawkes, T. (1977). *Structuralism and Semiotics*. London: Methuen.

Hawthorne, N. (1965). *The Scarlet Letter*. New York: Harper and Row.

Hayhurst, R. *et al.* (1972). *Organizational Design for Marketing Futures*. London: George Allen and Unwin.

Heidegger, M. (1977). *The Question Concerning Technology and Other Essays*, translated by W. Lovitt. New York: Harper and Row.

Heider, F. (1958). *The Psychology of Interpersonal Relations*. New York: Wiley.

Henry, J. (1966). *Culture Against Man*. London: Tavistock.

Heritage, J. (1977). Aspects of the flexibility of natural language use: a reply to Phillips, *Sociology*, 79–103.

Heron, J. (1981). Philosophical basis for a new paradigm. In P. Reason and J. Rowan (eds) *Human Inquiry: A Source Book of New Paradigm Research*. Chichester: Wiley.

Hersey, P., Blanchard, K. H. and Natemeyer, E. (1979). Situational leadership, perception and the impact of power, *Group and Organization Studies* **4** (4), 417–428.

Hodeir, A. (1956). *Jazz: Its Evolution and Essence*. London: Secker and Warburg.

Holland, W. E. (1972). Characteristics of individuals with high information potential in Government R and D organizations, *I.E.E. Transactions of Engineering Management* **EM–19**.

Holton, G. (1973). *Thematic Origins of Scientific Thought*. Cambridge, Mass: Harvard University Press.

Holzner, B. (1968). *Reality Construction in Society*. Cambridge, Mass: Schenckman.

Jameson, F. (1972). *The Prison-House of Language*. Princeton: Princeton University Press.

Jary, D. and Smith, G. (1976). Review of *Frame Analysis*, *The Sociological Review* **24** (4), 917–927.

Jay, A. (1967). *Management and Machiavelli*. London: Hodder and Stoughton.

Jehenson, R. (1974). Social construction of reality and the special distribution of knowledge in formal organisations, Paper presented at the American Sociological Association Meeting, Montreal, August.

Jewkes, J., Sawyers, D. and Stillerman, R. (1958). *The Sources of Invention*. London: St Martin's Press.

Johne, F.A. (1982). Innovation, organization and the marketing of high technology products, PhD thesis, University of Strathclyde.

Johne, F.A. (1984). Innovation in the marketing of high technolgy products, *Quarterly Review of Marketing* **9** (3), 1–7.

Johnson, J.M. (1977). Behind rational appearances. In J.D. Douglas and J.M. Johnson (eds) *Existential Sociology*. London: Cambridge University Press.

Jones, K.A. and Wilemon, D.L. (1972). Emerging patterns in New Venture Management, *Research Management*, November, 14–27.

Jones, S. (1985). The politics of problems: Intersubjectivity in defining powerful others, *Human Relations* **37** (11), 881–894.

Jones, S. (1986). Addressing internal politics: a role for modeling in consultant–client interaction, *Small Group Behaviour* **17** (1), 67–82.

Kaplan, A. (1964). *The Conduct of Enquiry*. San Francisco: Chandler.

Katz, E. (1961). The social itinerary of technical change: two studies on the diffusion of innovation, *Human Organization* **20**, 70–82.

Kelly, G.A. (1955). *The Psychology of Personal Constructs*, Vols 1 and 2. New York: Norton.

Kelly, G.A. (1963). *A Theory of Personality*. New York: Norton.

Kelly, G.A. (1977). The psychology of the unknown. In D. Bannister (ed.) *New Perspectives in Personal Construct Theory*. London: Academic Press.

King, S. (1973). *Developing New Brands*. London: Pitman.

Kirwan, C. (1978). *Logic and Argument*. London: Duckworth.

Koyre, A. (1965) The significance of the Newtonian Synthesis. In *Newtonian Studies*. Cambridge, Mass: Harvard University Press.

Lane, M. (ed.) (1970). *Structuralism; A Reader*. London: Cape.

Langer, E. (1978). Rethinking the role of thought in social interaction. In H. Harvey, W. Ickes and R. Kidd (eds) *New Directions in Attribution Research*, Vol. 2. Hillsdale, New Jersey: Erlbaum.

Langrish, J. (1969). Innovation in industry: some results of the Queen's Award study, Research Report No. 15, Department of Liberal Studies in Science, University of Manchester, September.

Langrish, J., Gibbons, M., Evans, W.G. and Jevons, F.R. (1972). *Wealth from Knowledge*. London: Macmilllan.

Laplanche, J. and Leclaire, S. (1966). *The Unconscious*. Yale French Studies No. 48.

Law, J. and Williams, R.J. (1982). Putting facts together: a study of scientific persuasion, *Social Studies of Sciences* **12**, 535–558.

Lawrence, P.R. and Lorsch, J.W. (1967). *Organization and Environment*. Boston: Harvard University Press.

Layton, C. (1972). *Ten Innovations*. London: George Allen and Unwin.

Lerner, A.W. (1976). *The Politics of Decision-Making: Strategy, Co-operation and Conflict*. London: Sage Publications.

Levinson, S.C. (1983). *Pragmatics*. Cambridge: Cambridge University Press.

Lewin, K. (1947). Frontiers in group dynamics: channel of group life: social planning and action research, *Human Relations* **1** (2), 143–53.

Likert, R. (1967). *The Human Organization: Its Management and Values*. New York: McGraw-Hill.

Lippitt, R., Watson, J. and Westley, B. (1985). *The Dynamics of Planned Change*. New York: Harcourt Brace.

Lofland, J. (1976). *Doing Social Life*. New York: Wiley.

Lukes, S. (1975). *Power: A Radical View*. London: Macmillan.

Lyman, S. M. and Scott, M. B. (1968). Accounts, *American Sociological Review* 33 (1).

Macksey, R. and Donato, E. (eds) (1970). *The Structuralist Controversy: The Languages of Criticism and the Sciences of Man.* Baltimore: John Hopkins.

McCall, G. J. and Simmons, J. L. (1966). *Identities and Interactions.* New York: Free Press.

McCaskey, M. (1982). *The Executive Challenge.* Marshfield, MA: Pitman.

McDermott, R. P. (1977). Kids make sense: an ethnographic account of the interactional management of success and failure in one first-grade classroom, Ph D thesis, Stanford University.

McHugh, P. (1968). *Defining the Situation.* New York: Bobbs-Merrill.

McLean, A., Sims, D., Mangham, I. and Tuffield, D. (1982). *Organization Development in Transition: Evidence of an Evolving Profession.* Chichester: Wiley.

Mangham, I. L. (1978). *Interactions and Interventions in Organizations.* Chichester: Wiley.

Mangham, I. L. (1979). *The Politics of Organizational Change.* London: Associated Business Press.

Mangham, I. L. (1982). The management of creativity. In J. Beck and C. Cox (eds) *Advances in Management Education.* Chichester: Wiley.

Mangham, I. L. (1986). *Power and Performance in Organizations: An Exploration of Executive Process.* Oxford: Blackwell.

Mangham, I. L. and Overington, M. A. (1987). *Organizations as Theatre: A Social Psychology of Dramatic Appearances.* Chichester: Wiley.

Manning, P. K. (1980). Goffman's framing order: style as structure. In J. Ditton (ed.) *The View from Goffman.* London: Macmillan.

Manning, P. K. (1983). Queries concerning the decision-making approach to police research, Paper presented to the British Psychological Society.

Mansfield, E. (1963). Size of firm, market structure and innovation, *Journal of Political Economy* LXXI, 556–576.

Mansfield, E. M. (1972). *Research and Innovation in the Modern Corporation.* London: Macmillan.

March, J. G. (1972). Model bias in social action, *Review of Educational Research* 42 (4), 413–429.

March, J. G. (1976). The technology of foolishness. In J. G. March and J. P. Olsen *Ambiguity and Choice in Organisations.* Bergen: UniversitetsforLaget.

March, J. G. and Olsen, J. P. (1976). *Ambiguity and Choice in Organisations.* Bergen: UniversitetsforLaget.

March, J. G. and Simon, H. A. (1958). The dysfunctions of bureaucracy. In D. S. Pugh (ed.) (1971) *Organization Theory.* Harmondsworth: Penguin.

Maruyama, M. (1974). Endogenous research versus 'experts' from outside, *Futures* 6, 389–394.

Maslow, A. H. (1954). *Motivation and Personality.* New York: Harper and Row.

Mead, G. H. (1934). *Mind, Self and Society.* Chicago: University of Chicago Press.

Meehl, P. E. (1965) The creative individual: why it is hard to identify him. In G. A. Steiner (ed.) *The Creative Organization.* Chicago: University of Chicago Press.

Mehan, H. and Wood, H. (1978). *The Reality of Ethnomethodology.* New York: Wiley Interscience.

Meltsner, A. J. (1979). Don't slight communication: some problems of analytical practice, *Policy Analysis* 3, 367–392.

Merelman, R. M. (1968). On the neo-elitist critique of community power, *American Political Science Review* 62, 45–460.

Merleau-Ponty, M. (1970). *Phenomenology of Perception.* New York: Humanities Press.

Messinger, S. L., Sampson, H. and Towne, R. D. (1962). Life as theatre: some notes on the dramaturgical approach to social reality, *Sociometry*, September, 98–110.

Miles, R. E. and Snow, C. C. (1978). *Organizational Strategy, Structure and Process.* New York: McGraw-Hill.

Miller, G. R. and Nilsen, T. R. (eds) (1966). *Perspectives on Argumentation.* Chicago: Scott Foresman.

Mintzberg, H. (1979). *The Structuring of Organisations.* Englewood Cliffs, New Jersey: Prentice-Hall.

Mintzberg, H. (1983). An emerging strategy of 'direct' research. In J. Van Maanen (ed.) *Qualitative Methodology.* Beverly Hills: Sage.

Mitroff, I. A. (1983). *Stakeholders of the Organizational Mind.* San Francisco: Jossey-Bass.

Mitroff, I. (1984). If Applied Systems Analysis is 'true', must it also be 'bad' and 'ugly'. In Tomlinson and Kiss (eds) *Rethinking the Process of Operational Research and Systems Analysis.* Oxford: Pergamon.

Moore, D. G. and Renek, R. (1955). The professional employee in industry, *Journal of Business* **XXVII** (1), January.

Moore, R. (1977). Becoming a sociologist in Sparkbrook. In C. Bell and H. Newby (eds) *Doing Sociological Research.* London: George Allen and Unwin.

Morris, I. (1980). *The Nobility of Failure: Tragic Heroes in the History of Japan.* Harmondsworth: Penguin.

Morris, M. (1977). *An Excursion into Creative Sociology.* Oxford: Blackwell.

Mumford, E. and Pettigrew, A. M. (1975). *Implementing Strategic Decisions.* London: Wiley.

Myers, S. and Marquis, D. G. (1969). *Successful Industrial Innovation.* National Science Foundation, NSF 69–17.

Nadler, D. A. and Tushman, M. L. (1980). A model for diagnosing organizational behaviour, *Organizational Dynamics*, Autumn.

National Economic Development Office (1972). *Organizing R and D.* London: NEDO, HMSO.

National Science Foundation (1966). *Technology Transfer and Innovation.* Conference Proceedings, NSF.

Neisser, U. (1976). *Cognition and Reality: Principles and Implications of Cognitive Psychology.* San Francisco: Freeman.

Nelkin, D. (ed.) (1979). *Controversy: Politics of Technical Decisions.* Beverly Hills: Sage.

Newcomb, T. M. and Turner, R. H. (1965). *Social Psychology: The Study of Human Relations.* New York: Holt, Rinehart and Winston.

Newton, F. (1959). *The Jazz Scene.* Harmondsworth: Penguin.

Norris, C. (1982). *Deconstruction: Theory and Practice.* London: Methuen.

Norris, C. (1983). *The Deconstructive Turn.* London: Methuen.

O'Keefe, D. J. (1979). Ethnomethodology, *Journal for the Theory of Social Behaviour* **9** (2), 187–219.

Organisation for Economic Cooperation and Development (1971). *The Conditions for Success in Technological Innovation.* Paris: OECD.

Overington, M. (1977). Kenneth Burke and the method of dramatism, *Theory and Society* **4** (1), Spring, 131–156.

Parsons, T. (1951). *The Social System.* Glencoe, Illinois: Free Press.

Parsons, T. (1960). *Structure and Process in Modern Societies.* New York: Free Press.

Parsons, T. (1968). Social interaction. In D. Sells (ed.) *International Encyclopedia of the Social Sciences*, Vol. 7. New York: Macmillan.

Pearson, K. (1937). *The Grammar of Science.* London: Everyman.

Peck, M.J. (1962). Invention in the post war aluminium industry. In National Bureau of Economic Research *The Rate and Direction of Inventive Activity*. NBER.

Pepper, S.C. (1942). *World Hypotheses*. Berkeley: University of California Press.

Perelman, C.H. and Olbrechts-Tyteca, L. (1969). *The New Rhetoric: A Treatise on Argumentation*. Notre Dame: University of Notre Dame Press.

Perinbanayagam, R.S. (1974). 'The definition of the situation: an anlaysis of the ethnomethodological and dramaturgical view, *The Sociological Quarterly* **15**, Autumn, 521–541.

Perrow, C. (1972). *Complex Organizations*. Chicago: Scott Foresman.

Perrow, C. (1982). Disintegrating social sciences, *Phi Delta Kappan* **63** (10), 684–688.

Peters, B. (1974). Overcoming organizational constraints on creativity and innovation, *Research Management*, May, 29–33.

Peters, T.J. and Waterman, R.H. (1984). *In Search of Excellence*. New York: Warner Books.

Pettigrew, A.M. (1973). *The Politics of Organizational Decision-Making*. London: Tavistock.

Pettigrew, A.M. (1977). Strategy formulation as a political process, *International Studies of Management and Organisation* **VII** (2), 78–87.

Pfeffer, J. (1981). *Power in Organizations*. Boston: Pitman.

Pfeffer, J. (1982). *Organisations and Organisation Theory*. Boston: Pitman.

Phillips, J. (1976). Some problems in locating practices, *Sociology* **12**, 56–77.

Phillips, L.D. (1984). Decision support for top managers. In H.J. Otway and M. Pelta (eds) *The Management Challenge of New Office Technology*. London: Butterworth.

Pittenger, R.E., Hockett, C.F. and Danehy, J.J. (1960). *The First Five Minutes: A Sample of Microscopic Interview Analysis*. New York: Paul Martineau.

Plato. *Phaedrus*, modern translation by W. Hamilton (1977). Harmondsworth: Penguin.

Polti, G. (1916). Quoted by T. Sarbin in V.L. Allen and K.E. Scheibe (eds.) *The Social Context of Conduct*. New York: Praeger.

Pomerantz, A. (1985). Agreeing and disagreeing with assessments: some features of preferred/dispreferred turn shapes. In J.M. Atkinson and J. Heritage (eds) *Structures of Social Action*. Cambridge: Cambridge University Press.

Porter, D.E. and Applewhite, P.B. (1966). *Studies in Organizational Behaviour and Management*. Glasgow: International Textbook Company.

Porter, D.E., Applewhite, P.B. and Misshauk, M.J. (1971). *Studies in Organizational Behaviour and Management* 2nd edn. Scranton: Intext Educational Publishers.

Presthus, R. (1978). *The Organizational Society*, revised edition. New York: St Martin's Press.

Price, W.J. and Bass, L.W. (1969). Scientific research and the innovative process, *Science*, 16th May, 802–806.

Propp, V.Y. (1968). *Morphology of the Folk Tale*. Austin: University of Texas Press.

Radford, K.J. (1977). *Complex Decision Problems*. Reston, VA: Reston.

Raiffa, H. (1968). *Decision Analysis*. Reading, Mass: Addison-Wesley.

Ramos, R. (1978) The use of improvisation and modulation in natural talk: an alternative approach to conversational analysis. In N.K. Denzin (ed.) *Studies in Symbolic Interaction*. Greenwich, Connecticut: JAI Press.

Ramsey, H. (1977). Cycles of control: worker participation in sociological and historical perspective, *Sociology*, 481–506.

Ranson, S., Hinings, R. and Greenwood, R. (1980). The structuring of organizational structures, *Administrative Science Quarterly* **25**, 1–17.

Rapoport, R.H. (1970). Three dilemmas in action research, *Human Relations* **23** (6), 499–513.

Reardon, K.K. (1981). *Persuasion: Theory and Context.* Beverley Hills: Sage.

Riccoboni, L. (1728). *Histoire du Theatre Italien.* Paris.

Rokeach, M. (1973). *The Nature of Human Values.* New York: Free Press.

Roloff, M.E. and Miller, G.R. (eds) (1980). *Persuasion: New Directions in Theory and Research.* Beverly Hills: Sage.

Roszak, T. (1972). *Where the Wasteland Ends.* New York: Doubleday.

Rothwell, R. and Robertson, A.B. (1973). The role of communications in technological innovation, *Research Policy* no. 2, 204–225.

Ryan, B. and Gross, N. (1943). The diffusion of hybrid seed corn in two Iowa communities, *Rural Sociology* **VIII**, March.

Sacks, H. (1963). Sociological description, *Berkeley Journal of Sociology* **8**, 1–17.

Sacks, H., Schegloff, E.A. and Jefferson, G. (1974). A simplest systematics for the organization of turn-taking in conversation, *Language* **50** (4), 696–735.

Said, E. (1978). The problem of textuality: two exemplary positions, *Critical Inquiry* **4**, Summer, 673–714.

Said, E. (1979). The text, the world, the critic. In J.V. Harari (ed.) *Textual Strategies.* London: Methuen.

Salter, W.E.G. (1960). *Productivity and Technical Change.* Cambridge: Cambridge University Press.

Sandford, N. (1981). A model for action research. In P. Reason and J. Rowan (eds) *Human Inquiry: A Sourcebook of New Paradigm Research.* Chichester: Wiley.

Sarbin T. (1982) Contextualism: A world view for modern psychology. In V.L. Allen and K.E. Scheibe (eds) *The Social Context of Conduct.* New York: Praeger.

Saren, M.A.J. (1979). The characteristics of the innovating firm, PhD thesis, University of Bath.

Saren, M.A.J. (1984). A classification and review of models of the infra-firm innovation process, *R & D Management* **14** (1), 11–24.

Saunders, P.R. (1979). *Urban Politics: A Sociological Interpretation.* London: Hutchinson.

Saussure, F. de (1972). Course in general linguistics. In R. and F. de George *The Structuralists.* New York: Anchor.

Saussure, F. de (1974). *Course in General Linguistics,* translated by Wade Baskin. London: Fontana.

Sayles, L.R. (1974). The innovation process: an organizational analysis, *Journal of Management Studies* **II** (3), October, 190–204.

Schank, R. and Abelson, R. (1977). *Scripts, Plans, Goals and Understanding.* Hillsdale, New Jersey: Erlbaum.

Scheflen, A.E. (1973). *Communicational Structure: Analysis of a Psychotherapy Transaction.* Bloomington: Indiana University Press.

Schegloff, E.A. (1972). Notes on a conversational practice: formulating place. In D. Sudnow (ed.) *Studies in Social Interaction.* New York: Free Press.

Schegloff, E.A. and Sacks, H. (1973). Opening up closings, *Semiotica* **7** (4), 289–327.

Schmookler, J. (1957). Inventors, past and present, *Review of Economics and Statistics* **39**, August, 321–333.

Schon, D.A. (1967). *Technology and Change.* London: Pergamon.

Schorer, M. (1968). *The World We Imagine: Selected Essays.* New York: Farrar, Straus and Giroux.

Schumacher, E. (1974). *Small is Beautiful.* London: Abacus.

Schumpeter, J. (1928). The instability of capitalism, *Economic Journal* **XXXVIII**, 361–386.

Schutz, A. (1962). *Collected Papers.* M. Natanson (ed.) The Hague: Nijhoff.

Schutz, A. (1970). *On Phenomenology and Social Relations*. Chicago: University of Chicago Press.

Science Policy Research Unit (1972). *Success and Failure in Industrial Innovation*. London: Centre for the Study of Industrial Innovation.

Scott, M. B. and Lyman, S. M. (1970). *The Sociology of the Absurd*. New York: Meredith Corporation.

Sharron, A. (1985). The mainstream of consciousness: an interactionist analysis of a phenomenological concept, *Symbolic Interaction* **8** (1), 47–62.

Sheppard, H. A. (1967). Innovation–resisting and innovation–producing organizations, *Journal of Business*, 40(4).

Shibutani, T. (1961). *Society and Personality*. Englewood Cliffs, New Jersey: Prentice-Hall.

Silverman, D. (1970). *The Theory of Organizations*. London: Heinemann.

Silverman, D. (1985). *Qualitative Methodology and Sociology*. Aldershot: Gower.

Silverman, D. and Jones, J. (1973). Getting in: the managed accomplishment of 'correct' selection outcomes. In J. Child (ed.) *Man and Organisation*. London: Allen and Unwin.

Silverman, D. and Jones, J. (1976). *Organisational Work: The Language of Grading / The Grading of Language*. London: Collier/Macmillan.

Silverman, D. and Torode, B. (1980). *The Material World: Some Theories of Language and its Limits*. London: Routledge and Kegan Paul.

Sims, D. (1978). Problem construction in teams, PhD thesis, University of Bath.

Sims, D. (1979). A framework for understanding the definition and formulation of problems in teams, *Human Relations* **32**, 909–921.

Sims, D. (1986). *Problem Construction in Organizations*. Chichester: Wiley.

Sims, D. and Smithin, T. (1982). Voluntary operational research, *Journal of the Operational Research Society* **33**, 21–28.

Smith, P. B. (1973). *Groups within Organizations: Applications of Social Psychology to Organizational Behaviour*. London: Harper and Row.

Smithin, T. (1982). Stranger in a strange land: a working guide to cognitive mapping, *Journal of Management Development* **1** (1), 34–43.

Smithin, T. and Eden, C. (1985). Issues in the design of computer decision support for senior managers. Working Paper, School of Management, University of Bath.

Smithin, T. and Sims, D. (1982). Ubi caritas? — modelling beliefs about charities, *European Journal of Operational Research* **10** 237–243.

Soloman, R. C. (1976). *The Passions*. Garden City, NY: Doubleday Anchor.

Starbuck, W. H. (1982). Congealing oil: Inventing ideologies to justify acting ideologies out, *Journal of Management Studies* **19**, 3–27.

States, B. O. (1985). *Great Reckonings in Little Rooms*. Berkeley: University of California Press.

Staw, B. M. (1980). Rationality and justification in organizational life. In B. M. Staw and L. L. Cummings (eds) *Research in Organizational Behaviour*, Vol. 2. Greenwich, Connecticut: JAI Press.

Stebbins, R. (1967). A theory of the definition of the situation, *The Canadian Review of Sociology and Anthropology* **4**, 148–164.

Stebbins, R. (1969). Studying the definition of the situation: theory and field research strategies, *Canadian Review of Sociology and Anthropology* **6** (4), 193–211.

Stebbins, R. (1970). The meaning of disorderly behaviour: teacher definitions of a classroom situation, *Sociology of Education* **V 44**, Spring, 217–236.

Stein, J. G. (1977). Freud and Descartes: the paradoxes of psychological logic, *International Journal* **33** (3), 429–451.

Stein, M.I. (1975). *Stimulating Creativity, Vol. 1: Industrial Processes*. New York: Academic Press.

Strauss, A. (1978). *Negotiations, Varieties, Contexts, Processes and Social Order*. San Francisco: Jossey-Bass.

Stryker, S. (1980). *Symbolic Interactionism: A Social Structural Version*. Menlo Park, California: Benjamin/Cummings.

Summer, J.A. (1972). Business and research — uneasy strangers in the same house, *Research Management*, March, 60–66.

Taylor, L. (1979). Vocabularies, rhetorics and grammar: problems in the sociology of motivation. In T. Downes and P. Rock (eds) *Deviant Interpretations*. London: Martin Robinson.

Thomas, W.I. (1937). *The Unadjusted Girl*. Boston: Little Brown.

Thomas, W.I. (1951). *Social Behaviour and Personality*. New York: Social Science Research Council.

Thomas, W.I. and Thomas, D.S. (1928). *The Child in America: Behavior Problems and Programs*. New York: Knopf.

Thomas, W.I. and Znaniecki, F. (1927). *The Polish Peasant in Europe and America*. Chicago: Chicago University Press.

Thorndike, E.L. (1931). *Human Learning*. New York: Appleton Century Crofts.

Toulmin, S.E. (1958). *The Uses of Argument*. Cambridge: Cambridge University Press.

Toulmin, S., Rieke, R. and Janik, A. (1979). *An Introduction to Reasoning*. New York: Macmillan.

Travers, A. (1981). The stalking ground: some varieties of human conduct seen in and through a frame of ritual, PhD thesis, School of Management, University of Bath.

Travers, A. (1982). Ritual power in interaction, *Symbolic Interaction* 5 (2), 277–286.

Trigg, R. (1973). *Reason and Commitment*. Cambridge: Cambridge University Press.

Turner, R.H. (1968). The self-conception in social interaction. In C. Gordon and K.J. Gergen (eds) *The Self in Social Interaction*, Vol. 1. New York: Wiley.

Turner, R. (1972). Some formal properties of therapy talk. In D. Sudnow (ed.) *Studies in Social Interaction*. New York: Free Press.

Tushman, M.L. and Moore, W.L. (1982). *Readings in the Management of Innovation*. Cambridge, Mass: Billinger.

Urban, G.L. and Hauser, J.R. (1980). *Design and Marketing of New Products*. Englewood Cliffs, New Jersey: Prentice-Hall.

Utterback, J.M. (1971). The process of innovation: A study of the origination and development of ideas for new scientific instruments, *I.E.E. Transactions on Engineering Management*, EM–18.

Van Maanen, J. (1979). *Qualitative Methodology*. Beverly Hills: Sage.

Vernon, G.M. (1965). *Human Interaction: An Introduction to Sociology*. New York: Ronald Press.

Vesper, K.H. and Holmdahl, T.G. (1973). How venture management fares in innovative companies, *Research Management*, May, 30–32.

Wallace, K.R. (1963). The substance of rhetoric: good reasons, *Quarterly Journal of Speech* 49, 239–249.

Weber, M. (1947). *The Theory of Social and Economic Organizations*. New York: Free Press.

Weber, M. (1974). The general character of charisma. In *From Max Weber*. London: Routledge and Kegan Paul.

Weick, K. (1977). Repunctuating the problem. In P.S. Goodman and J.M. Pennings (eds) *New Perspectives in Organisational Effectiveness*. San Francisco: Jossey-Bass.

Weick, K. (1979). *The Social Psychology of Organizing*, 2nd edn. Reading, Mass: Addison-Wesley.

Weick, K. (1985). Sources of order in underorganized systems: Themes in recent organiz-ational theory. In Y. Lincoln *Organizational Theory and Inquiry: The Paradigm Revolution*. Beverly Hills: Sage.

Weisblat, D.I. and Stucki, J.C. (1974). Organizing and planning for effective research: Goal-oriented organization at Upjohn, *Research Management*, January, 34–37.

Weiss, J. (1980). Script processes in organizations. *Organizational Dynamics*, September.

Westerlund, G. and Sjostrand, S-E. (1979). *Organizational Myths*. London: Harper and Row.

Westwood, R.I. (1983). Contests in meaning: the rhetoric of participation. Unpublished PhD thesis, University of Bath.

Whitley, R.D. (1977). Concepts of organization and power in the study of organizations, *Personnel Review* **6** (1), Winter, 54–59.

Weider, D.L. (1969). The convict code: a study of a moral order as a persuasive activity, PhD thesis, University of California, Los Angeles.

Wilensky, H.L. (1967). *Organizational Intelligence: Knowledge and Policy in Government and Industry*. New York: Basic Books.

Wimsatt, W.K. (1970). *The Verbal Icon: Studies in the Meaning of Poetry*. London: Methuen.

Winick, C. (1961). The diffusion of an innovation among physicians in a large city, *Sociometry* **24**, 384–396.

Wolfe, T. (1979). *The Right Stuff*. London: Jonathan Cape.

Woodward, J. (1965). *Industrial Organization*. London: Oxford University Press.

Wootton, A. (1975). *Dilemmas of Discourse*. London: George Allen and Unwin.

Wooton, A.J. (1981). The management of grantings and rejections by parents in request sequences, *Semiotica* **1** (2), 59–89.

Wynne, B. (1982). *Rationality and Ritual: The Windscale Inquiry and Nuclear Decisions in Britain*. Chalfont St Giles: British Society for the History of Science.

Young, K. (1977). Values in the policy process, *Policy and Politics* **5**, 1–22.

Young, R. (ed.) (1981). *Untying the Text: A Post-Structuralist Reader*. London: Routledge and Kegan Paul.

Index